The Elements of Export Practice

The Elements of Export Practice

ALAN E. BRANCH
M.C.I.T., A.M.I.Ex., A.I.T.A.

Shipping Executive/Lecturer/Chief Examiner
Shipping and Export Practice/Shipping and Export Consultant/
Author of The Elements of Shipping *and*
A dictionary of Shipping/International Trade Terms and Abbreviations

CHAPMAN AND HALL
LONDON

First published 1979
by Chapman and Hall Ltd
11 New Fetter Lane, London EC4P 4EE

© 1979 Alan E. Branch

Typeset by Inforum, Guildhall Square, Portsmouth
and printed in Great Britain by
J.W. Arrowsmith Ltd, Bristol

ISBN 0 412 15610 5

Distributed in the U.S.A. by
Halsted Press, a Division of John Wiley & Sons, Inc.,
New York

TO
MY SON
DAVID

Foreword

by Sir Frederick Catherwood,
Chairman of the British Overseas Trade Board

The Foundation Course in Overseas Trade is now in its fourth year and is attracting hundreds of students to many centres throughout the United Kingdom. Much of its success is owed to the subject specialists who at the outset assisted the British Overseas Trade Board and the professional institutes concerned in drawing up the syllabus. Mr Branch, as the specialist on transportation and documentation, and subsequently as a moderator on this subject, has made a major contribution to the course.

For students and businessmen alike, there is a need to know more about export practice and I am sure this book will be of considerable help towards providing a more professional approach by all concerned. I wish it every success.

Preface

This book has been written to provide a basic overall understanding of the theory and efficient, practical, professional technique of exporting goods involving the complete, competitive, profitable export business contract. It is written in simple language and deals with documentation, Customs, export finance, packing, cargo insurance, the export office, the contract of affreightment, market research, dangerous cargoes, marketing, transport distribution analysis, freight rates, export facilitation organizations, together with many other aspects of this extensive subject.

It is intended not only for the student preparing for the export examination, but also for the person employed in the export/shipping office who wishes to further his or her knowledge of the subject. In short, it is an 'aide memoire' to those engaged in the industry and may be regarded as the 'exporters handbook.'

I was one of the four subject specialists responsible for the evolvement of the Foundation Course in Overseas Trade introduced in 1975, and sponsored by the HM Government under the aegis of the British Overseas Trade Board. My subject was transportation and documentation. This book covers all the aspects of this subject and, therefore, is specifically recommended to students taking this course.

The book is also particularly commended to students taking export/shipping/transport examinations sponsored by the Institute of Export, Institute of Freight Forwarders Ltd, Institute of Marketing, Institute of Materials Handling, Institute of Traffic Administration, Institute of Road Transport Engineers, Institute of Chartered Shipbrokers, Chartered Institute of Transport, London Chamber of Commerce and Industry, University of London Diploma in Transport Studies, and the shipping certificate sponsored by the City of London Polytechnic and City of Liverpool College of Commerce. The book is also ideal for the student or export/shipping executive taking the short export induction courses often sponsored by local Chambers of Commerce.

In writing this book I am greatly indebted to the various organizations who have helped me so enthusiastically in their various contributions. These organizations appear under 'Acknowledgements' and I am grateful for their help.

At my request, Mr D.W. Disley was responsible for Chapter 7 on export customs practice, and Mr H.B. Jackson, B.Sc. (Econ), F.I.Ex, FIB, for Chapters 1 and 9 on international trade and export finance respectively. Mr H.B. Jackson was a subject specialist colleague responsible for the International Trade and Payments under the Foundation Course in Overseas Trade and formerly Chief Executive Barclays Export and Finance Co. Ltd. Likewise Mr D.B. Cox was responsible for the diagrams. I am most grateful to all of them for their very significant contribution which has enriched the contents of the book.

Finally, I would like to record my grateful thanks for all the secretarial help given by lifelong family friends Mr and Mrs Splarn, who have undertaken similar tasks for my four previous publications. As always, I record with gratitude the help rendered by my wife in proof reading and her tolerance and enthusiasm involving many lost weekends.

A.E.B.

19, The Ridings,
Emmer Green,
Reading,
Berkshire.
January 1979.

Contents

Contents

Diagrams

Acknowledgements

British Airways

British Overseas Trade Board

British Railways Board

British Shippers Council

British Standards Institution

Central Office of Information

Confederation of British Industry

Department of the Environment

Department of Transport

Export Credits Guarantee Department

Foreign and Commonwealth Office

Freight Liners Ltd

HM Customs and Excise

International Air Transport Association

Inter-Governmental Maritime Consultative Organisation

London Chamber of Commerce and Industry

Lufthansa Airline

Overseas Containers Ltd

Ozalid (UK) Ltd

Post Office — Overseas Post Division

Road Haulage Association

Simplification of International Trade Procedures Board

CHAPTER 1

International Trade

Scope of book. Function of international trade. Survey of international trade. Commodity trades. Flow of manufactured goods. Multinational companies. Balance of trade and balance of payments. International organizations. Major trading areas of the world.

SCOPE OF BOOK

This book is written primarily for the student or businessman (export/shipping executive) who knows little or virtually nothing of export practice involving the processing of international trade. It aims to provide a basic overall understanding of the theory and efficient, practical, profitable technique of exporting goods involving the complete, competitive, export business contract. With this in mind, it deals with the salient aspects of the subject embracing transportation, documentation, rates, Customs, principal export facilitation organizations, export/shipping office, contracts of sale/affreightment, export packing, export agents, shipping/international trade terms/abbreviations, export research and marketing. It also examines cargo insurance and export finance also involving the Export Credits Guarantee Department.

Overall, it is written in a simple but lucid style. It reflects the author's very wide experience in the export industry spanning many years. This embraces not only work in the industry itself, but also as a lecturer/chief examiner of the subject at home and overseas, and as a member of a special four-man subject specialist team brought together to evolve for HM Government a Foundation Course in Overseas Trade sponsored by the British Overseas Trade Board. This was implemented in September 1975. Above all, the theme of export practice must be to develop international trade on a profitable basis and this book sets out to achieve this objective. Successful exporting is only realized through complete professionalism in the development and processing of international trade.

FUNCTION OF INTERNATIONAL TRADE

There are several reasons why nations began to trade with one another. The distribution of natural resources around the world is somewhat haphazard: some nations possess natural ores and chemical deposits in excess of their own requirements while other nations have none. For example, Britain has large reserves of coal but lacks many minerals such as nickel, copper, aluminium etc, whereas the Arab states have vast oil deposits but little else. In the cultivation of natural products climate plays a decisive role. Some products will only grow in tropical climates whereas others, such as citrus fruits, require a Mediterranean climate. Moreover, some nations are unable to produce sufficient of a particular product to satisfy a large home demand, for example, Britain and wheat. These are the reasons why international trade first began but, with the development of manufacturing and technology, there arose another incentive for nations to exchange their products. It was found that it made economic sense for a nation to specialize in certain activities and produce those goods for which it had the most advantages, and to exchange those goods for the products of other nations which had advantages in different fields. This trade is based on the 'law of comparative costs'.

Economists maintain that it will be advantageous for mankind if people specialize in those occupations at which they have the greatest comparative advantage, or the least comparative disadvantage, leaving others to produce the goods and services for which they have little aptitude. This principle is the basis of specialization into trades and occupations. Today it is paramount in the theory of international trade. At the same time, complete specialization may never occur even when it is economically advantageous. For strategic or domestic reasons, a country may continue to produce goods for which it does not have an advantage. The benefits of specialization may also be affected by transport costs: goods and raw materials have to be transported around the world and the cost of the transport narrows the limits between which it will prove profitable to trade. Another impediment to the free flow of goods between nations, in accordance with the principle of comparative advantage, is the possible introduction of artificial barriers to trade, such as tariffs or quotas.

The benefits derived from the development of international trade are (i) cheaper goods because of the advantages possessed by the supplying country; (ii) a greater variety of products available to the consumer; (iii) wider markets for the producing country conferring the economies of large scale production; and (iv) the overall growth of trade due to the reciprocal advantages.

SURVEY OF INTERNATIONAL TRADE

There is evidence of trading between nations as far back as the sixth century B.C. In those early days, the exchange of goods was conducted on a 'barter' basis now known as 'compensation trade.' Solomon exchanged food with the Lebanon against delivery of timber for the building of the Temple and early Phoenicians brought fabrics and dyestuffs to Cornwall in exchange for tin. A medium of exchange in the form of coins was introduced early in the fifth century B.C. These coins were exchanged weight for weight one country against another, where sufficient confidence existed in the metallic values. This, however, was not a foreign exchange system in the modern sense. In Roman times, some trading was carried on by exchange of coin and is the first evidence of a foreign exchange system. Money changers such as those ejected from the Temple were carrying on the dual function of bullion dealing and foreign exchange which now form distinct but related markets. From the end of the Roman Empire there was a considerable reversion to barter or the exchange of metallic coin by weight but, by the eleventh century A.D., money changing once more became an important profession. Money changers were found in places like Genoa and, during the time of the Papal Court in France, Avignon became the centre of foreign exchange where the wide variety of coins brought by visitors from all parts of the Christian world were freely exchanged. Medieval English coins made their way to the Low Countries and world expansion made foreign exchange important even in India and China.

From the thirteenth century onwards, bills of exchange gradually took the place of coin and the market in bills of exchange remained almost unchanged until the end of the eighteenth century. Throughout this period, the importance of London was increasing, although in the sixteenth and seventeenth centuries Antwerp and Amsterdam were probably more important. In the sixteenth century, there also appeared a system of forecasts of future exchange rates which in Holland, Belgium and Spain was mainly in the form of betting. From the French Revolution onwards, although bills of exchange remained of greatest importance, mail transfers came into being and, throughout the nineteenth century, there was some development of forward exchange dealing. At that time, London lagged behind such centres as Vienna, Berlin, Trieste and St. Petersburg. This was mainly because, with the growing influence of Great Britain on world trade, a large proportion of that trade was expressed in sterling and London merchants had no need to buy or sell currencies, whilst abroad the need for a market in sterling against other currencies was obvious.

The conduct of international trade developed from a system of barter to the settlement for goods exchanged by means of an independent commodity, that is, metallic coinage, and then on to the bill of exchange and the bank note. At the same time, the medium of exchange was organized until the foreign exchange markets as we know them today were developed. As banking techniques and services were developed, the banks provided facilities for the smooth conduct of international trade: the foreign exchange markets enabled traders to conduct their business in any currency and exchange currencies freely one for another; and worldwide banking networks made the transfer of monies easier and quicker and provided economic and credit information. The activities of merchants made everyone more aware of what was available in other lands and so the desire to exchange goods became greater. Just as the means of payment had developed, so did the means of transport. With the development of shipping from the clipper through to steam, then oil-driven vessels and now the growth of container transport, the transfer of goods from one part of the world to another became quicker and safer. Alongside this grew the development of cargo insurance.

The basic requirements for the growth of international trade were provided and there then developed a variety of methods and expertise to assist in the conduct of that trade, for example, the services of export houses who were specialists in certain markets; the appointing of agents overseas; selling direct by travelling sales staff; setting up of branch offices or subsidiary companies in overseas markets; and group marketing to share expenses.

Everything would suggest that the 'law of comparative costs' could operate to its fullest extent to the benefit of all. Unfortunately, the pressures both economic and political under which individual nations exist have tended to impose barriers to the free flow of goods. Home industries are protected by tariffs and quotas, Customs duties are imposed for revenue, the import of goods from certain countries prohibited, for example, the activities of the Arab nations against those firms selling to Israel, the formation of Customs Unions, for example, EFTA and the EEC. On the other hand, there have been the attempts by the more prosperous countries to facilitate the sale by the underdeveloped countries of their primary products.

COMMODITY TRADES

A commodity is any article of commerce of any kind, that is, anything that is for sale — goods, merchandise or produce. In modern marketing, however, the term is employed in a more restricted sense and as the opposite of 'manufactured goods'. It is used to describe any primary product or any raw material marketed internationally, either in its original state, for example, mineral ores, corn, cotton etc, or after the initial process which makes it acceptable as an industrial raw material, for example, metal ingots.

As already mentioned above, the essential factors of climate, topography and accessibility have led to commodites surplus to local requirements being produced for export, from certain areas of the world. Primary producers are increasingly aware of the importance of studying the requirements of their buyers, and adjusting their product accordingly. Whereas the producers of manufacturered goods will assist in the marketing of their goods and often deal direct with the retailer, very few primary producers go further in the marketing process than to place their offers through intermediaries such as the merchant, broker or jobber. Moreover, in the marketing of manufacturers the 'market' is the chain of retailers nationwide but for the primary products (commodities) there are market places where buyers meet the sellers (or the merchants or brokers who deal for the sellers), and bargains are struck which conform to the self-imposed rules and regulations of the members of the market. Membership of the latter is exclusive.

Some of the most important commodity markets of the world are in England and particularly in London. The prices fixed in the London markets are reported daily in the financial press, which also comment on what is happening in foreign terminal markets such as New

York (for example, coffee).

Three different types of sale are practised in the London markets: sale of actual bulk of physical goods, sale by sample and sale by specification. Thus fruit, fish etc. is sold in bulk after inspection; imported frozen meat is sold by auction against sample at Smithfield; wool from Australia and New Zealand is auctioned on the Wool Exchange after inspection in warehouse; and at the daily meeting of the London Metal Exchange members buy and sell by specification such metals as copper, lead, tin and zinc. The Bullion Market meets twice daily, and the dealers both buy and sell gold and silver on behalf of their clients. All orders are tabled and the price is fixed to reflect the forces of supply and demand.

In markets where sale is by specificiation, the members have evolved through their associations standard specifications to which all conform. On the Metal Exchange 'lead' is defined as 'good soft pig lead' and on the Baltic Exchange there are international standards for grain. Rubber is in the form of 'latex' or 'sheet' conforming to standards laid down by the Rubber Trading Association.

Membership of any of these markets involves the firms concerned in compliance with established discipline as follows:

(1) Although transactions are verbally conducted, where the commodity is not immediately transferred to the buyer against payment, written confirmations are exchanged between buyers and sellers. These take the form of standard 'contracts' which have been evolved over time and must be employed by all parties.

(2) In the event of a dispute between any buyer and his seller, this is submitted to arbitration as laid down by the market authorities.

(3) Where any commodity is sold by specification, the established practice is for the actual quantity delivered by the seller to be inspected and the price adjusted to allow for divergences from standard.

Many of these markets have evolved an important form of 'futures' contract, usually for three months ahead. A 'future' is a contract by which the seller undertakes to deliver and the buyer undertakes to take delivery of a stipulated quantity of a standard commodity at a future date, the date and related price being fixed at the time the contract is entered into. This procedure enables dealers to safeguard their position against the risk of price fluctuations. It also enables dealers who are carrying stocks to 'hedge' against the risk of a decline in value.

Of the two types of intermediary in the markets the merchant buys from one or more suppliers and on-sells to his client in the same way as an export merchant, whilst the broker buys and sells on behalf of a principal and is paid a 'brokerage'. In some markets, there are those who act as buying brokers and others who act as selling brokers. Where the commodity is sold by auction, the auctioneer is considered to be the agent of both buyer and seller. In many commodity transactions, the goods are sold whilst still in transit and then the buyer, in effect, purchases the documents of title and not the goods themselves. The main document is the bill of lading.

FLOW OF MANUFACTURED GOODS

As the developed countries began to specialize increasingly in manufacture, they reached a point where they no longer produced enough raw materials for their industries or food for their peoples. In consequence, they exported their manufactured goods in exchange for raw materials and foodstuffs. The increase in specialization and the growth of technology resulted in the exchange of technical products between the more industralized countries so that manufactures were exported, not only to buy raw materials and food, but also in exchange for other technical products.

As a result of scientific research and technological development, the extent and variety of manufactured goods has increased enormously. This has meant a rapid growth in the exchange of manufactured goods between industralized countries, but also has produced synthetic substitutes for many natural products, for example, synthetic rubber, plastics, man-made fibres etc. This has led many primary producers to seek to acquire manufacturing expertise and become at least partly industralized.

There are then a multiplicity of factors affecting the growth and direction of international trade: comparative advantage which will encourage a country to specialize increasingly on certain products; political factors where governments seek to control the movement of imports and exports either to protect the value of the currency or for strategic reasons; the desire to diversify the economy, especially where the country has been dependent on a single product; and finally, a monopoly by one country of the supply of an essential product.

MULTINATIONAL COMPANIES

With the scale of world trade increasing with a corresponding increase in risks, many firms experienced pressures for adoption of international strategy. Where they had previously pursued a policy of putting in a plant whenever an export market reached sufficient size to carry the investment, they now made sure that they had a plant wherever market analysis indicated a potential need. This change in policy has led to the creation of large multinational companies. As one company put it, 'we are no longer a British company with some international business but a British-based international organization'. The economic factors which have influenced the development of multinational corporations are: (i) the use of local products; (ii) savings in freight costs; (iii) local labour may be cheaper; (iv) possible tax concessions and available finance; (v) technical collaboration to spread development costs and to secure new products; (vi) the provision of more reliable demonstration, installation, delivery, repair and maintenance service from local facilities; and (vii) higher profits.

Strategic motives are: (i) the need to control facilities of a certain size so as to gain market power and avoid dispersion — control over resource allocation; (ii) economies of scale in central services and research; (iii) fiscal advantages obtained by transferring goods at the most advantageous prices for minimizing tax; (iv) investment grants; and (v) shifting liquid capital to hedge against devaluations. Host countries welcome the establishment of multinational group companies because they bring employment, new technology and increased growth. They may or may not increase exports and/or imports. At the same time, the host country is wary of the possibility of price adjustments between members of the group, particularly in order to show profits where tax is lowest.

The expansion in the activities of multinational corporations and the development of new ones has added the exchange of skills and technology to the exchange of goods and services which make up international trade.

BALANCE OF TRADE AND BALANCE OF PAYMENTS

When a country engages in international trade there arises what is called the 'balance of payments' problem. The people of every country require to be paid eventually for the goods they make or the services they render in their own currency — that is, all they can use legally in their own country. If we buy goods or services from the USA we must pay in dollars, if we buy from Germany we must pay in deutschemarks. The best way to obtain these currencies is to sell some of our own goods and services to the USA and to Germany. If we can sell to them exactly as much as we want to buy from them, then we have a simple balance of payments with those countries. It does not, of course, work out so simply as we may want more, or less, from a country than it requires from us, and so we cannot achieve a balance of payments with that country. Fortunately, in most cases we can overcome the problem by paying in some other currency which is acceptable to them. Because our balance with different countries may be in our favour or in their favour, and because of the interchangeability of currencies, we have to consider our balance of payments against all the other countries of the world in total. The balance of payments then is the relationship between the total sales of a country's goods and services to other nations, and the total purchases it makes of goods and services from abroad. It is composed of three elements: the balance of trade, the balance of invisibles, and the balance of capital items. The balance of trade is quite simply the difference between the total of 'visible' items exported and those imported, that is, items which can actually be seen passing through our docks and airports. The 'invisible' items are services rendered to foreigners or services received from foreigners. The chief 'invisibles' are banking, shipping, insurance, air transport, tourism and interest on foreign investment. To these can be added remittances home by emigrants, cost of maintaining diplomatic posts and troops abroad, brokerages, specialist fees etc.

Capital items in the past were a very small and unimportant section of the balance of payments but this is no longer the case. Today, there are thousands of millions of pounds moved around seeking a secure investment with a high rate of interest. This is known as 'hot' money. As the term implies, it moves easily and quickly in response to economic conditions and can leave a country as quickly as it came in. Other capital items arise from loans made by the government to other countries — usually underdeveloped countries — and long term borrowing by large corporations or local authorities. The balance of trade plus the balance of 'invisibles' together make up the 'current account' section of the balance of payments as distinct from the capital account.

At the end of the year, when all the figures have been worked out and adjusted a balance is struck and if this shows a deficit the government has to borrow enough money from other financial bodies around the world to keep the account straight. Where a country has a balance in surplus, this may be placed in reserves or used to lend to other countries in deficit.

The problems arising from the balance of payments are a matter for the Government and the Treasury. They dictate the policy and the exporter and importer can only operate within the framework laid down. Basically, the only way to solve a balance of payments deficit is to increase our income and reduce our expenditure, that is, increase our exports of goods and services, and curtail our imports. Moreover, take whatever steps are necessary internally to bring that about, and encourage the inflow of money on capital account by maintaining economic stability and adjusting interest rates. Latterly the UK has tended to rely on a 'floating' pound to encourage exports.

The large sums of money which are today transferred around the world, as mentioned above, have upset the once orderly conduct of international trade and exchanges. This has led on the one hand to restrictive measures which have hindered trade development, and on the other resulted in the formation of various international organizations with a view to controlling these measures.

INTERNATIONAL ORGANIZATIONS

In 1944, a conference was held at Bretton Woods attended by representatives from the Governments of 44 countries, where plans were drawn up for the formation of the International Monetary Fund (IMF). Its purposes were as follows:

(1) To promote international monetary co-operation through a permanent institution which provides the machinery for consultation and collaboration on international monetary problems.

(2) To facilitate the expansion and balanced growth of interna-

tional trade and to contribute thereby to the promotion and maintenance of high levels of employment and real income and to the development of the productive resources of all members.

(3) To promote exchange stability and maintain orderly exchange arrangements among members and to avoid competitive exchange depreciation.

(4) To assist in the establishment of a multilateral system of payments in respect of current transactions between members and in the elimination of foreign exchange restrictions which hamper the growth of world trade.

(5) To give confidence to members by making the fund's resources temporarily available to them under adequate safeguards thus providing them with opportunity to correct maladjustments in their balance of payments without resorting to measures destructive of national or international prosperity.

At the Bretton Woods conference it was recognized that some system better than the gold standard and better than the flexible exchange rate method was necessary. The volume of world trade was out of line with the amount of gold to back it. On the other hand, freely fluctuating exchange rates made trade subject to sudden and unpredictable changes which ruined the profitability of enterprises. What was needed was a system of 'managed flexibility' and this led to the creation of the Fund. By an agreed date all members were to declare a par value of their currency and this agreed rate should be permitted to fluctuate by up to 1% on either side of the parity rate. Members in balance of payments difficulty and whose rate of exchange was, therefore, under pressure could apply to the Fund for permission to devalue the par figure, for example, the UK in 1949 and 1967. As members found it increasingly difficult to maintain their exchange rates within the prescribed limits these were widened to 2¼% either side of parity at the Smithsonian Agreement in 1971. In spite of this, the UK found the drain on the reserves in trying to maintain the sterling rate was too great, and in June 1972 the pound was allowed to float, that is, to fluctuate in the market in accordance with supply and demand. Many other countries followed the UK lead in 1973.

The Fund itself is a huge reserve of currency and gold collected on a quota basis from all the members. These resources are available to provide temporary assistance to countries in balance of payments difficulty, for example, the UK in 1976. One major change made by the IMF is the introduction in January 1970 of the special drawing rights. These are a new kind of reserve asset to increase the supply of international liquidity. The unit is a 'cocktail' of 16 currencies weighted according to the importance of the currency in international transactions. They are allocated to members who may change them for foreign currencies with permission from the IMF.

At the same time as the IMF, there was set up the International Bank for Reconstruction and Development (IBRD). Its original purpose was to assist the reconstruction and development of member territories by facilitating capital investment and encouraging less developed countries. It also promoted private foreign investment by guarantees or participation in loans and investments made by private investors. Now that the damage created by the war has largely been made good the main purposes of IBRD are as under:

(a) To facilitate the investment of capital for productive purposes.

(b) To promote private investment and to make loans when private capital is not available.

The IBRD has two offshoots: the International Finance Corporation (IFC) and the International Development Association (IDA). The IFC aims to encourage private enterprise in less developed countries without government guarantee, whereas the main purpose of IDA is to extend credits for longer periods, say up to 50 years, for priority projects in the less developed countries generally free of interest.

The IBRD together with its affiliates IFC and IDA has been able to operate more actively than the IMF. It had been responsible for the emergence of development projects for which finance could not otherwise have been found.

It is said that the potential of world output for the satisfaction of the wants of mankind is almost limitless, and it is rather a paradox that a growing appreciation of long-term world problems is developing side by side with an increasing spread of nationalism especially in the less developed countries. Wars and rumours of wars, industrial and political unrest, intense nationalism aiming at the self-sufficiency of the national economy, natural disasters such as floods, droughts and earthquakes, all militate against the ideal of complete freedom between communities for the exchange of goods and services and the movement of capital. Hindrances to trade imposed by governments take many forms. These include tariffs and export bounties, quotas and licences and currency restrictions. Following the discussions at Bretton Woods, a Conference was set up at Geneva in April 1947. It was attended by 23 nations and they drew up a General Agreement on Tariffs and Trade. This summarized the results of certain tariff negotiations arranged on a multilateral basis between members of the Conference and also laid down certain general rules covering other aspects of trade relations. A document was drawn up called the 'Charter of the International Trade Organization.' The Charter aimed at raising standards of living all round; at ensuring full employment; and at developing the full use of resources of the world by 'reciprocal and mutually advantageous arrangements directed to the substantial reduction of tariffs and other barriers to trade and the elimination of discriminatory treatment in international commerce'.

Subsequent amendments to the Charter caused the USA to withdraw and the proposed International Trade Organization became almost a dead letter. The General Agreement on Tariffs and Trade, however, continued and commanded more and more support. Its general rules may now be summarized as follows:

(1) Members undertake to concert together to achieve a mutual reduction of tariff barriers and preferences and the greatest possible development of mutual trade.

(2) The principle of 'general most-favoured nation treatment' is accepted and members undertake that any concessions granted to any one member country shall immediately and unconditionally be granted to all the others.

(3) Discrimination by means of tariffs against foreign products which compete with home products shall be avoided in future and any existing discrimination of this nature shall be reduced and eventually abolished as soon as possible.

(4) Quantitative controls shall also be abolished as quickly as circumstances permit, both externally and internally, and existing systems of import licensing shall be reduced to a minimum.

(5) Existing restrictions imposed by exchange controls shall be removed as quickly and as completely as may be practicable but only in regard to current trading transactions.

It will be seen that in general these rules follow the principles laid down at Bretton Woods for the IMF. Although several of these rules have been given practical application in the liberalization of trade, the objectives of GATT, in the present world conditions, must remain a counsel of perfection.

Another body with similar objectives is the Organization for Economic Co-operation and Development whose aims are as follows:

(1) To achieve the highest possible rate of economic growth and employment consistent with financial stability;

(2) to contribute to the sound economic expansion of member countries; and

(3) to encourage the expansion of world trade on a multilateral non-discriminatory basis.

MAJOR TRADING AREAS OF THE WORLD

There are in the world three main types of economy as follows:

(1) Free enterprise economies where there is a minimum of government control, and trade and industry are largely run by private enterprise. The best example of this is the USA, although many of the developing countries have this type of economy.

(2) Mixed economies where there are some State-run industries but many industries and most trading activities are in the hands of private firms. A good example of this type is the UK but to some extent all advanced nations and many developing nations have at least some State-run industry.

(3) Controlled economies where the complete economy is State-run, including all the trading activity except for tiny pockets of free enterprise such as the peasant who is permitted to grow a few vegetables and sell them for cash. This sort of economy is generally communist controlled and its international trade is carried on by state trading enterprises.

The manner in which international trade is conducted will vary according to which type of economy is involved. If we are trading with a free enterprise nation we may expect to meet many nationals of that country moving freely around the world, prepared to visit us to do business or to welcome us abroad. With a controlled economy we shall expect to do business only with accredited representatives of their state trading organization.

Since the end of the War, there has been a gradual change in the trading patterns between countries. The Western nations had in the past specialized in industrial products to exchange for the raw materials, and food they required whilst the primary producers relied upon their sales of natural produce to buy the industrial products they needed. Some countries with the right climate were able to combine industrial growth with the production of much of their food requirements.

The UK is probably the best example of a country which relied almost entirely on its manufactures to export in exchange for raw materials and food. The colonial system made this a very satisfactory arrangement for the UK but with the end of the Empire the newly-independent nations began to shop around both for buyers of their produce and suppliers of their industrial needs. At the same time they sought to diversify their economies and develop some industry.

The original basic pattern of geographical produce remains because the climate and existing raw materials, such as minerals, are still the same, that is, Western Europe and North America producing industrial goods; South America producing coffee and rubber (Brazil); wheat and beef (Argentine); minerals such as copper (Peru); Near East — rubber and tin; Australasia — wool and mutton; and Africa — timber, cocoa, vegetable oils etc. However, these divisions are no longer so sharply defined. Japan has entered the list of manufacturing countries in a big way; the Arab nations have developed their oil production; and countries of South America (especially Brazil), Africa, and the Near East have begun to establish industries. At the same time, the Western nations have sought to become more self-sufficient in food and to intensify the search for minerals at home, for example, the UK encouragement of agriculture and the search for oil, and the development of fruit and vegetable cultivation by those countries on the Mediterranean. Thus the interchange of goods between nation and nation grows and expands with increasing diversity and no longer follows the old clearly defined paths.

CHAPTER 2

The Export and Shipping Office

THE EXPORT OFFICE ROLE

Exporting today is a highly skilled and professional operation. To be successful in this field requires an adequate and effective organization designed to enlarge the company product market share overseas. Above all, the exporting results must be profitable and, accordingly, it is most desirable that the export personnel are of a high calibre, adequately qualified and rewarded, to attain this objective.

The size of the company, its products, and scale of export business will largely influence the form of export organization. Moreover, cognisance must be taken of company structure and organization, and how the export role can best be injected into it. In broad terms, the industrial company has three functions — production, finance and sales. Additionally, there are various other subsidiary activities which significantly contribute to the running of the company, which include personnel, administration, research/development, training, purchasing, etc.

If the company is rather small with only an element of export business, it is likely that an export manager with a secretary and a clerk would be adequate but, as the export trade grows, it will soon become necessary to have a properly structured export organization with qualified specialist staff designed to exploit the export trade potential. One can no longer rely on inexperienced unqualified personnel in the export field (whether it be marketing, sales, or shipping), as standards will tend to be low, overseas product reputation poor and the overall financial results probably very indifferent. Exporting is a highly professional activity which is increasing annually in terms of its overseas market competition.

The export department has two main functions: marketing and shipping. The former is responsible for sales, pricing enquiries, quotations, recording and checking orders, and other marketing functions such as promotion, research etc, whilst the latter is responsible for transportation/distribution and the relevant documents involved, packaging, costings for distribution etc. There must be at all times close liaison with the accounts department particularly on credit control, costings and financial documentation/information. Overall, the export department objective is to ensure that the export order processes smoothly from start to finish to obtain complete customer satisfaction and produce a modest profit to the company. Unless the profit motive is present throughout the export activities of the company, it will produce indifferent results with no disciplines/techniques. Hence, all the aspects of an export operation are interlinked with clearly defined functions and responsibilities of either a horizontal or a vertical export department organization with efficient and well trained specialist and professional staff.

THE EXPORT OFFICE ORGANIZATION AND STRUCTURE

The smallest export department may consist of an export manager, shipping clerk, typist and accounts clerk. At first, the department may be engaged merely in shipping orders secured by the sales organization, but as the export trade develops the department will enlarge and have its own sales organization, attend to their shipment and collect payment. Hence, it will become a self-contained department.

In such circumstances, the overall aim of the export department is to collect sufficient data to enable them to quote promptly and accurately a competititve CIF, or other delivery term price for any consignment to the important centres of the world. This involves an evaluation of the most suitable method of despatch and requires knowledge of rates, services, routes, terminal charges, insurance, packaging, documentation etc.

The department must study the needs of different markets, their trends and likely future developments together with possible methods of increasing overseas sales. This involves the scrutiny of overseas agents and branch reports and provision of adequate publicity of overseas journals/publications. Additionally, close liaison must be maintained with trade associations and relevant Government departments on overseas market development opportunities. Moreover, a continuing dialogue must be maintained with overseas representatives on all developments at home. This involves manufacturing and technical aspects of the commodity, distribution methods and future developments, that is, a new product range. Such an exchange of information is vital to the future well-being of the company and any reports indicating shortcomings in product, distribution, inadequate packing, faulty products etc. should be acted on quickly and remedial measures taken.

The export department not only has the task of obtaining and executing the export orders, but also of ensuring payment is received without undue delay in accord with the terms of sale as prescribed in the export contract. Enforcement of rights in foreign courts of law is often a troublesome business and tends to create a bad public image for the company. It is prudent to liaise closely with and/or use the export services provided by banks and the Export Credits Guarantee Department on financial matters.

In the larger export orientated company a greater degree of specialization is essential which usually involves the appointment of an export marketing manager, an export sales manager, and a shipping manager each with defined responsibilities. In the small to medium-sized firm an export manager is usually found dealing alone with all sections of his company's export business. In the larger firm, on the other hand, the work is split up between the three appointments in the following manner:

(1) The export marketing manager has overall executive control usually under a export marketing director. He controls and co-ordinates the activities of the other two functions, deals with policy, and usually represents the export department at internal sales conferences.

(2) An export sales manager is generally responsible to the export marketing manager and in a limited way is involved with sales inasmuch as he controls the agents and representatives and promotes actual sales to customers everywhere. His job is done when the export order is obtained and passed on to the export office for issuing to the factory or, in the case of a merchant, to the manufacturer. This involves the following stages:

(i) Receiving the enquiry, ascertaining its feasibility, ensuring that the price is calculated and preparing the quotation.

(ii) Ascertaining the despatch date by the specified mode of transport.

(iii) Obtaining sanction of credit controller and approval of quotation before it is sent to the customer.

(iv) Ensuring the quotation is sent to the customer and following it up, initiating investigations into orders presumed to be lost.

(v) Receiving the order from the customer and checking it against the quotation. Where the order is received without earlier quotation much of (i)-(iii) has to be done at this time.

(vi) Obtaining production controller's sanction, priority rating and credit controller's permission (if applicable).

(vii) Acknowledging the order and informing the local agent (if necessary), of the order.

(viii) Arranging for the preparation and issue of the works order.

(ix) Informing records or statistics department of the details of the order. This will permit the preparation of returns for ECGD (Export Credits Guarantee Department).

(x) Confirming date of despatch to clients, agents or distributors and notifying any unavoidable changes.

(xi) Progress chasing.

(xii) Handing over the order to the shipping department to arrange the delivery procedure.

Overall one can conclude by saying the export sales office function is to deal with enquiries and orders up to the point of despatch.

(3) The export shipping manager is informed of any orders booked usually by a copy order and later receives definite notice from works/manufacturer when the goods are nearing completion. This involves the following stages:

(i) Linking with export sales, checking that the order complies with import/export controls and establishing from letters of credit relevant details of items which have to be reconciled with the ultimate forwarding arrangements (See also Chapter 13).

(ii) Deciding on the method of transportation (if not already specified).

(iii) Issuing instructions for packing and marking (if not already given).

(iv) Chartering or booking shipping (or air etc.) space.

(v) Pre-entering at customs (if necessary).

(vi) Issuing instructions to works, transport office, and freight forwarders.

(vii) Drawing up all the necessary documents and later collecting, collating and cross-checking all documents after shipment.

1. Vertical organization

Export marketing manager
controlling departments dealing
with individual aspects as under:

a) Credit control
b) Order processing
c) Production/Assembly
d) Packing
e) Transportation and Insurance   } for ALL MARKETS
f) Invoicing
g) Documentation
h) Filing
i) Finance/Accounting/Costing

2. Horizontal organization

Export marketing manager
controlling sections, each dealing
with all aspects for one market,
as under:

Group market 1	Group market 2	Group market 3	Group market 4	Group market 5	Group market 6
USA Canada	EEC EFTA	Africa	Middle East	Comecon	South America

I   Organization of export and shipping office

(viii) Passing documents to accounts dept. for collection of payment.

Overall, the export shipping function normally commences when the works order is issued and takes over fully when the goods ordered have been produced and are ready for despatch. It is a section where a sense of urgency is essential. He is responsible for obtaining shipping or air freight space, arranging despatch, documentation, insurance, possibly packing and customs clearance etc.

The export salesman involved in direct selling overseas in the field has a very demanding job requiring many aptitudes. He must be multilingual, ideally have good product knowledge, with good managerial potential and knowledge of export practice. Moreover, the person must be tenacious, with good judgement and sufficiently diplomatic to secure a most favourable export sales contract.

It cannot be stressed too strongly that the ultimate organization structure will depend on the size of the company and the nature/volume of export business. Likewise, the precise relationship and division of responsibilities between the foregoing three functions will vary from firm to firm.

Basically, there are two main forms of shipping office organization structure: the vertical and horizontal as detailed in DIAGRAM I.

The vertical type streamlines the documentation activities and thereby assists simplified documentation. Personnel are selected on the basis of their expertise, that is, transportation, insurance, packing etc. and, in total, efficiency in all the stages through which the export order must be processed are high. Hence the overall knowledge of export technique becomes limited to a specific area of activity, with the result that there can be a tendency for personnel to become disinterested in the total operation and frustration can set in.

The horizontal structure, however, produces total involvement and expertise in a group of markets and thus identification with the progress of the markets. The personnel will probably handle several aspects of the subgroups' activity thus avoiding boredom. Overall this type of system could produce unnecessary rivalry and overlap. See DIAGRAM I.

Basically there are three types of sales office as detailed below and in DIAGRAM II:

(1) Product orientated. This type tends to be warranted where the

(a) *Product orientated*

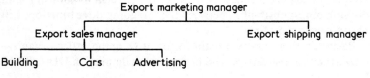

```
                        Export marketing manager
          ┌──────────────────┴──────────────────────┐
     Export sales manager                    Export shipping manager
   ┌─────────┼──────────────┐
Product group X  Product group Y  Advertising
```

(b) *Customer orientated*

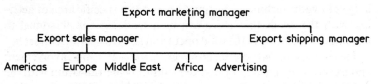

```
                        Export marketing manager
          ┌──────────────────┴──────────────────────┐
     Export sales manager                    Export shipping manager
   ┌─────────┼──────────────┐
Building        Cars        Advertising
```

(c) *Market group*

```
                        Export marketing manager
          ┌──────────────────┴──────────────────────┐
     Export sales manager                    Export shipping manager
   ┌──────┬──────┬──────────┬──────┬──────────┐
Americas  Europe  Middle East  Africa  Advertising
```

II Sales office organization

products are technically complex, or the number of products in the range is vast, or where the products are completely unrelated. It is ideal for the company who feel that product knowledge is paramount in the interest of giving a good customer service. For example, it is suitable for a company selling overseas medical equipment, cycles, bathroom fittings etc. Conversely, it can inflate cost as various representatives will call on the same customer which could cause customer irritation.

(2) Customer orientated. Under this system each representative specializes in a class of customer thereby gaining expert knowledge of the industry concerned, its technology, and decision patterns etc. Thus the salesman will get to know the specific customer needs and will be able to satisfy them more efficiently. Conversely, it does encourage duplication of journeys with increased cost of the export product when more than one representative visits the same area to see different types of companies. It tends to be used by the larger companies.

(3) Market group of area based organization. This involves allocating the salesman to a specific world area to service — as found in the horizontal system in the shipping office. It results in a clear definition of responsibility and interest in that area which will tend to lead to the cultivation of local business and personal ties. Travelling expenses will be kept to a reasonable level. This system works satisfactorily when the area is not too large, where the products and customers are homogeneous, but once the situation occurs where the company's products become diversified so that the representative is physically incapable of learning everything about the products, then this method becomes less effective.

For the export department to function efficiently, close co-operation with other sections of the business is imperative. The export manager should have powers to ensure prompt delivery of his orders from the factory, and compliance with instructions as regards packing and despatch. Moreover, he should be able to secure exactly the right type of goods. The dangers from lack of co-operation between all departments arise when the factory is asked to expedite urgent orders for both the home and export markets. An understanding between the department heads will obviate lack of attention to overseas needs in this respect.

For the whole business to work satisfactorily, someone must make it his business to co-ordinate the work of all departments and to adjust differences that may arise. If the export department complains that it is not being well served by the traffic department, the matter is best settled by a conference between the heads of both departments, supervised by a senior official of the business. The traffic manager is usually able to advise the export department as to the quantities most convenient for packing and transportation units. In an increasingly competitive overseas market, the need to ensure delivery dates are maintained is paramount otherwise orders will be lost and goodwill impaired.

EXPORT POLICY AND RECORDS

The proportion of a manufacturer's output to be exported is, nowadays, very often influenced by national policy, particularly by means of incentives. The chief concern of a company will be to combine stability with the highest financial return obtainable. In many industries this is achieved by a balance/mixture between home and overseas markets, but much depends on the product. This is important where:

(1) Exports may rely on the continued existence of one or two foreign markets, which may be cut off by changes in import licensing laws etc. of the countries concerned.

(2) Demand abroad may be seasonal for goods which require a constant market to make them pay.

(3) Overseas enthusiasm for a product may depend on the fact that it is in use in Britain.

Some businesses virtually exist solely for export with no significant home market. In such a situation, it is prudent where possible to have the export markets broadly based extending to several countries thereby lessening the impact of any change of export demand in any one of the countries.

Export marketing research is an important function and involves a fact-finding enquiry on which the marketing policy is based. It is more fully dealt with in Chapter 15, but it is appropriate to deal with its salient features within the context of the export department. Basically the functions are fourfold as detailed below:

(1) Statistical. This involves the determination of the total existing market insofar as the quantity brought, the price range and their loca-

tions. Additionally, it should indicate, where relevant, a comparison with the company's own sales in the area, and whether the total market is expanding or otherwise.

(2) Economic. This involves evaluation of the product market potential and its acceptable market price bearing in mind competition.

(3) Social. This indicates the public attitude towards the products and their adequacy in terms of design/durability/etc.

(4) Psychological. This involves what motivates the consumer to buy the product; an evaluation of measures which could be devised to further its market growth, and in what ways it is adversely influenced by competition/substitutes.

The results of research in the export market can be correlated with parallel activities on the home market so that an overall marketing policy may be formulated. However, the divergence of treatment called for by home and overseas markets makes a fusion of the export department with the home marketing organization under a general marketing manager most unwise.

With regard to accounting, there is no fundamental difference between the accounting methods adopted in an export company and those in any other concern. In a manufacturing or wholesaling business which maintains an export department certain accounts will be subdivided with the export department having separate sales, cash etc. returns.

A trading firm engaged solely in export business does so either (a) as an export merchant on its own account exporting its own goods to buyers overseas; (b) as commission agent for foreign importers; or (c) as export agent undertaking the export business of manufacturers in a variety of industries. Freight forwarders do not engage in the trade of goods, but undertake the transportation arrangements including sometimes a packaging service.

In the case of a manufacturer, it is usual for the export department to keep separate accounts. Hence, when an order is received from an overseas buyer, the goods will be subsequently invoiced giving details of the sale price. Where appropriate, further records will be maintained of other charges as insurance, freight, packaging etc. The usual method of charging export orders is to use serially numbered invoice sets. These give instructions to finished stores department, and advising and charging the customer. An alternative method is to issue warehouse instructions and process it through the various offices. The former is the most modern and is often computerized.

If the exporter does not manufacture his own products, he either buys the goods for export on his own account or exports on behalf of a manufacturer. An exporter on his own account may concentrate solely on the overseas trade or he may be a general wholesaler maintaining an export department. In the latter case, the accountancy of the export department will be similar to those in a manufacturing concern, the sole difference being that instead of producing merchandise for home and overseas markets, the business merely purchases the goods bulking or breaking bulk as the case may be. The organization of the export department is thus much the same in either type of concern.

There is no doubt today that the export and shipping office structure should be well thought out and adequate to exploit the company products overseas. It should be able to successfully market and develop the export market profitably, particularly in terms of identifying/processing/executing the export order. Moreover, close liaison should be maintained with all the various organizations, particularly Trade Associations and Government departments viz. British Overseas Trade Board, available to facilitate overseas market development. These additionally include the identity of new markets and opportunity to exhibit at overseas trade fairs/exhibitions.

Today, more and more small UK companies are getting into the export business. Usually it involves the appointment of an export manager with a small staff. Transportation arrangements are usually undertaken by the freight forwarder leaving the export management department to concentrate on sales, pricing enquiries/quotations, receiving and checking orders, together with other marketing functions. As the business prospers, the export department expands and the shipping office emerges. In some cases, the exporter actually provides his own transport to undertake the distribution task. This applies particularly within Europe.

Finally, the exporter must strive to attain high standards at all times. This applies not only to adequately qualified personnel, but also in the general marketing and shipping processes employed.

CHAPTER 3

Characteristics of International Transport Modes

The role and essentials of a transport system. Canals/inland waterways. International air transport. International road transport. International rail transport.

THE ROLE AND ESSENTIALS OF A TRANSPORT SYSTEM

Transport is an essential facility for the exploitation or development of economic resources on a national or international scale. It allows articles or materials to be conveyed from areas of low utility to areas of high utility.

Overall its provision arises for economic, social or political reasons. The presence of a steel works in South Wales is due to the local availability of coal and labour, and to reliable low cost sea transport which allows the import of iron ore through Port Talbot. Ore is mined in South Australia where it has little local value and is shipped to an area of steel production, such as, South Wales. Similarly, rail and sea transport enables Canadian wheat growers to ship substantial quantities of grain from the production areas (the prairies) to processing and consuming areas such as the UK or India. Likewise, reliable low cost transport services enable Japanese produced cars to be sold at competitive prices in the UK. The existence of an international air network facilitates tourism and business developments, so fostering world trade.

In a society where transport costs are relatively high, the need for a balanced social policy is paramount, otherwise isolated communities may cease to exist.

The political influence on transport is often considerable to the extent that many large transport operators are State owned. Moreover, such policies extend to the provision of uneconomical services for political reasons, such as an international air service retained for reasons of national prestige in the face of competition from other national airlines. Another example of the political influence on transport is flag discrimination practised in shipping whereby countries insist on certain imported cargoes being moved in ships of their own flag so sustaining their fleet.

An evaluation of the foregoing reveals that transport permits the development of economic resources to the full. It makes possible specialization in economic development whether it be mining, car manufacturing or farming. Without a low cost reliable and well managed transport system, goods or services would not be exchanged to the serious detriment of living standards worldwide.

Transport is a product which is consumed immediately it is produced. Hence it cannot be stored. Its intensive economic deployment is, therefore, paramount to help ensure its viability.

The essentials of a transport system embraces three elements: the way, the vehicle including motive power unit, and the terminal. The way may be, naturally occuring such as, the seas or river, or artificially made by man, such as, the railway, canal, or motorway. One can have a combination of these two circumstances embracing the inland waterway system where new canals have been built into an established river or lake network such as the St. Lawrence Seaway thereby offering a through inland waterway network. The way may be for general public use administered in user terms by the State as, for example, the vehicle registration licencing system in the UK and most other countries. Alternatively, the exclusive use system is found in the railway network. The latter has the distinct advantage of operating under a disciplined timetable to obtain maximum use of the network but conversely, unlike the road operator, is responsible for financing all the initial, maintenance and replacement cost of the railway system. Moreover, the railway company provides a policing system through a signalling complex, but the road user relies on traffic control which is financed by the State.

The transport unit may be either of the integral type embracing the carrying and motive power unit such as the aircraft or ship, or have an independent motive power unit such as the railway locomotive and carrying unit found in the road trailer and barge. A further refinement exists whereby the integral or separate motive power unit either carries its own energy fuel such as a car, ship and aircraft or relies on remotely-situated generated energy such as electric rail traction. The advantage of separate carrying and motive power unit is their independence and flexibility in operation. Moreover, whilst the carrying unit contents are being transhipped, the motive power unit can be operational elsewhere. A further factor is that the failure of the motive power unit does not immobilize the carrying unit, as one merely obtains a standby unit.

The terminal must be artificially made by man, and be well designed to ensure the most efficient operation/utilization of the transport unit using it. This is particularly important today when more and more emphasis is on more intensive unit operation. Basically, the terminal is the link in the transport chain and merges at an interchange point one or more forms of transport to offer the through transit such as airport, sea port. It must have adequate area for expansion and good layout to permit an unimpeded flow of traffic passing through it.

To conclude, the essentials of a transport system are the way, the vehicle, its motive power and the terminal. All must be so designed as to produce an efficient system, preferably capital intensive with a low labour content to encourage low tariffs and thereby facilitate traffic development to contribute to economic expansion and social development.

A study of the individual forms of transport now follows.

CANALS/INLAND WATERWAYS

The canal network in the UK extends to only 2000 route miles compared with 200 000 route miles of roads, some 1200 miles of motorway and 11 000 route miles of railway. Consequently, the UK canal network makes little impact on the International Trade scene particularly since the era of lighterage serving 'tween deck tonnage has ceased in many ports, such as London, following the development of deep-sea container services, and Ro/Ro services UK/Europe — Asia. The development of LASH may have a very marginal effect in stimulating the UK canal system facilities, but it is more likely to have a greater impact in the Continental canal network and similar modern canal systems where favourable market situations prevail.

In regard to the Continental canal network, we must bear in mind it is very modern and extensive serving most major ports. It forms a major transport distributor in Europe involving transits of considerable distances and covering a wide range of cargoes embracing general merchandise, bulk commodities and dangerous classified products such as oil. Moreover, barges of up to 3000 tons are found on it and, in many of the near Continental counties, that is, Belgium,

France, Holland etc, approximately 10% of merchandise is moved by canal compared with ½% in the UK. Hence it plays an important role in the distribution of international consignments and as such is often a very competitive method of transit.

The UK canal system was developed during the period 1760-1830 and the present network is based on this, albeit on a smaller scale, as some 2000 route miles of canal have become derelict or closed, with a similar mileage today open and operational. The only major canal developed since this period in the UK was the building of the Manchester Ship Canal. A significant feature of the network is what is called 'the cross' which, with Birmingham as the centre, links by canal London, Bristol, Humberside and Liverpool.

The UK canal system, in comparison with the Continental network, is very antiquated and no extensive modernization has taken place for many years. Undoubtedly a major reason for this is the competitive vulnerability of the network to road or rail — particularly the former. This applies not only to overall rates, but also transit time. A significant factor overall is the time consuming and expensive process of transshipment both at the port and alongside the canal situated destination warehouse. Moreover, few traders have warehouses situated on the canal network which again discourages use of the system. A further aspect is that the average transit in UK is 60-70 miles compared with up to 1000 miles or more in France.

Features of the UK canal network are as follows:

(1) It is narrow in many parts which in turn restricts the average lighter to some 60-70 tons capacity compared with up to 3000 tons on the Continent.

(2) Basically the transits are slow particularly compared with road transport offering a door to door transit. A significant factor is the narrow canal and manual lock system in many parts.

(3) Containerization has eliminated the need for lighterage.

(4) The network from an environmental standpoint is virtually noiseless, and non-polluting.

(5) The canal is ideal for movement of dangerous cargoes and indivisible loads such as those which cannot be broken down into separate segments to form a composite consignment.

(6) As much of the canal network is narrow, it inhibits the development of the higher capacity lighter which is more economical to operate and thereby aids competitive rate quotation. Meanwhile,

on the Continent, the average lighterage capacity continues to rise whilst in the UK the road transport unit is getting larger and faster with better utilization.

(7) The network is ideal for bulk cargoes such as oil, coal, timber etc.

(8) Coasters use the canal network involving vessels of up to 1000 gross and of limited draught. An increasing number of similar sized vessels plying from the continental inland waterway system use the UK canal network — primarily the more modern elements of it, particularly Humberside area, Sharpness Dock, etc.

(9) Few companies in the UK have their warehouse on the canal system thereby relying on road/rail for feeder/distribution service which in turn inflates cost and transit time.

The State-owned British Waterway Board who control much of the UK canal network continue to make strenuous effort to generate new international business to the system.

INTERNATIONAL AIR TRANSPORT

Air transport is one of the youngest forms of transport and undoubtedly continues to make a major contribution to the exploitation of world resources. The bulk of international passenger travel today moves by air and an increasing volume of air freight. At the moment, the latter constitutes 1% in volume and about 20-30% in value terms of total world trade.

The development of civil aviation was particularly fostered during the Second World War (1939-45) which aided very considerably the advancement of this mode of transport in technical terms. Initially, the passenger sector was developed, but from the mid 1950s air freight began to grow rapidly annually until 1973 when the escalation in fuel cost occurred. Air freight rates were increased to offset the additional operators cost and, coupled with the·subsequent minor world trade recession, the annual growth rate of some airlines almost diminished. Nevertheless, by 1978 the market was beginning to expand again — quite dramatically with some airlines — and coupled with a differing rates system, this trend should continue.

Advantages
(1) High speed and quick transits.

(2) Low risk of damage/pilferage with very competitive insurance rates.

(3) Simplified documentation system — one document: an air way-bill for throughout air freight transit interchangeable between IATA accredited airlines. The IATA air waybill is, therefore, acceptable on any IATA airline thereby permitting flexibility of through routing with no transhipment documentation problems at *en route* airports.

(4) Common code of liability conditions to all IATA accredited airlines.

(5) Virtually eliminates much packing cost. This is an important cost saving attributed to air freight and the shipper may find it worthwhile to engage professional packaging services to ensure the merchandise is having the correct packing specification for this mode of transport. Significant packaging cost savings can be realized to offset the higher air freight rate compared with surface transport.

(6) Ideal for palletized consignments. An increasing volume of merchandise is now moving on pallets which aids handling, reduces packing needs, facilitates stowage and lessens risk of damage/pilferage. Again for the shipper new to the export business, it may prove worthwhile to establish whether it would be advantageous to have the merchandise palletized.

(7) Quick transits reduces amount of capital tied up in transit. This facilitates prompt financial settlement of individual consignments thereby aiding the exporters cash flow situation. On this point much depends, of course, on the export sale contract terms of delivery.

(8) Quick reliable transits eliminates need for extensive warehouse storage accommodation provided by the importer; reduces risk of stock piling, that is, obsolescence, deterioration, and capital cost tied up in warehouse/stock provision. Moreover, it enables the importer to replenish quickly his stock, such as when demand for a commodity has become exhausted quicker than forecast.

(9) Ideal for a wide variety of consumer type cargoes, particularly consignments up to 1500-2000 kg. Moreover, the average consignment is increasing as larger air freighters are introduced.

(10) The existing very extensive air freight international network continues to expand which aids its development and increases its share of the international trade market. This in turn encourages new markets to the air freight sector thereby aiding international trade development. For example, in some large countries major car manu-

facturers guarantee a replacement spares service through the medium of air freight which in itself has a status symbol and thereby aids the exporter sales. Likewise air freight services generate new markets to the exporter such as day-old chicks being transported 3000 miles which obviously would not be possible or practicable by sea transport.

(11) Parity obtains on rates on IATA scheduled international services and competition exist only on service quality. This in the long term benefits the shipper as no rate wars arise to the detriment of the service and trade.

(12) Services are reliable and to a high quality.

Disadvantages

(1) Limited capacity of air freighter and overall dimensions of acceptable cargo together with weight restrictions.

(2) Very high operating expenses and initial cost of aircraft when related to overall capacity — average capacity 20 000-25 000 kg. It is for the latter reason that many air freighters are converted passenger aircraft. Moreover, some 45% of air freight is conveyed on passenger scheduled services to counter for the unsold/unoccupied passenger seats.

(3) Service is vulnerable to disruption when fog prevails, particularly in airports with less modern traffic control equipment.

(4) Consignments, until recently, tended not to be consolidated; consequently, most consignments were individually processed viz. handling/customs etc. which can be expensive to the shipper. Nowadays, an increasing volume of air freight is moving under consolidation and chartered arrangements. This will further aid development of the air freight market. Moreover, IATA specified containerized shipments are increasing. Again, the shipper new to the international market is advised to contact his freight forwarder to establish whether consolidation arrangements are available.

(5) Air freight relies in the main on road primarily as feeder/distributor services. Moreover, airports are sparsely located and not all have Customs clearance facilities as they only serve domestic flights. Additionally, not all airports are situated close to industrial areas. These factors tend to slightly inhibit air freight development and increase transit costs.

It must be recognized that an increasing volume of cargo is now conveyed on air freight charter flights and this latter market is tending to expand quite rapidly. Air freight is an expanding market and the trend to developing larger capacity air freighters will continue to meet such demand and facilitate optimum performance/operation. It is particularly ideal to the small exporter and this form of international distribution should be continuously borne in mind by the discerning shipper.

INTERNATIONAL ROAD TRANSPORT

The road vehicle is a low capacity but very versatile unit of transport which is most flexible in its operation. Since the early 1970s, the international road haulier has become increasingly dominant in the UK/Continental trade with some services extending to Asia and Middle East. It has the following features:

(1) One of its most significant advantages is the road vehicle distributive ability. Overall it can, therefore, offer a door to door service without intermediate handling.

(2) No Customs examination arises in transit countries provided the haulier is affilitated to TIR as the cargo passes under bond and the unit is passing through one of their countries. Insofar as transit countries within EEC are concerned, no Customs examination arises provided the appropriate community transit documentation is completed.

(3) It is very flexible in operation which is particularly useful when circumstances demand a change in routing through road works/blockage or disrupted shipping services.

(4) It is very competitive within certain distance bands compared with air freight and train ferry, both in terms of transit times and rates.

(5) Documentation is simple as under CMR a through consignment note is operative with a common code of liability conditions.

(6) The service tends to be reliable and to a high standard. Delays usually only occur when bad weather prevails or for some other exceptional circumstance.

(7) The TIR vehicle may be of 12 or 15 m length with an overall capacity of 40 tonnes. Hence, initial cost is low when related to an air freighter. Moreover, limited capacity imposes certain weight and dimensional restrictions on the traffic which can be carried.

(8) It is ideal for general merchandise and selective cargo in bulk in small quantities conveyed in a specialized road vehicle. The service is renowned for its groupage flow under a freight forwarders sponsorship and, therefore, ideal for the small exporter. An increasing number of shippers are now using their own vehicles to distribute their own goods.

(9) Packing costs are less when compared with conventional shipping ('tween deck tonnage) services.

(10) The driver accompanies the vehicle throughout the road transit thereby exercising personal supervision and reducing risk of damage and pilfering. Accordingly, the operator can control his vehicle at all times as the driver usually 'reports in' to his company control office at staged points *en route*.

During the past ten years, roll on/roll off traffic between the UK/Continent has developed very substantially under CMR/TIR conditions conveyed on vehicular ferries. The freight forwarder has featured greatly in this development offering groupage services to many countries under scheduled services usually working in correspondent with a Continental based freight forwarder. Such services have developed much faster than originally envisaged and in some cases to the detriment of the air freight, container and train ferry services in the UK/Continental trade. In some countries, the environmental lobby has slowed down the roll on/roll off (Ro/Ro) expansion and some Continental countries restrict the times/periods/routes over which such traffic may be conveyed. Moreover, vehicle permits are difficult to obtain in some countries for such operations as they are usually restricted. A problem to the road operator is to obtain balanced working, that is, a full profitable load in each direction.

The Ro/Ro operation is ideal for the small exporter and is worthy of enquiry to a freight forwarder for a particular stream of international consumer type traffic insofar as rates/transit time/routing/schedules etc. are concerned.

INTERNATIONAL RAIL TRANSPORT

In the UK, the railways developed in the 1850s in an era of steam traction. Today they are a formidable transport system exploiting the economic features of a high capacity disciplined transport network using an exclusive way.

The modern railway system is a high capacity form of transport operating on a disciplined, controlled, reliable, exclusive artificial way. It is capable of attaining relatively high speeds and is most economical under the complete train load concept as distinct from the individual wagon load involving frequent marshalling. In the UK, the freight railway system falls under the following classification for export traffic:

(1) The development of the block train load system has been significant in the past ten years, many of them from private sidings/terminals of custom-built requirements, with the wagons privately owned as distinct from British Rail ownership. For example, such block train load movement includes cars, ore, oil, timber, coal etc. to/from the ports.

(2) The freightliner concept is based on the carriage of high capacity containers on high speed custom built wagons. These operate in UK in fixed formation trains to provide fast and reliable services. The majority of the containers carried are to ISO specification which aim to make possible the most efficient combination of rail/road/sea transport.

Today, the freightliner network consists of 37 terminals of which seven are situated at ports to meet the increasing ISO container market need.

The principles of the freightliner system are that the trains are run in fixed formation between terminals to a prescribed timetable in the same way as a passenger train. The wagons are tailor-made to carry only containers. The transfer from road to rail (or ship) is carried out at specially built terminals and it is smooth, safe and fast. The method of transfer is by means of 'portal' type cranes, which can operate over the whole length of specially laid rail sidings.

In addition to its activities within Great Britain, freightliners offer services to Ireland and Europe thereby providing through container services. Moreover, it serves all the major UK ports operating deep-sea services and thereby conveys a very large volume of maritime ISO containers for shipping lines operating from these ports, that is, OCL, ACT, Dart Line, etc. Freightliners also have a container base direct distribution facility which eliminates intermediate warehousing.

Features of the freightliner system are detailed below:

(a) High speed regular reliable rail container distribution network serving some 37 terminals operating throughout UK. A reservation system exists to ensure space is available on trains available on a pre-booking system.

(b) Simplified documentation system.

(c) Door to door service with the rail and ship undertaking the trunk movement and the road the distribution role.

(d) Low risk of damage and pilferage.

(e) No intermediate handling and with ISO containers engaged on international transits. They travel in bond usually under TIR arrangements. Moreover, the containers to and from the major ports frequently travel under bond to the ICD.

Undoubtedly during the next decade the freightliners will become more dominant particularly with the maritime ISO container distribution.

(3) A number of train ferry wagons have been built specially for use both on the Continental and UK rail networks. This permits through transits to be undertaken between UK and the Continent with no intermediate handling at the ports as the wagons are merely shunted on or off the train ferry vessel. Services operate between Dover/Dunkirk and Harwich/Zeebrugge.

Overall there are some three hundred train ferry terminals in the UK and the most important ones include Stratford-London (LIFT), Manchester (MIFT), Birmingham, Glasgow (GIFT), and Paddock Wood.

Features of the train ferry system are as follows:

(1) A simplified documentation system involving the CIM consignment offering a common code of liability for the throughout consignment.

(2) No intermediate handling at the ports or in the transit countries as the consignment is under customs bond throughout.

(3) Ideal for a wide range of consumer products and some bulk cargoes conveyed in purpose built wagons such as chemicals. The exporter may have exclusive use of a wagon or patronize a groupage service sponsored by the freight forwarder.

The latter service is very popular with the small exporter and very prominent at LIFT.

(4) Reliable service and very competitive — both in rates and transit times — within certain distance bands. This is particularly so

when it is siding to siding traffic, thereby offering a door to door service.

(5) The train ferry wagons form a common pool wagon fleet which lessens the problem of obtaining balanced working involving a loaded wagon in each direction of the transit.

(6) Packing cost are low and insurance rates are competitive reflecting the low risk of damage/pilferage.

(7) Customs clearance may be undertaken at the port in UK or at one of the inland clearance depots.

The train ferry wagon in recent years, following escalation in international road transport cost plus more stringest regulations regarding their operation, has tended to increase their market share. Indeed, some large industrial companies have built their own wagons to convey their products on the service. The freight forwarder features very much in the train ferry business both in UK and on the Continent. This applies not only to groupage services, but also the full wagon load traffic on behalf of the shipper.

CHAPTER 4

Characteristics of International Transport Modes (continued)

Containerization. Container bases. Inland clearance depots. Sea transport. Pipelines. Palletization.

CONTAINERIZATION

Containerization is a method of distributing merchandise in a unitized form thereby permitting an inter-modal transport system to be evolved providing a possible combination of rail, road, canal and maritime transport. The system is long established and was in being at the turn of the century in a somewhat modified form to that which exists today. It became particularly evident in the North American coastal trade in the 1930s when the vessels were called 'Van ships'. Today, we are in the process of seeing a third generation of container ships being evolved as the benefits of containerization become more attractive in a large number of countries, thereby aiding rising living standards and facilitating trade expansion.

In more recent years, IATA has encouraged the introduction of containers to facilitate air freight distribution and in so doing have permitted airline operators to offer concessionary rates. Regretfully, for a variety of reasons, they have not proved exceptionally popular, but with the development of more consolidation of air freight this may encourage their use.

Undoubtedly, long term containerization will be virtually the only method of general merchandise distribution in major deep-sea trades, and already some 75% of such trades are containerized.

These developments have brought a new era in international trade distribution both to the small and large exporter. In fact, in some trades, the shipper actually owns the container as distinct from the container operator or freight forwarder. The exporter may use a complete ISO container or despatch his merchandise to a container base/ICD for it to be consolidated with other compatible cargo to a similar destination country or area for despatch as a full container load. In the case of IATA containers, these are usually consolidated at the air freight terminal. It is uncommon for the ISO container to be conveyed by air freighter.

Features of containerization can conveniently be summarized as follows:

(1) It permits a door to door service which, with the ISO or IATA container, may be from the factory production site to the retail distributors store — an overall distance of some 6000 km.

It must be appreciated that many airline operators today convey cargo on the air freighter under the unit load device (ULD). This permits concessionary rates being given to shippers.

(2) No intermediate handling at terminal transhipment points viz. the sea port or airport.

(3) Low risk of cargo damage and pilferage enables more favourable cargo premiums to be obtained compared with conventional cargo shipments such as 'tween deck tonnage and individual airfreight consignments.

(4) The absence *en route* of intermediate handling plus quicker sea transits compared with 'tween deck tonnage permits less risk of damage and pilferage. This also applies to IATA containers.

(5) Elimination of intermediate handling at maritime terminal transfer points, that is, seaports, enables substantial dock labour savings to be realized. In industrial countries, where there is a high income per head, this can realize considerable financial savings.

(6) Less packing needs for containerized consignments. In some cases, particularly with specialized ISO containers such as, refrigerated ones or, tanks (liquid or powder), no packing is required. This produces substantial cost savings of the international transit and raises service quality.

(7) The elimination of intermediate handling coupled with the other inherent advantages of containerized shipments tends to permit the cargo to arrive in a better condition thereby aiding quality of service.

(8) Emerging from the inherent advantages of containerization, rates are likely to remain more competitive. A significant reason is that containerization is, in the main, a capital intensive transport network, compared with the individual consignment distribution system which tends to be more labour intensive. This is particularly so with maritime container distribution which has produced substantial labour cost savings.

(9) Maritime container transits are much quicker compared with

conventional ('tween deck) tonnage. This is usually achieved through a combination of circumstances, viz. faster vessels/rationalization of ports of call/substantially quicker transhipments. For example, on the UK/Australia service the schedule has been reduced by half to less than four weeks.

(10) Emerging from faster transits and the advantages under items (7) and (8), it encourages trade development and permits quicker payment of export invoices.

(11) Maritime containerization has permitted maritime fleet rationalization producing substantial capital cost replacement savings as fewer ships are needed. However, these ships must be more intensely operated and of overall larger capacity. On average, one container ship — usually of much increased capacity/faster speed — has displaced up to six 'tween deck vessels on deep sea services. This development has been facilitated by the rationalization of ports of call.

(12) Container vessels attain much improved utilization and generally are very much more productive than the 'tween deck tonnage.

(13) Faster transits usually coupled with more reliable maritime schedules, and ultimately increased service frequency is tending to encourage many importers in selective shipping trades to hold reduced stocks/spares. This produces savings in warehouse accommodation needs, lessens risks of obsolescent stock and reduces importers working capital. These are good selling points to bear in mind by the shipper when deciding on the mode of transport to be used.

(14) Containerization produces quicker transits and encourages rationalization of ports of call. This in many trades is tending to stimulate trade expansion through much improved service standards. This is resulting in increased service frequency which will aid trade development.

(15) Provision of through documentation (consignment note) viz. air waybill or bill of lading.

(16) Provision of a through rate. For example, this embraces both the maritime and surface transport cost of the ISO container. Again, this aids marketing the container concept.

(17) More reliable transits — particularly disciplined controlled transit arrangements in maritime schedules. Most major container ship operators have computer equipment to facilitate the booking

and control of containers.

(18) New markets have emerged through container development and its inherent advantages.

(19) Maritime containerization is a capital intensive project and as such is beyond the financial limit of many shipowners.

(20) Not all merchandise can be conveniently containerized. The percentage of such traffic falls annually as new types of maritime containers are introduced.

(21) Maritime containerization has greatly facilitated the development of consolidated or break bulk consignments. This particularly favours the small exporter unable to originate a full container load which is consolidated through a container base.

Overall, there is no doubt the foregoing features of containerization confirm it has much to offer to the shipper as an international trade distributor.

It would be appropriate to examine the size and types of both ISO and IATA containers which now follows.

The range of ISO container types tends to expand annually to meet the increasing market demands on this fast growing primarily deep-sea international method of distributing merchandise. Basically, the majority of containers used are built to ISO (International Standards Organization) specification thereby permitting their ease of ubiquitous use on an international scale. Many of the containers are built to a standard outlined by one of the major ship classification societies, such as, Lloyds Register of Shipping. The basic container most commonly built of steel or aluminium modual size is 2.45 m (8 ft) x 2.45 m (8 ft) but there exist some of 2.45 m (8 ft) x 2.60 m (8 ft 6 in) which tend to be applicable to the North American Trade. Their length is 3.05 m (10 ft), 6.10 m (20 ft), 9.15 m (30 ft), 10.70 m (35 ft), or 12.20 m (40 ft). The 3.05 m (10 ft) and 10.70 m (35 ft) are not very common and the former is usually found in the short sea trades. The most popular size is the 6.10 m (20 ft) or 12.20 m (40 ft) length with a modular of either 2.45 m (8ft) x 2.60 m (8 ft 6 in) or 2.45 m (8ft) x 2.45 m (8 ft). More recently, containers of a modular of 2.45 m (8 ft) x 2.75 m (9 ft) have emerged but their use is limited due to the extra height clearance, particularly by rail. The 6.10 m (20 ft) and 12.20 m (40 ft) length containers with a modular of 2.45 m (8 ft) x 2.45 m (8 ft) have a cubic metre capacity of 30 and 66.5 and a maximum load weight of 18 000 kg and 27 070 kg respectively. Similar respective details relative to the 2.45 m (8 ft) x 2.60 m (8 ft 6 in) module are in cubic metre capacity terms 31 and 68.1, with a maximum load capacity of 18 720 kg and 27 580 kg. In some countries, the 12.20 m (40 ft) container cannot be used to the full capacity due to road weight restrictions.

Cargo is usually stowed in air freighter under a unit load device (ULD). This may involve a pallet, container or igloo. Usually the container or igloo is accommodated in a pallet which is stowed in the aircraft. A pallet container stowed on the main deck of a 747 Freighter would be 2.45 m (8 ft) x 2.45 m (8 ft) x 3.05 m (10 ft) with a maximum gross weight of 6800 kg and usuable internal volume of 17.2 m³ (609 ft³). Numerous types of ISO containers exist and these are detailed in DIAGRAM III. It must be appreciated usually such containers are to ISO IATA specification and accommodate usually consolidated consignments as distinct from a full container load consignment.

Details of the main ISO container types are given below:

(1) Covered (dry) container. This is the most popular container type and is particularly suitable for a wide range of merchandise such as consumer commodities shipped in cartons. These containers usually have end doors for easy access and floors fully stressed for mechanical aids, that is, palletized products; flush panelling throughout, alloy interior skirting boards, ventilators and flush mounted bars for interior roping. This type of container is ideal for the consolidated shipment.

(2) Insulated and refrigerated container. This is a specialized container type and is, particularly, suitable for perishable cargoes such as, meat, dairy products, fruit, drugs and photographic material. Such containers are connected to a duct system on the container vessel. Some refrigerated containers are self-refrigerated for prolonged periods.

(3) Top loader container. This type is usually designed with a pull back plastic waterproof cover roof thereby permitting cargo to be loaded from the top. Such a container is particularly suitable for large awkwardly shaped cargoes such as heavy pieces of machinery.

(4) Bulk liquid container. This type is ideally suitable for liquid cargoes such as wine, spirits, oil, chemicals etc.

(5) Bulk powder container. This type is ideal for bulk powder shipments such as fertilizers, cement etc. Again a very specialized type suitable for industrial company ownership/distribution. This type

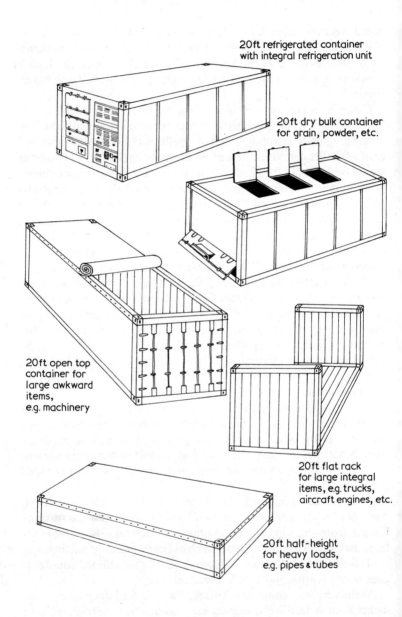

20ft refrigerated container
with integral refrigeration unit

20ft dry bulk container
for grain, powder, etc.

20ft open top
container for
large awkward
items,
e.g. machinery

20ft flat rack
for large integral
items, e.g. trucks,
aircraft engines, etc.

20ft half-height
for heavy loads,
e.g. pipes & tubes

III   Types of containers

of container is frequently interchangeable in use with the previous one, subject to it being suitably equipped and adequate cleansing facilities being available.

(6) Bin type of container. Ideal for bulk grain, coal or powder-type cargoes. Again a specialized container increasing in popularity and helping to expand the container trade market. Additionally, a half bin type exists suitable for drum work.

(7) Skeleton type container. Such a container is equipped with a specially strengthened floor and profile of similar outline to the covered dry container. It is ideal for shipment of drums, wire, cables and certain commercial vehicles.

(8) Open containers with hinged drop-side gates and removable stanchions give full length access for side loading. Suitable for timber lengths, metal, machinery etc.

(9) The flat rack container is the basic 'flat' with panelled-in ends. It is ideal for long lengths of heavy and awkward pieces of cargo such as trucks, buses, aircraft engines, etc.

(10) The open sided containers are fixed with a roof and there are open sides and end-opening doors. Some types are fitted with wire mesh non-load-bearing gates and are covered by heavy duty waterproof tarpaulin side curtains. Another type involves the sides which are 'closed' by full height gates which may be unshipped and stowed within the container at each end if not required. These types are suitable for timber, plywood and cargoes classified as hazardous.

(11) The half height container is ideal for the carriage of heavy, dense cargoes such as steel, pipes and tubes etc. The sides are fixed but the end doors may be opened.

Many of the foregoing container types are found in DIAGRAM III.

Undoubtedly, further types of ISO containers will emerge as container trades expand particularly with the third generation of container ships.

· Associated with ISO containerization is the container base and to a lesser degree the inland clearance depot which we will now examine.

CONTAINER BASES

The function of a container base is to consolidate break bulk cargoes (that is, less than full container load consignments) into full container loads. The container base may be under the management of a consortia of ship operators; a container operator(s) engaged in freight forwarding business, a consortia comprising freight forwarders, road hauliers etc., and others engaged in such business, such as, a local port authority. It can be situated in the port itself; the port environs; or an industrial area which can support the facility in generating adequate quantities of containerized import/export traffic through it. The container base is road served and often the larger ones also have rail facilities.

The object of the facility is to consolidate break bulk compatible cargoes destined for the same area/country into full container loads and thereby provide a service in that area particularly for the small importer/exporter. Consequently, the process of stuffing (loading) and unstuffing (unloading) containers is performed at the container base. Many of the larger container bases are inland clearance depots which have the added facility of customs clearance for both import and export cargoes.

The major advantages of the container bases is to provide a service to the importer/exporter situated in the container base hinterland and relieve the port authority of local customs clearance of import/export cargoes. This latter advantage tends to reduce the problems of port congestion, that is, containers awaiting clearance due to non-availability of documents, and enables the throughput of the container berth to be maximized. Ultimately, it speeds up the transit, as no inordinate delay is usually experienced at the port, and thereby encourages the development of international trade. Undoubtedly, the number of container bases will increase as the container trade expands.

INLAND CLEARANCE DEPOTS

Inland clearance depots (ICDs) are situated at convenient points — usually in industrial and commercial areas often outside the limits of any port or airport. They are operated by a consortium or other approved body and provide facilities for the entry, examination and clearance of goods imported or exported in containers, railway train ferry wagons, unit loads or other approved methods. This facility has been inaugurated in recent years to reduce to a minimum the formalities that have to be observed at ships side. It enables importers and exporters to gain full advantage of the use of such services in UK as freight liners, TIR (Transport International Routier), Ro/Ro vessels and containerization. By 1978, there were some thirty inland clearance depots in England and Scotland.

SEA TRANSPORT

During the past fifteen years, there has been a radical change in the techniques adopted in the distribution of international trade insofar as maritime transport is concerned. Basically, some 98% of world trade in volume terms is conveyed by sea transport and the following developments have emerged since the mid 1960s which have aided a more economical distribution thereby encouraging the exploitation of the world resources.

(1) Containerization displacing the conventional 'tween deck tonnage has transformed the international distribution of general merchandise introducing a door to door service. Moreover, it has substantially improved transit times and raised service quality.

(2) Ro/Ro services conveying road haulage vehicles on international transits again offers a door to door service. Likewise, it speeds up transits and has raised service standards. This mode of distribution is very popular in the fast expanding UK/Continental trade.

(3) Provision of numerous types of purpose built specialized bulk cargo carriers. These include liquefied natural gas carriers (LNGs); vehicular carriers for shipment of trade cars, cab chassis, lorries; banana carriers; cement ships etc. Moreover, existing long established vessel types such as oil tankers, ore carriers, timber vessels, have been dramatically improved in terms of their design with particular emphasis on speed of handling cargo transshipment and quick turn round time in port.

Sea transport is basically a capital intensive method of distribution and involves vast investment sums as, for example, the inauguration of the UK/South African container service which totalled £575 million investment in 1977. Consequently the life of the ship spans some 15-20 years but, as vessels become more intensely used coupled with the advancement of marine engineering technology, the ships life may become 10-15 years. The problem facing the shipowner, and to a lesser degree other types of transport, is the degree of inflation inherent in ship replacement.

It is appropriate to mention that vessels generally in the past decade have tended to become faster; of much increased capacity; rather more specialized and purpose-built for particular cargoes; much more intensely used with overall rather small crew complements; and finally, offering a much improved quality of service. All these factors have aided the development of international trade and in so doing has enabled sea transport to remain competitively priced.

An examination of the more important types of vessels follows, but the reader who wishes to know more about these aspects should study Chapters 2, 3 and 4 of my book by the same publisher entitled *The Elements of Shipping*.

(1) The oil tanker represents almost half of the world merchant fleet in deadweight capacity terms. In fact, some of the world's larger vessels are tankers, some of which exceed 500 000 d.w.t. Crude oil is transported from the oil fields to refineries, and petroleum and fuel oil from refineries to distribution centres and bunkering ports, so that there is a world-wide network of tanker routes. Vessels exceeding 200000 d.w.t. are called very large crude carriers (VLCC) and those above 350 000 d.w.t. ultra large crude carriers (ULCC).

(2) Coasters are all purpose cargo carriers operating around our coast.

(3) A container vessel is a basically cellular vessel with crew and machinery situated aft. Each hold of a cellular ship is fitted with a series of vertical angle guides adequately cross braced to accept the container. The third generation container vessel has a speed of 22 knots with up to 2500 container capacity. A prominent shipowner is Overseas Containers Ltd.

(4) LASH. Lighter aboard the ship. This new type of vessel enables lighters to be conveyed from one port to another thus combining inland waterway with ocean transportation. Advantages of the service include through rates/bills of lading; no intermediate handling during transfer from the ship, thereby reduding cost and permitting competitive rates to be quoted and faster transits attained; lower insurance premiums, less damage/pilferage; low risk of cargo delay as barges are lowered into the water immediately on arrival at each port and the barges are likewise loaded on the LASH vessel; it reduces time spent in port or its environs to a minimum. By 1978, there was little evidence of this type of vessel increasing her

fleet size and undoubtedly it has proved vulnerable competitively to container distribution.

(5) LNG. The liquefied natural gas carrier fleet will be quite formidable by the early 1980s. This product is fast becoming an important form of world energy and international distribution is essential to exploit its potential.

(6) OBO. (Ore/bulk/oil) ships are multi-purpose bulk carriers designed for switching between bulk shipments of oil/bulk grain, fertilizer and ore trades. Many of such vessels exceed 200 000 d.w.t.

(7) Ro/Ro type of vessels are designed to carry private cars with passengers, coaches, road haulage vehicles and non-motorist passengers. Such vessels are also termed multi-purpose vehicle ferries and an increasing number of them operate in the UK/Continental trade.

The important feature of the Ro/Ro vessel is that the vehicles are driven on or off the ship by means of a ramp at the port berth thereby permitting an unimpeded transhipment movement.

(8) The SD14 is a modern tramp vessel and designed to convey the traditional tramp bulk cargoes such as grain, timber, ore, coal etc. Another similar type of ship is called the Freedom. Both vessels are multi-purpose, dry cargo carriers and engaged under a document called a charter party on a time or voyage basis.

(9) Train ferry vessels carry railway passenger and freight rolling stock. Access to and from the vessel is over a ramp thereby permitting an unimpeded transhipment offering through transits.

(10) The 'tween deck vessel is a general cargo vessel engaged primarily on deep-sea liner cargo services. This type of vessel has other decks below the main deck called 'tween decks and all run the full length of the vessel. Currently, this type of vessel is being displaced in many trades by the container ship.

(11) In recent years, the hovercraft and hydrofoil craft have emerged primarily operative in UK/Continental trade conveying passengers and accompanied cars. Currently classified as an aircraft, they are unlikely to capture any significant international trade distribution market. A number are operating in estuarial services and in the Baltic, plus some being used in various parts of the world for land exploration work in rivers/swamps.

The type of merchant vessel employed on a trade route is determined basically by the traffic carried. Broadly there are three main divisions: liners, tramps and specialized vessels such as tankers.

The liner vessel operates on a scheduled service between a group of ports. Such services offer cargo space or passenger accommodation to all shippers and passengers who require them. The ships sail on scheduled dates/times irrespective of whether they are full or not. Container vessels in deep-sea trades and Ro/Ro vessels in the short sea trades feature prominently in this field. The passenger market is now only relevant to the UK/Continental trade and similar short sea trades in other parts of the world. The deep-sea liner services often operate under the aegis of the liner conference system. The bill of lading features very prominently as the consignment note used in the liner cargo service with the exception of the international road haulage shipment which attracts the CMR document and rail which attracts the CIM consignment note.

The tramp or general trader as she is often called, does not operate on a fixed sailing schedule, but merely trades in all parts of the world in search of cargo primarily bulk shipments. Such cargoes include coal, grain, timber, sugar, ores, fertilizers, copra etc. which are carried in complete shiploads. Many of the cargoes are seasonal. Tramp vessels are engaged under a document called a charter party on a time or voyage basis. Such negotiations usually are conducted by shipbrokers on behalf of their principals. The fixture rate is determined by the economic forces of demand and supply insofar as cargoes seeking shipping space and the availability of vessels is concerned. Such vessels occasionally are chartered to supplement existing liner services to meet peak cargo shipment demands, or by the shipper with a substantial shipment of cargo, that is, trade cars/chassis.

The specialized vessel such as the oil tanker, ore carrier, timber carrier, etc. may be under charter or operated by an industrial company, that is, oil company, motor manufacturer etc. to suit their own individual/market needs.

PIPELINES

Pipeline networks in the UK are mainly confined to oil and gas distribution. In the case of oil, the pipelines link the oil refinery — usually a port terminal — with various distribution depots.

The basic advantage of a pipeline is the low cost of distribution with virtually no labour content in the distribution network. Cost of installing the pipeline system may be moderately high, but are relatively low insofar as distribution is concerned. A further basic advantage is the 24 hour availability of the pipeline and its low maintenance.

Conversely, the pipeline has a fixed capacity which inhibits market growth unless a further pipeline is installed. It has many advantages from an environmental point of view with virtually no noise or fumes. Little disruption is caused to the environment during installation compared with road or rail development. Moreover, it permits more than one type of product to be distributed through it.

PALLETIZATION

Palletization is the process of placing or anchoring the consignment to a pallet or base made of wood or metal. It is a very common technique in air freight where the pallet accompanies the consignment throughout the transit from the factory premises to the retailer. It may be a stillage involving base plates, the box pallets where one side can be dropped, or the skeleton pallet for lightweight cargoes.

Palletization is also used in container shipment in the process of general freight forwarding insofar as surface transport is concerned. Basically, palletization aids cargo handling, reduces packing, facilitates stowage, and mechanises the technique of cargo handling involving the pallet truck and fork lift truck. To the shipper involved in general merchandise distribution, an enquiry into the possible use of pallets may prove worthwhile. Some shipowners and port operators offer rates concession on palletized cargo.

CHAPTER 5

Freight Rates

Theory of freight rates. The constituents of the freight rate. Factors influencing formulation of freight rates. Air freight rates. Canal/inland waterways freight rates. International train ferry rates. International road haulage freight rates. Maritime container rates. Sea freight rates. Overseas postal services tariffs.

THEORY OF FREIGHT RATES

Freight is the reward payable to the carrier for the carriage and arrival of goods in a mercantile or recognized condition ready to be delivered to the merchant.

The pricing of air or sea transport services, usually in combination with land transport services, is dependent on the forces of supply and demand, but the factors affecting both supply and demand are perhaps more complicated than in the case of most other industries and services. The demand for a particular international transport service mode(s) is basically derived from the demand for the commodities carried, and is, therefore, affected by the elasticity of demand for these commodities.

The demand for sea or air transport is affected by both direct competition between carriers and, because it is a derived demand, by the competition of substitutes or alternatives for the commodity carried. On any particular route, the shipowner or airline is subject to competition from carriers on the same route, and also from the carriers operating from alternative supply areas. The commodities carried by the latter may be competitive with the commodites from his own supply area and, to that extent, may affect the demand for his services. On many routes there is also competition from more than one form of transport.

The elasticity of demand for sea or air transport varies from one commodity to another. In normal times, an important factor affecting elasticity of demand for sea or air transport, is the cost of transport in relation to the market price of the goods carried. Although it may be small, the cost of sea or air transport is often a significant element in the final market price of many commodities.

The price eventually fixed for a chartered vessel or aircraft depends largely on the relationship between buyers and sellers.

Where both groups are numerous and have equal bargaining power, and where demand is fairly elastic, conditions of relative perfect competition prevail. Under these conditions for chartered tonnage, prices are fixed by the 'haggling of the market' and are known as contract prices. The market for tramp charters operate under such conditions and the contract is drawn up as an agreement known as a charter party.

Under these conditions, the rate structure for tramps is a very simple product and emerges from the competitive interplay of supply and demand. From the economists point of view, rates made in this way represent the most efficient method of pricing; for when price is determined under conditions of perfect competition, production is encouraged to follow consumer wishes and price itself does not deviate to any great extent from average total cost. A similar criteria applies to air freight charterers. It must be borne in mind, however, that the air charter market extends both to the very large shipment offering, for example, an indivisible load urgently required such as a ship's propellor, and the smaller split charter involving consignments of 500-2500 kgs. Many air freight forwarders have their own charter subsidiaries and the Exporter is advised to examine this market.

Chartering can also extend to Ro/Ro vehicles in the UK/European trade and markets beyond. The shipper/freight forwarder can charter a portion of the vehicle from the road operator either on a regular or spasmodic basis.

In general terms the shipper must critically examine, including alternatives, the total freight cost of the transit and reconcile it with the distance. Generally, the shorter the total journey distance, the greater the need to ensure the cost is proportionate to the distance otherwise it could quickly price the goods out of the overseas market. Generally, documentation, and Customs entry cost do not vary greatly.

In the liner conferences which include container trades, the shipowners control fairly large concerns, and although some of their shippers may be very large firms, the bulk of their traffic comes from the numerous small shippers. In these conditions it is more convenient for the shipowner to estimate how much his customers are prepared to pay and fix his own rate. Such prices are known as tariff prices which the liner conference issues.

In regard to air freight rates operative on regular scheduled international services, these are decided collectively by the airlines attending their usual twice yearly traffic conferences. These are held under the aegis of the International Air Transport Association who adopt a policy of parity on level of rates on individual services/routes thereby not permitting rates competition amongst airlines. The rates reflect market conditions and service cost.

Overall, a properly compiled tariff should encourage the movement of all classes of cargo to ensure the best balance between revenue production and the full utilization of the transport unit.

THE CONSTITUENTS OF THE FREIGHT RATE

Basically, the tariff raised for a consignment can embrace a number of elements other than the sea, air, plus inland transport tariff and these are detailed below:

(1) Tariff cargo rate. In the case of air freight it will be between the relevant airports. Likewise for maritime transport, it will be the port to port container, Ro/Ro vehicle, or general cargo rates. The same criteria applies to a chartered aircraft or ship. The charter party will determine the extent the charterer bears the cargo handling transhipment cost included in the overall fixture rate.

(2) The customs clearance charge is usually based on the local port authority or airline tariff. Charges vary between import/export, commodity type, quantity, and the degree of ultimate customs physical 'turn out' examination of the consignment. The latter is usually a separate charge. It includes the presentation of the requisite documents/entry to customs. The HM Customs have the legal authority to examine all imported consignments, but in reality only random inspection is made at the discretion of the local customs officer. Customs clearance may be undertaken at an inland clearance depot with the goods travelling under bond to/from the seaport. The actual presentation of the goods to customs and their ultimate clearance will be undertaken on behalf of the shipper by the port authority or airline, or the freight forwarder acting on behalf of his client.

(3) Freight forwarders commission. Many small exporters engage the services of a freight forwarder to look after the distribution arrangements of the consignment. The role of the freight forwarder is explained in Chapter 16 page 306 and accordingly raises a commis-

sion charge with the exporter/importer. This is usually 5% of the total freight account.

(4) Customs duty will vary according to commodity specification and applies to imported consignments. It also extends to Value Added Tax or something similar depending on the importing country.

(5) Disbursements. These embrace a variety of items including freight services, telephone calls, telex messages, currency surcharge, fuel surcharge, cost of feeding livestock, additional cost to police valuable consignment, etc. Again it will depend on the nature of the cargo and the particular circumstances obtaining at the airport, sea port, or inland clearance depot.

(6) Cargo insurance premium. Usually the premium is lower for air freight than for sea transport but much depends on the latter method of forwarding viz. container, train ferry, Ro/Ro, or general freight in 'tween deck tonnage.

(7) Delivery/collection charge. The collection and delivery of the cargo is usually undertaken by road transpot. The rate is normally assessed on distance within a zonal rating. This is related to the weight or cubic measurement of the consignment. This task may be undertaken by the exporter and/or importer's own vehicles. In other circumstances, the delivery and/or collection may be included in the through rate.

(8) Transhipment charge. This arises when cargo is transhipped *en route* to continue its transit. It may occur at an airport or sea port. Again it could be an inclusive charge within the through rate, but much depends on the circumstances. When the cargo involves special arrangements being made to tranship it due to its awkward shape, excessive weight or size, or general nature of the commodity i.e. livestock, additional charges are normally raised.

(9) Documentation charge. Circumstances arise when it is necessary to obtain a certificate of origin to accord with the importing country customs requirement to establish/verify the place of manufacture of the goods. This document obtained by the exporter is obtained from the local Chamber of Commerce, or if a consular invoice is required from the consulate of the importing country. A charge is raised by the consulate office for this service which can be as much as £30 in some cases.

(10) Demurrage. Cargo detained at an airport, seaport or inland

clearance depot beyond a prescribed period attracts a daily demurrage charge. The cargo may be delayed due to wrong presentation of customs clearance documents, non-availability of export/import licence, pending payment of customs duty, awaiting collection by consignee etc.

(11) Handling cost. This embraces cost of handling the cargo at the terminal. It is sometimes included in the throughout rate. In the case of containers, it is usually based on a tariff per container lift, ship to shore and vice versa. It can vary by container type, empty or loaded. Extra charges are raised for special lifts i.e. indivisible load.

(12) Wharfage charge. This is a charge raised by the port authority for cargo transhipment.

(13) Cargo dues. Again a cost raised by the port authority for goods passing over the quay.

(14) Rebate. In the case of sea freight, exporters originating substantial quantities of traffic are granted a rebate provided they adhere to the shipowner/liner conference conditions. It may be an immediate rebate offering 10% on the published tariff or possibly 10½% on a deferred rebate payable six months after the traffic passed. Basically, a deferred rebate is a device to ensure that shippers will continue to support a conference or shipping line. Hence the shipper has an inducement to remain loyal to the liner conference or shipping line insofar as he stands to lose the rebate by a non-conference vessel.

The level of rebate is usually negotiated between the shipper and shipowner. It is very evident in the liner conference trades and also the Ro/Ro services between the UK/Continent where up to 37½% has been granted in exceptional cases.

Obviously the ultimate rate, mode of transport, route will be much influenced by the Export Sales contract and the delivery terms contained therein.

FACTORS INFLUENCING FORMULATION OF FREIGHT RATES

We will now examine the salient factors which influence the formulation of freight rates.

(1) Competition. Parity on rates exist on air freight IATA scheduled services, but keen competition exists in the trade from various

modes of transport. For example, in the UK/Europe trade competition exists amongst air freight agents offering consolidated services, train ferry services, ISO containerization and international road haulage.

(2) The nature of the commodity, its quantity, period of shipment(s) and overall cubic measurements/dimensions/value.

(3) The origin and destination of the cargo.

(4) The overall transit cost.

(5) The nature of packaging and convenience of handling.

(6) The susceptibility of the cargo to damage and pilferage.

(7) The general loadability of the transport unit.

(8) Provision of additional facilities to accommodate the cargo viz. heavy lifts, strong room, livestock facilities etc.

(9) The mode(s) of transport.

(10) Actual routing of cargo consignment. Alternative routes tend to exist particularly in air freight with differing rates structure and overall transport cost.

We will now examine the varying methods of available freight rates by mode of transport.

AIR FREIGHT RATES

The formulation of air freight rates is controlled by the International Air Transport Association (IATA) insofar as major world airlines are affiliated to it, which represent about 98% of international air freight services. IATA has no influence on internal, that is, Glasgow/London domestic flight air freight tariffs or charter flights. The significant aspect of the IATA affiliated airlines is that no competition is permitted on air freight rates, that is, parity obtains, and competition is permitted only on service quality, frequency, etc.

Basically, there are six types of air freight rates in existence each of which is designed to stimulate traffic by various ways. Moreover, it is relevant to say the same individual rates do not necessarily apply in both directions thereby reflecting the differing market situations. For example, a commodity rate for product type 'A' may exist from London to New York but not in reverse direction. Moreover, routing of cargo is significant both in terms of transit time and tariff.

If two routes are available, the shorter route in distance terms is likely to be the cheapest, but may be the longer in transit time due to the less frequent and slower schedules/connections.

Air cargo is charged by weight except where the volume is more than 427 in³/kg. In such cases, volumetric charges apply and each unit of 427 in³ is charged as 1 kg. To calculate this, the maximum dimensions of the piece should be multiplied together to give a volume in cubic inches. This volume must be divided by 427 and the result will be the volumetric weight. If this is more than the actual weight, then the volumetric weight will be the chargeable weight. Where the consignment consists of pieces varying in density, the volumetric calculation will be based on the whole consignment. For metric measurements, 7000 cm³ = 1 kg.

Air cargo rates are quoted per kilogram (gross weight or volume equivalent) except in the case of specific commodity rates to certain European countries and Ireland which are quoted per 100 kg. The 100 kg rates apply from airport of departure to airport of destination and do not include charges for cartage, customs entry and clearance, etc.

For mixed cargo containing a number of different commodities which do not qualify for the same rate and conditions, such consignments are based on the applicable general cargo rate. Where the shipper declares separately the rate or volume and the contents of each package in the consignment, charges are based on either the appropriate commodity rate or the general cargo rate of each package. The packaging of the whole or part of the consignment will be charged on the basis of the consignment.

A brief examination of each air freight rate classification now follows:

(1) Specific commodity rates. These reduced rates apply to a wide range of commodities and to qualify the shipper must comply precisely with the commodity specifications as found in the tariff. Likewise, only between the specified airports of departure and arrival — it is not possible to send goods at these preferential rates to alternative destinations even where the alternative airport is on the same route and nearer to the airport of origin. The minimum quantity allowed at each rate is 100, 300, 500 and 1000 kg (shipping above the limit is allowed but not below it). Hence a consignment of 85 kg would be charged at the minimum kilogram rate, that is, 100 kg at 0.65 p which equals £65.00. This type of rate has done much to stimulate air freight development and by encouraging quantity shipments

has produced cost savings in documentation/handling/packaging.

(2) Classification rates. This applies to the following commodities if no such commodity rate is available:

(i) Live animals — generally 50% above the minimum charge for general cargo. Stringent regulations apply regarding documentation/ travel facilities and conditions. A shippers certificate for live animals is required and prior arrangements must be made.

(ii) Newspapers, periodicals and books — special reduced rates are usually available on application to the airline.

(iii) Human remains — regulations and rates vary by route — prior application necessary to each airline.

(iv) Valuable cargo — certain types of gold and platinum, diamonds, rubies, emeralds, sapphires and pearls, legal bank notes, shares and coupons, charged at the under 45 kg air cargo rate plus a 100% surcharge with a minimum charge operative. Quantity rates are not applicable.

(v) Valuation charge — if the declared value for carriage is more than £7.6754 / kg (operative rate November 1977), charges for carriage will be on a weight or volume basis plus a valuation charge based on the amount by which the value for carriage exceeds £7.6754 / kg that is, £0·400 per £100 pro rata of declared amount.

(3) General cargo rates. These are the basic rates and fall into three categories as below:

(i) Minimum charges.

(ii) Normal rate — the under 45 kg rate.

(iii) Quantity rate — applicable on the various minimum quantities shipped, called break-points. It is permissible to charge a consignment at a higher weight rate if a lower charge results overall.

(4) Unit load device (ULD) rates. This applies to any type of container, container with an integral pallet, or aircraft pallet whether or not owned by an IATA member, and whether or not considered to be aircraft equipment. Two basic types of rates exist which are attractive to shippers moving cargo in such a form. Long term, this type of rate should become more popular as a method of stimulating air freight in containerized/unit load form with favourable rates/ease of handling etc. An important condition is that the cargo must travel in the ULD throughout the transit to qualify for the rate.

(5) Economy pack rates. On a number of European routes, special rates exist for cargo having density of 155 in^3 (2500 cm^3)/kg or more.

The cargo must be loaded and securely fastened in a normal warehouse pallet in such a way the complete unit can be fork-lifted without the load shifting and/or tipping. The pallet size must not exceed 40 x 48 in (100 x 120 cm) and the load must not overhang the pallet.

(6) Cabotage. The term used for movement of air freight when points of origin and destination are both within UK and special domestic rates apply.

All these air freight rates exclude customs clearance charges duty, road/rail collection/distribution, warehousing — demurrage, etc. In addition to the foregoing, for special/large consignments, an aircraft can be chartered. Rates vary according to market conditions and other factors. The shipper conducts his negotiations through an air charter broker found on the Baltic Exchange or direct with an airline or air freight forwarder. As indicated earlier, a certain degree of bargaining can emerge to settle the ultimate charter rate for the larger air freighter. Much depends whether prospects exist for the aircraft to be chartered on the next flight otherwise the operator will be faced with an empty aircraft to fly to the next assignment. Little room exists for bargaining for split charters for small consignments varying between 500 kg and 3 tonnes. The charterer may need to wait a few days in such circumstances to combine with other cargo thereby obtaining a favourable rate based on a full aircraft.

Today an increasing volume of air freight is moving under consolidation arrangements developed by air freight forwarders in consultation with major airlines. Under such arrangements the air freight forwarder consolidates the cargo from various shippers and presents it to the airline to convey as one consignment. The freight forwarder usually quotes an inclusive rate to include collection and sometimes delivery charge, customs clearance etc. Many air freight forwarders usually have a pre-booked arrangement with airline operators reserving cargo space on regular specified flights. The airlines welcome this development particularly as it improves aircraft loadability, reduces handling as the consignments are in unit loads, and eliminates the airline involvement with the shipper as the contact is through the air freight forwarder. Rates are competitive and ideal for small exporters.

CANAL/INLAND WATERWAYS FREIGHT RATES

The portion of the international transit conveyed by canal will have a tariff based on distance/commodity type/trans-shipment cost/ handling charges and any other miscellaneous charges. For example, if the consignment is an indivisible load, it may involve some special, heavy lifting equipment. Special rates usually exist for containers, palletized cargoes and special contract tariffs are available for regular shipments. The tariffs and range thereof vary by individual country and canal authority. They exclude customs clearance charges. The rates are based on either a weight or measurement assessment.

In some trades the lighter aboard ship (LASH) concept has been developed. This type of ship enables lighters to be carried from one port to another thus combining inland waterway with ocean transportation. Each ship has a capacity of about 73 barges each of 400 tons capacity. The rates are usually port to port.

Distribution of international trade by inland waterway based on the major European ports is very extensive on the continent for a variety of reasons. Rates again are based on weight or cubic measurement and vary by commodity and trade. It is a very competitive method of distribution for certain commodities/trades and one of continued expansion as the system is modernized/further developed.

INTERNATIONAL TRAIN FERRY RATES

British Rail under CIM conditions operate through UK/Continental freight rail services. The rates are based on the origin and destination of the consignment and a per wagon charge to encourage good loadability. Special rates exist for particular streams of traffic and between selective countries. A number of privately-owned train ferry wagons exist and in such cases special rates apply.

Additionally, a substantial volume of cargo passes in groupage wagon consignments under forwarding agent sponsorship. To the agent, the rate is based on the wagon unit. To the shipper the charge is based on the weight or cubic measurement of the consignment whichever produces the greater revenue.

Overall, the rates are very competitive and the popularity of the service is increasing, as new wagon types are being introduced by private operators.

INTERNATIONAL ROAD HAULAGE FREIGHT RATES

The development of the international road haulage market UK/

Europe — Asia — Middle East has been outstanding in recent years
particularly UK/Continent under CMR conditions. Undoubtedly
the UK entry into the European Economic Community has facilitated this development.

The rates charged to the international road freight forwarder to
convey the vehicle/trailer on the vehicular ferry are based on the trai-
ler/vehicle length, and whether it is empty or loaded, accompanied
or unaccompanied. Additional charges are raised for excessive
width and/or height. Special rates usually exist for declared valuable
cargoes. Rebates are given to hauliers/agents who originate substantial quantities of traffic annually to an operator for a particular
route/service. These rates are exclusive of customs clearance charges
etc. Keen competition exist amongst operators particularly on rates
and fringe benefits viz. free cabin/meals for drivers, together with
free passage for drivers. An increasing number of large and indeed
medium sized exporters now undertake their own International distribution by road. It has many advantages particularly if the cargo
flow can be balanced in each direction.

To the shipper using the international road freight forwarders service — much of which is groupage traffic — the actual rate is based
on the cubic measurement or weight of the cargo whichever produces the greater revenue. This is related to the commodity classification, and origin and destination of the cargo. The cargo
measurement is 40 ft³ equals one ton. Rates are very competitive particularly compared with air freight and train ferry within an overall
distance band of 900-1000 km. To improve vehicle crew utilization in
an era of rising cost, an increasing number of the larger road haulage
operators despatch their vehicles unaccompanied on the vehicular
ferry. This enables the driver to deposit his trailer at the ferry terminal and collect another one waiting. It avoids driver lodging allo-
wance cost being incurred and enables better vehicle control to be
achieved with improved reliability and lower cost.

MARITIME CONTAINER RATES

The general practice is to formulate individual rates by container
type, capacity, and the actual origin and destination of the merchandise. The through rate will embrace the inland transportation cost
known at the time of despatch embracing collection and terminal

handling expenses, but it will usually exclude customs clearance charges, demurrage etc. Much of course depends on the trade. This practice applies to full container load (FCL) traffic. Some of the containers are stuffed and unstuffed at the Container Base which may be an inland clearance depot.

Some large multi-national companies run ISO containers. They are usually of a specialized type offering a two way traffic flow. The tariff for such traffic is usually specially negotiated contract rates.

A very substantial volume of traffic which is conveyed in containers is less than container load (LCL) traffic. The cargo is assembled and stuffed into a container at a container base or inland clearance depot with each individual consignment attracting separate rates. Such rates are calculated on a weight or cubic measurement basis whichever produces the greater revenue. They naturally reflect the origin and destination of such merchandise, together when practicable likely disbursement charges viz. handling, customs clearance etc.

For consignments requiring special facilities such as livestock or indivisible loads requiring heavy lifts, additional charges are raised.

Maritime container rates are very competitive and this mode of transport now constitutes a substantial volume of deep-sea world general merchandise cargo.

SEA FREIGHT RATES

We will now examine the sea freight tariff formulation relative to liner cargo rates involving shipowners operating 'tween deck tonnage and ship chartering. It should be mentioned that the terms tariff and rate are synonymous inasmuch as various forms of transport use either, according to circumstances.

Liner rates are based partly on cost, and partly on value. Many freight rates are quoted on a basis of weight or measurement at ship's option. This means that the rate quoted will be applied either per ton of 2240 lb (weight) or on 40 ft^3 (cubic measurement) per ton, whichever will produce the greater revenue. The reason for this method of charging is that heavy cargo will bring a vessel to her loadline before her space is full, while light cargo will fill her space without bringing her down to her maximum draught. To produce the highest revenue a vessel must be loaded to her full internal capacity, and immersed to her maximum permitted depth. In most trades, cargo measuring under 40 ft³ ton weight is charged on a weight basis, whilst cargo measuring 40 ft³ or more per ton is charged on a measurement basis. With the spread of the metric system, many freight rates are quoted per 1000 kg or m³ (35.5 ft³).

Liner tariffs quote rates for many commodities which move regularly. These rates are based on the stowage factor (rate of bulk to weight), on the value of the cargo and on the competitive situation. Many tariffs publish class rates for general cargo not otherwise specified. Some tariffs publish class rates whereby commodities are grouped for charging into several classes. On commodities of very high value, *ad valorem* rates are charged at so much per cent of the declared value. When commodities move in large quantities, and are susceptible to tramp competition, shipowners often employ 'open rates', that is, the rate is left open, so that the shipping line can quote whatever rate it determines. For heavy lifts and extra lengths it is usual to make additional charges in order to cover the special handling of such cargo.

Insofar as chartered vessels are concerned the negotiation is usually undertaken by a shipbroker who may be on the Baltic Exchange communicating with other shipbrokers having a vessel available to hire. Alternatively, the shipbroker may go direct to the shipowner.

The rates are not pre-determined but are based on economic forces of supply and demand. A voyage charter is a contract for a special voyage, while a time charter is a contract for a period of time which may cover several voyages. Therefore, the voyage charter rate is a short-term rate, while the time charter rate is often a long-term rate. When trade is buoyant and voyage rates are rising, charterers, in anticipation of further rises, tend to charter for longer periods to cover their commitments; when rates are expected to fall, they tend to contract for shorter periods. Therefore, the current time charter rate tends to reflect the expected trend of voyage rates in the future. If rates are expected to rise, it will tend to be above the current voyage rates; if they are expected to fall, it will tend to be below the current voyage rates. Generally speaking, the two rates move in the same direction but because time charter rates depend on market expectations, they tend to fluctuate more widely than voyage rates. When conditions are improving, long-term rates tend to rise more rapidly than voyage rates; when conditions are deteriorating, voyage rates tend to fall more rapidly.

It is relevant to mention the bill of lading is the document usually associated with liner cargo and the charter party with chartered vessels.

This study of sea freight rates would not be complete without an examination of the types available. The true test of the shipowners' right to freight is whether the service in respect of which freight was contracted to be paid has been substantially performed, or, if not, whether its performance has been prevented by any act of the cargo owner. Details of the various types are given below:

(1) Advance freight is payable in advance, before delivery of the actual goods. This is generally regarded as the most important type of freight, and is extensively used in the liner cargo trades and tramping. It must not be confused with 'advance of freight' which may be a payment on account of disbursements or an advance to the Master, in which case the charterer would be entitled to a return of the monies advanced. Such a payment is really in the nature of a loan.

(2) Lump sum freight is the amount payable for the use of the whole or portion of a ship. This form of freight is calculated on the actual cubic capacity of the ship offered, and has no direct relation to the cargo to be carried. Lump sum freight is payable irrespective of the actual quantity delivered.

(3) Dead freight is the name given to a damage claim for breach of contract by, for example, the charterer to furnish a full cargo to a ship. Such a situation would arise if the charterer undertook to provide 500 tons of cargo, but only supplied 400 tons. The shipowner would, under such circumstances, be entitled to claim dead freight for the unoccupied space. Alternatively, a shipper may fail to provide all the cargo promised and for which space has been reserved on a particular sailing, in which case the shipowner would again claim dead freight for the unoccupied space.

(4) Back freight arises when goods have been despatched to a certain port, and on arrival are refused. The freight charged for the return of the goods constitutes back freight.

(5) *Pro rata* freight arises when the cargo has been carried only part of the way and circumstances make it impossible to continue the voyage further. For example, ice formation may exist at the original port of delivery, and the owner may decide to accept delivery of the cargo at an intermediate port. The point then arises whether the freight calculated *pro rata* for the portion of the voyage actually accomplished becomes payable. It will only do so when there is a clear agreement by the cargo owner to pay.

(6) *Ad valorem* freight arises when cargo is assessed for rate purposes on a percentage of its value. For example, a 2% *ad valorem* rate on a consignment valued at £1000 would raise £20.

OVERSEAS POSTAL SERVICES TARIFFS

A significant volume of international trade is distributed by overseas postal services which may be by air or surface. It is particularly ideal for the small exporter.

Overall the Post Office is a member of the Universal Postal Union totalling some 157 countries and enjoys a special relationship with more than 200 countries and territories. It is against this background the Post Office is able to offer the UK exporter a wide range of international services with the basic following advantages:

(1) Door to door service. Free collection can be arranged from factory or warehouse for bulk postings. At the overseas destination, parcels may be delivered to the customers address or held at a local depot for collection. In some countries a small charge is made for delivery, but this with any Customs charges due, can be prepaid by the FDD or Franc de Droits service where this service exist for the particular country.

(2) Inclusive charges. All costs in UK are easily predetermined and are included in the price of postage with no extra handling charges or UK Customs clearance charges. In the country of destination, Customs clearance and local delivery charges if any are minimal.

(3) Prestige treatment. Air parcels particularly are treated as Royal Mail in most countries and receive priority handling including separate Customs clearance.

(4) Daily service to main trading destinations by air mail.

(5) No minimum weight penalties (contract bulk air services are the only exceptions requiring a minimum of 15 kg/destination).

(6) Customs documentation is straightforward. The necessary forms are obtainable from Post Offices and can easily be completed by the sender.

Apart from the basic air and surface parcel and letter services, there are modern business aids like ASP (accelerated surface post), BAM (bulk air mail) and International Datapost — the gold-badge guaranteed service.

The accelerated surface post ASP is the service that gives printed papers a flying start to destinations outside Europe. It has links with about 80 countries and uses a combination of air transport for speed and surface transport for economy. ASP offers quick transits and sometimes can cost little more than surface mails. It can mean that all sorts of printed material can be speeded direct to overseas destinations in a matter of days. It provides a useful 'happy medium' between existing air mail and surface mail services as it handles its consignments as surface mail in the UK and in the country of destination. In between, the mail goes by air.

When bags of ASP arrive at their overseas destination, individual packages are fed into the postal system. Large consignments can often, if wished, be delivered complete. It is a direct delivery without the need for forwarding agents or delivery charges.

The bulk air mail BAM is used for bulk consignments of printed paper items sent to Europe. Delivery is, as far as possible, within two to three days of postings. Both regular and occasional consignments of printed papers can be sent. Multi-address items can be sent to a number of the nearer European countries.

For both services there is a minimum weight requirement of 15 kg per destination. Individual items may be of any weight up to 2 kg (up to 5 kg for books) and thus most requirements can be met. Cost varies according to destination and size and frequency of consignments, but postage is assessed on a 'pence per kilo' basis for a complete shipment. Both services are available for regular or one-off postings and customers are asked to sort, bag and label the goods themselves.

International Datapost, like its parent, the home-based Datapost, is a reliable door to door service which delivers with fast transit and security and gives users individual treatment. Consignments of business papers, documents, data and, to some countries, machine parts, medical samples, etc, travel with the utmost security. They are checked by special staff at every stage of the journey.

It has now links with most major towns and cities in the USA, Japan, France, Belgium, Argentina, Kuwait, Australia plus a large number of places in Brazil, Hong Kong, Singapore, Switzerland, W. Germany, South Africa and the Netherlands.

Costs are negotiated individually according to weight, frequency of use, destination and timing. On a contract basis they are most competitive. There are no weight limits except that individual packages should not weigh more than 15 kg.

The international service has proved to be suitable for business papers, but it now carries anything that can go through the normal post to Australia, Hong Kong and the Netherlands. The service is continually being extended to take in more countries. International Datapost is for customers who sign contracts with the Post Office Corporation and have regular shipments. The newer International Datapost 'D' (the on-demand service) is for those customers who have an irregular need for Datapost services overseas.

Additionally the following supplementary services exist:

(1) Overseas registration — provides proof of posting and a record of delivery.

(2) Insured letters and insured parcels service — low cost overseas insurance gives proof of posting, a record of delivery and additional security during transit. In the event of loss or damage, compensation of up to £600 may be payable according to destination.

(3) Compensation — uninsured parcels — in the service with most countries, a small amount of compensation may be paid for loss or damage; no extra fee is payable for this.

(4) Cash on delivery service (parcels). Not available to every country, but it provides for the collection on delivery of the trade charge, specified by the sender and remitted to him by money order.

(5) Express overseas service can provide accelerated service in the country of destination.

(6) Franc de Droits (parcels) allows senders to pre-pay customs charges and any other charges arising in the country of destination and is available to many overseas countries. Senders must pay a deposit on account of the charges and undertake to pay the balance later. The balance includes a fee for this service.

The Post Office air parcel service provides fast, convenient, reliable and economic transmission and is ideal for small and medium-sized goods being sent to almost every country in the world. The surface parcel service also operates to almost every country in the world and is suitable for the exporter of goods which do not require the speed and priority of the air service, and the cost is therefore usually much less. For letters and commercial documents associated with commercial transactions, the simplest and speediest service is the letter or letter-packet post. Full details of the Overseas Services provided by the Post Office are given in the Post Office Guide, and all overseas services rates and fees (except for contract services) are given in the Postal Rates Overseas Compendium.

CHAPTER 6

Export Cargo Packaging, Stowage and Marking

Factors influencing type of cargo packaging. Types of packing. Stowage of cargo. Marking of cargo. Dangerous cargo.

FACTORS INFLUENCING TYPE OF CARGO PACKAGING

Packaging techniques today are becoming increasingly sophisticated to meet a market which is seeking continuous improvements in the following areas:

(1) Improved standards to reduce risk of damage and pilferage. This in turn encourages competitive cargo insurance premiums and maintains good relations with the importer. Cargo received in a damaged condition seriously impairs the exporters product overseas market prospects as it lessens much good will with the importer. Moreover, the exporter is ultimately obliged to replace the damaged goods which can be a costly task.

(2) A better utilization of transport capacity to lower distribution cost. This is particularly relevant to the ISO container use when ideally suitably sized packaged cargo can be firmly stowed in it with no broken stowage. This reduces risk of damage, and ensures all container capacity is utilized subject to the total weight limitations not being exceeded. Moreover, it reduces need to use dunnage and by attaining higher utilization/load factor of container capacity lowers the freight cost of each unit distributed.

(3) Improved cargo handling. Cargo packaging in design viz. dimension and configuration, should facilitate the most economical method of handling. This is particularly relevant to awkward shaped cargo. Moreover, it applies from the time the goods are packaged which may be in the factory until it reaches the importers warehouse/ distribution centre. Mechanical cargo handling equipment is now in extensive use to reduce labour cost and speed up cargo handling.

(4) Packaging cost amongst various manufacturers are now very competitive. The shipper is very conscious of containing packing costs and the exporter is well advised to engage a specialist packag-

ing company to obtain professional advice and have the best results. Packaging specification varies by transport mode, commodity and transit routing. Each overseas sales contract cargo needs to be individually considered to obtain the best results and sustain/develop overseas markets.

An examination will now be made of the various factors influencing the nature of packaging for an international consignment:

(1) Value of the goods. In the main the high value consignment usually attracts more extensive packing than the low value merchandise. Much, of course, depends on the nature of the commodity. If packing is inadequate, bearing in mind transit and declared cargo valuation, problems could be experienced in carriers liability, acceptance, and adequate cargo insurance coverage. Moreover, high value consignments, such as a valuable painting, require adequate security and likewise attracts higher freight rates. Such packing must be done professionally.

(2) Nature of the transit. Certain forms of transport, particularly air and ISO containerization, require usually less extensive packing. This is a strong marketing feature of their service. Air transport particularly encourages palletized consignments with cargo strapped/anchored to it throughout the transit. Fibre board cartons for consumer products are both very popular with air and ISO container shipments. In regard to consignments despatched in conventional 'tween deck tonnage involving several transhipments at the ports and other points *en route*, more elaborate robust packing is required. Despite this type of tonnage being displaced by containerization, such vessels still carry a formidable volume of world trade. Train ferry and Ro/Ro consignments require modest packing requirements, but much depends on their collection and delivery arrangements and the degree of robust packing needed. Packing needs for cargoes despatched in purpose-built transport units are usually minimal. This is particularly so with containerization. Packing needs are obviously modest for transport services offering a door to door service with no transhipment *en route*.

(3) Nature of the cargo. This factor together with item (2) are the two major factors which determine the type of packing of an individual consignment. In the main, cargo shipped in bulk requires little or no packing, whilst general merchandise needs adequate packing. For example, apples can be consigned in cases, boxes, cartons or pal-

let boxes. Cement on the other hand may be shipped in five- or six-ply paper bags, containers or in bulk. Motor vehicles are usually shipped unpacked to reduce freight with each vehicle individually secured and stowed. Grain, ores, and coal are all shipped in bulk. Electrical equipment such as cathode ray tubes would be accommodated in a skeleton wooden case and usually conveyed by air. Computer equipment falls into a similar category.

(4) Compliance with Customs or statutory requirements. This is particularly relevant to dangerous cargo where strict regulations apply both by air and sea concerning the acceptance, packing, stowage, documentation, marking and carriers liability. This aspect will be examined later in this chapter.

In some countries, straw is an unacceptable form of packing due to the risk of insects being imported. Quarantine regulations are particularly extensive in Australasia where materials such as wood products, rice husks, straw and similar plant material may not be used as packaging material or dunnage. This ensures that all packing materials are free from soil and contamination from animal products which can harbour pests, particularly insects, which are capable of causing wholesale devastation in forests. If the exporter does use wood it is advisable to have it suitably treated viz. fumigation, kiln drying, or impregnation, and to obtain a certificate to this effect for despatch to the importer. If in doubt the exporter is advised to consult his agent.

(5) Resale value, if any, of packaging material in the importer's country. In some developing countries, large drums, wooden cases, or bags have a modest resale value. This helps to offset the packaging cost.

(6) General fragility of cargo. In the main, the more fragile the cargo becomes, the greater the degree of packaging required. This is very much related to the mode of transport, particulary air freight which has only limited packaging needs and value of consignment. A judgement must be made on the most acceptable form of packaging to adopt and if in doubt advice must be sought.

(7) The international consignment delivery terms of sale. Again the actual packing specification may be contained therein and who bears the cost. This is usually the exporter.

(8) Variation in temperature during the course of the transit. Temperature variation can be quite extensive during transit and packag-

ing needs must take account of this to permit the cargo to breathe and avoid excessive condensation/sweating. Again advice should be sought when necessary from the airline or shipowner.

(9) Ease of handling and stowage. Awkward shaped cargoes packed in cartons or containers can greatly facilitate stowage, particularly in a container and using mechanical cargo handling equipment. Stowing cargo and obtaining the maximum practicable utilization of available transport unit capacity is an area worthy of study to lower unit distribution cost. Likewise, awkward shaped cargoes conveniently packed speed cargo handling. Moreover, some cargoes of awkward shape can attract additional handling charges and a freight surcharge in some circumstances. Furthermore, such cargoes are more vulnerable to damage and could attract higher cargo insurance premiums.

(10) Insurance acceptance conditions. Cargo which is particularly fragile or which has a bad record in terms of damage/pilferage may be subject to a prescribed packing specification. Otherwise, the insurance company or underwriter will refuse to cover them at a competitive cargo insurance premium.

(11) The size of the cargo and its weight. Basically there are three main considerations to be observed when determining the form that a package should take and these include size, shape and strength.

(i) The size of the package will be governed by the size of the marketable unit as, for example, a sliced loaf and a packet of 20 cigarettes. Comparison between the sizes of marketable units of various products frequently reveals the phenomen that products of low bulk command relatively higher prices than those of greater bulk. The reasons for this are two-fold. Firstly, a readily saleable unit of an expensive product tends to be small in order to come within the means of the average consumer, for example, ladies perfume. Secondly, the purchase of a large quantity of a product normally results in an overall reduction in the cost per basic marketable unit. This means that the customer pays less for the product, or alternatively is able to buy a larger quantity for the price he is prepared to pay. An example is found in the retail shop when the basic-sized package of a household product may cost 25p, while the family size containing almost twice the quantity 37p.

(ii) Shape to a large extent is determined by the shape of the goods to be enclosed within the package. Loose goods, the shape of which is flexible, may be accommodated within a package designed to meet one or more of a range of requirements, for example, the cylindrical shape of the package containing a household bleach cleaner makes it convenient to use with one hand, yet the package is self-balancing upon a flat and stable base. More rigid products, such as a pair of tailors scissors must be packaged within a container of a more regular shape - in this instance, an oblong package.

(iii) Coupled with the considerations of size and shape is that of strength. Some products by their very nature need protection by the package, for example, eggs, while others lend support to the package material, for example, metal ashtrays. Some products possess a rigid natural shape, but need cushioning by the package to protect a delicate mechanism, for example, a model electric train, while others rely upon the package for protection and retention of shape, for example, tinned fruit.

Finally, one must bear in mind that the final shape/dimension/weight of consignment, will determine level of freight rate.

(12) Marketing considerations. An overriding consideration, certainly for consumer goods and increasingly so for industrial products, is that the package should fit into the overall marketing concept. On a company strategic level, it must enhance and reinforce the company's image with the customer, whilst, on a lower level, it must sell positively by putting across three cardinal points: the nature, the price, and the advantages of the product. Moreover, it must endeavour to generate further sales with the same customer by performing satisfactorily whilst the product is in use. Additionally, one must bear in mind any advertising motif to be accommodated in the packaging.

(13) Facilities available at the terminals viz. airport, sea port, container base, inland clearance depot, warehouse, etc. Lifting equipment at some sea ports and particularly airports may be of limited capacity. Accordingly, relative to an indivisable load, the shipper may be compelled to despatch it in two parts instead of one integral unit. Moreover, not all airports have customs clearance facilities and this could lead to an alternative air terminal being used with differing handling equipment capacity.

(14) Type and size of container, train ferry wagon, pallet, Ro/Ro vehicle or aircraft. The configuration of the transport unit together with access thereto will influence the actual ultimate dimension of

Sling here

Fragile—handle with care

Use no hooks

This way up

Keep away from heat

Centre of gravity

IV Recognized international cargo marking symbols

the packaging, its maximum weight and shape.

(15) Marking of cargo packaging. Each package must bear a marking code and use a symbol to ease handling. See DIAGRAM IV.

(16) Cost of packaging. This is becoming an increasingly important aspect in deciding on the type of packaging. In a world where overseas markets are becoming more competitive the exporter is constantly exploring ways and means of reducing distribution cost and improving marketing techniques. Packaging features very much in this evaluation.

Packaging, therefore, is not only designed as a form of protection to reduce the risk of goods being damaged in transit, but also to prevent pilferage and aid marketing. It is, of course, essential to see not only that the right type of packing is provided, but also that the correct quality and form of containers is used. There are numerous types of packing and a description of the more important ones follow.

TYPES OF PACKING

Many goods have little or no form of packing and are carried loose. These include iron and steel plates, iron rods, railway sleepers, and steel rails. Such cargoes are generally weight cargoes with a low stowage factor. Heavy vehicles, locomotives and buses are also carried loose, because of the impracticability and high cost of packing.

Baling is a form of packing consisting of a canvas cover often cross-looped by metal or rope binding. It is most suitable for paper, wool, hay, peat, cotton, carpets and rope. Basically, it is a cheap and effective form of packing which aids handling. It affords limited protection to cargo.

Bags made of jute, cotton, plastic, or paper are a cheap form of container and are ideal for a wide variety of products including cement, fertilizer, flour, oil cakes, animal feeding products, chemicals and many consumer products. Their prime disadvantage is that they are subject to damage by water, sweat, leakages or, in the case of paper bags, breakage. The bags can be stacked on pallets to facilitate handling.

Barrels, hogsheads and drums are used for the conveyance of liquid or greasy cargoes. The main problems associated with this type of packing is the likelihood of leakage if the unit is not properly sealed, and the possibility of the drums becoming rusty during transit. Acids can also be carried in plastic drums and bottles. Such a form of packing, particularly drums, can have a resale value in certain countries overseas, whilst others are used indefinitely in various transits, particularly hogsheads.

Boxes, cases and metal-lined cases are also used extensively particularly in 'tween deck tonnage and liner cargo type of services. It is an expensive form of packing and has a certain resale value in certain countries overseas. Overall, this type of packing gives complete protection and lessens risk of pilferage plus an aid to handling. Basically, this form of packing is wooden in construction and varies in size and capacity. Moreover, it may be strengthened by the provision of battens and metal binding. Many of them, such as tea chests, are lined to create airtight packing, so as to overcome the difficulties that arise when passing through zones of variable temperature. This form of packing is particularly prominent with surface transport and is used for much machinery and other items of expensive equipment. However, it is becoming less popular as the cost of timber has risen sharply in recent years and containerization has lessened the need for such elaborate robust packing in certain trades.

Carboys, or glass containers enclosed in metal baskets have a limited use and are primarily employed for the carriage of acids and other dangerous liquids transported in small quantities. Again, it is a packing form found primarily in sea transport.

Cartons are a very common form of packing in all modes of international distribution involving particularly consumer type of products. They may be constructed of cardboard, strawboard or fibreboard. This form of packing is very much on the increase as it is relatively inexpensive, expandable, aids marketing, handling and stowage. It is particularly ideal for containerization and palletized consignments — the latter featuring prominently in the air freight field with the cartons affixed by metal bands to the pallet. The principal disadvantage is its susceptibility to crushing and pilfering. It is a very flexible form of packing and, therefore, prevents the breakage which may occur if rigid containers are used. Polystyrene now features more and more as a packing aid in cartons.

Crates or skeleton cases are a form of container halfway between a bale and a case. They are of wooden construction. Lightweight goods of larger cubic capacity such as machinery, domestic appliances like refrigerators, cycles and certain foodstuffs, for instance oranges, are suitable for this form of packing. This form of packing is used both in air and sea transport.

Palletization is closely associated with packing. The pallet may be of steel or wooden construction. A typical size is 1000 mm x 1200 mm, has a capacity of two tonnes and in appearance is like a platform on which the cargo is placed. An aperture is provided at each side to enable the fork life truck to mobilize/handle the pallet. Wooden pallets by which the cargo is anchored are very common in air freight thereby facilitating cargo handling on a unitized basis. The pallet accompanies the cargo throughout the transit. Wooden pallets are regarded as expended equipment when provided by the shipper who anchors the cargo to it. The pallet is manoeuvred by the fork lift truck described on page 78 and illustrated in DIAGRAM V.

Packaging is now universally recognized as a decisive selling point in the realm of household consumer goods and similar products. Mass production, marketing, consumer advertising, display, design, presentation, protection hygiene and self-service retailing have made mechanical wrapping an almost universal necessity for small consumer goods. Modern packaging materials combine with modern handling equipment to make stacking at greater height possible resulting in saving of floor space. Improvements are constantly becoming possible in the durability and protective quality of the package as technology progresses.

To the UK exporter who is anxious to improve his packaging distribution technique, it is suggested he consults the Packaging Division of the Research Association for the Paper and Board, Printing and Packaging Industries (PIRA) of Leatherhead, Surrey. This organization provides the following for which a fee is raised:

(1) Evaluation in laboratory conditions the performance of filled packages.

(2) Arranged consultancy facilities on, for example, the development of packaging for new products, ways of reducing packaging costs and of improving the protection provided by existing packs, and how best to organize packaging activity in your firm.

(3) To provide information on packaging suppliers regulations and appropriate standards.

(4) To measure, test or analyse the properties of packing materials to enable the client to (i) prepare specifications; (ii) to check the mate-

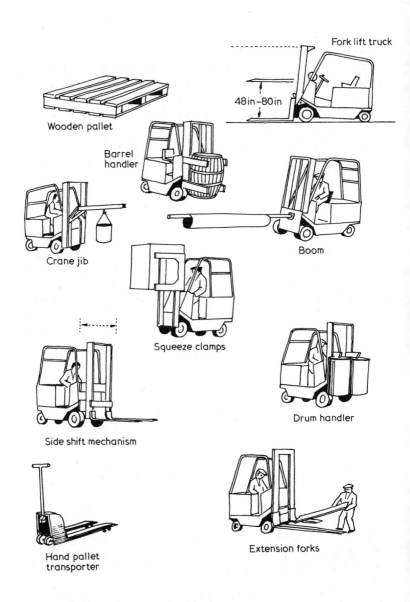

Wooden pallet

Fork lift truck

48 in - 80 in

Barrel handler

Crane jib

Boom

Squeeze clamps

Side shift mechanism

Drum handler

Hand pallet transporter

Extension forks

V Fork lift trucks

rials conform to packaging requirements to recognized standards; (iii) to assess their ability to withstand transit conditions; and (iv) to detect and prevent any harmful effects on a product of a specific packaging material.

Finally, the shipper must continuously review the form of packaging used in the light of the foregoing factors and the need to remain competive coupled with rising standards.

STOWAGE OF CARGO

To the exporter, it is important he is aware of the principle of cargo stowage, particularly in an era where more shippers are stuffing containers or operating their own TIR international road haulage vehicle between UK and Continent and beyond. Overall, the prime consideration is the safety of the transport unit employed which may be a container, vessel, aircraft or road vehicle. It is the overriding factor to be borne in mind throughout the transit that the merchandise does not impair the general safety of the transport unit and likewise it is not a danger to others. Moreover, one must bear in mind that stowage standards are rising all the time and the shipper should always seek prior advice if in doubt. This is particularly relevant to containerization where most major container operators provide a free advisory service on the principles of container stowage.

Basically there are four main factors to consider in the stowage of cargo:

(1) The best possible use should be made of the available dead weight or cubic capacity. It may be a container, road vehicle, ship or aircraft. Broken stowage which is space wasted by cargo of irregular shaped packages or irregularity of cargo spaces, should be kept to a minimum consistent with the general stability of the transport unit. Generally 10-15% of the total cubic capacity is allowed for broken stowage.

A stowage plan detailing the cargo location can greatly facilitate achieving a good utilization of available space compatible with safety standards and is so used extensively in shipping, air freight cargo hold distribution, containerization and the large TIR international road haulage vehicle used by a freight forwarder. Then, as far as practicable, full use should be made of the cubic capacity of the transport unit. If there is not an even distribution of cargo, it could result in an unstable load and it encourages cargo movement throughout the transit. In the case of a vessel, an uneven distribution of cargo can be compensated by ballasting the portion of the ship empty of cargo.

(2) Allied to the previous item is the need to prevent damage to the ship, road vehicle, aircraft or container. Not only must there be a proper distribution of cargo to ensure adequate stability and trim, but also it must be properly secured to prevent shifting. If there is a movement of the cargo during the transit, it will tend to cause the transport unit to become unstable thereby creating a serious hazard. In the case of a vessel, she will tend to list, which is particularly relevant to movement of bulk cargoes such as grain, small coal, flintstone, or iron ores. The situation is more serious when dangerous cargoes are involved irrespective of the transport mode. To reduce risk of cargo movement, dunnage is provided. This is in the form of foam rubber, polystyrene, timber boards, mats or inflatable bags which are placed between the cargo to prevent movement during the transit. The shipper must be careful of the type used for some countries, particularly in Australasia, where stringent regulations exist prescribing the dunnage material which may be used, for example, does not permit timber. Again one cannot stress too strongly the need to have total regard to safety of the transit which is the prime consideration.

(3) Similarly, cargo which is fragile, taints very easily, is liable to leakage, scratches easily, has strong odours, or is liable to sweat requires proper segregation, otherwise the carrier will be faced with heavy claims and possible loss of much goodwill amongst shippers. Obviously a crate of oranges with a penetrating odour cannot be stowed adjacent to a consignment of tea, which taints easily, and machinery cannot be placed on top of chinaware.

(4) Finally, a proper segregation of different consignments for various destinations/areas/ports/countries must be made to prevent delay in distribution and avoid double handling. This is a task primarily for the shipowner, airline, container operator, or freight forwarder — the latter two being particularly involved in consolidated/groupage consignments. Again the stowage plan has a significant role to play in such a situation.

Our study of cargo stowage would not be complete without an

examination of the principles of ISO container stowage, which is an increasingly popular method of international distribution. The container specification is found on pages 42-45 and the relevant diagram on page 44. Moreover, an increasing number of exporters are using the full container load consignment and undertaking their own stowage. Details of the principles of container stowage are detailed as follows. Again it cannot be stressed too strongly that safe container transport depends primarily on a correct and immovable cargo stow and an even weight distribution.

(1) The container must be stowed tightly so that lateral and longitudinal movement of the cargo within is impossible. Tight stowage can be achieved by making the shape and the dimensions of the package an optimum module of the container. Alternatively, if a unit load is being used such as a pallet, the base of it must form a module of the container.

(2) As an alternative to item (1), the cargo must be effectively restrained within the container. This is necessary for a variety of reasons including: (a) to prevent collapse of the stow while packing, unpacking, or during transit, for example, rolls of linoleum on end; (b) to prevent any movement during transit of part-loads or if single heavy items, for example, large pieces of machinery, (the heavier the item the more damage it will do if allowed to move); and finally, (c) to prevent the 'face' of the stow collapsing and leaning against the container doors, that is, to prevent it from falling out when the doors are opened at final destination or for customs inspection.

(3) The consignment must be adequately secured. Details of the various techniques are given below:

(i) Shoring — bars, struts and spars located in cargo voids to keep the cargo pressed against the walls or other cargo.

(ii) Lashing — rope, wire, chains, strapping or net secured to proper anchoring points within the container and tensioned against the cargo.

(iii) Wedging — wooden distance pieces, pads of synthetic material, inflatable dunnage to fill voids in the cargo and keep it immobile against the container walls.

(iv) Locking — cargo built up to give a three dimensional brick wall effect.

Basically, there is no simple formula to apply when securing cargo in a container and only experience can aid perfection and solution.

Each cargo must be treated on its merits — the type of cargo, the way in which it is stowed, the cargo handling equipment available and the permanent fittings in the container. The built-in securing points, dunnage brackets etc. should be used extensively. Any timber dunnage used must be dry and comply with any quarantine regulations. Any shoring which presses against the container wall should have extra timber laid longitudinally between the wall and point of support to spread the weight over two or more side posts. Useful filler pieces for wedging or preventing chafe include old tyres, polyurethane slabs, macerated paper pads, and for light packages, rolled-up cardboard. Unless an identical stow is anticipated on the return container journey, it is best if the lashing equipment be chosen and considered as expendable. Where synthetic strapping material is used terylene is preferable to nylon for heavy loads as it is less liable to stretch.

To restrain cargo various techniques exist. Again it depends on the commodity involved. Top heavy articles should be wedged, shored and lashed to prevent toppling. Heavy weights should be secured to stout ring-bolts (sited in the container floor and side walls) and/or be shored with timber. Chain or wire with bottle screws may be used. Wheeled vehicles should be chocked, and lashed with Spanish windlasses, with the chocks chamfered or padded to protect the tyres. If the floor is of extruded aluminium, portable securing devices must be used. Resilient loads can cause lashings to slacken. This may be overcome by introducing elasticity, for example, rubber rope into the lashing pattern. No securing of pallets is necessary, provided the load is properly secured to the pallet, if the distance between pallets and container walls is 100 mm (4 in) or less. Pallets must not be allowed any longitudinal movement. If securing is necessary, stow pallets against container walls and wedge wood blocks between pallets. It may be necessary to insert sheets of board between pallet loads to protect against chafe and prevent bags, cartons, etc. interweaving and jamming the stow.

In many instances there is a space 400-2400 mm (1-24 in) remaining between the face of the cargo and container doors. Cargo must be prevented from collapsing into this space. It can be achieved in a variety of ways detailed as follows:

(1) Use of suitably positioned lashing points with wire, rope, strapping etc. woven across.

(2) A simple wooden gate for the wider gaps and heavier cargo.

(3) Use of filler pieces, that is, macerated paper pads, polystyrene, wood wool pads etc. for the narrower gaps and lighter cargoes, for example, cartons of biscuits.

Care must be taken to ensure that there is no 'fall out' when the container doors are opened. This is particularly relevant to a container which has been completely packed such as with cartons or sacks. Although this can sometimes be achieved by interlocking tiers of packages, it is better to make sure by using any fixing points located in the door posts of the container. Nylon strapping, polypropylene or wire threaded through such points form an effective barrier.

To ensure there is adequate and correct overall distribution of cargo within the covered container, the goods must be secure within their packages. Moreover, the pack itself must be as full as possible so as to resist pressures external to it. Packages must be sufficiently rigid to withstand the weight imposed upon them when stacked, usually to a minimum height of 2.10 m (8 ft). If more than one type of cargo is stowed in the container, it is essential they are all compatible and cannot contaminate or be contaminated. Heavy items and liquids should be placed at the bottom with light and dry ones on the top. Within practical physical limitations of handling, the unit package should be as large as possible since this can reduce costs by up to 20% and increase volumetric efficiency by up to 10%. Consult when practicable the consignee about the proposed method of loading and sequence. This will facilitate discharge at the destination. Where relevant, stowing should be carried out in sequence which will permit rapid checking and stowage operations during and subsequent to unloading. In the event of the consignment being subject to Customs pre-entry procedures, it would facilitate Customs examination, should this occur and obviate unloading, if such cargo was stowed at the door end of the container. Shippers should avoid having a gap in the stow along the centre line of the container or at the sides as this will generate cargo movement in the transit and possible cargo damage.

Undoubtedly much of the foregoing cargo stowage principles relative to ISO covered container can likewise be applied in many areas to stowage in other transport modes particularly train ferry wagon and the TIR international road haulage unit conveying consolidated/groupage cargo in a covered enclosed transport unit.

It would be appropriate to deal briefly with the equipment used in container stowage and discharge particularly as many exporters/importers have such cargo handling equipment in their factory/warehouse. Basically, the handling method used should be the one which gives the greater efficiency with economy and makes full use of any existing facilities and equipment available.

The most versatile tool for tiering/stacking cargo in a warehouse/container base etc. and for transporting loads up to a maximum of 2000 kg is the fork lift truck. Its general characteristics such as capacity, height of lift, speed etc. will depend on overall work factors. The fork lift truck specification required for container work includes: a maximum collapsed mast height of 80 in; a free lift minimum of 48 in; its motive power must be either battery, electric or gas depending on circumstances; the mast tilts must be as large as possible; the gradient capacity laden minimum 1 in 10; cushion tyres; and spot light and wheel loadings in accord with maximum permitted load.

A wide variety of fork lift types exist and these include the following which are illustrated on page 78 in DIAGRAM V.

(1) Side shift mechanism. This moves the forks laterally either side of centre and thus considerably reduces the necessity to manoeuvre the fork lift truck inside the container.

(2) Extension forks. These are used for handling awkward loads and to obtain extra reach. They are particularly useful, if the fork lift truck is of sufficient capacity, for clearing a space equivalent to the depth of the pallets on each side of a trailer mounted container, thus providing easy operation of the pallet transporters.

(3) Boom. Ideal for carpets, pipe etc.

(4) Barrel handler. In addition to clamping the barrel with two sets of upper and lower arms, it also revolves so that the barrel can be picked up and handled in the roll, or in the upright position.

(5) Crane jib. This converts the fork lift truck into a mobile crane.

(6) Drum handler. This permits the fork lift truck to handle one or two drums at a time.

(7) Squeeze-clamps. This is used for handling unit loads and individual items without the aid of pallets. The design and application of this attachment must be selected carefully since the operation of the clamp arms may be impeded by the container walls.

The foregoing types demonstrate the versatility of the fork type truck.

MARKING OF CARGO

Associated with packing is the marking of cargo. Basically, the export shipping mark and number is vital in the correct identification of the shipment irrespective of the transport mode. Moreover, it must be simple, easily identifiable and not masked with irrelevant information or old markings.

When goods are packed, they are marked on the outside in a manner which will remain legible for the whole of the transit. First of all, there is some mark of identification and then immediately underneath this for a maritime consignment, the port mark is shown. For example, the merchant may be T. Smith Ltd and the goods are being shipped in the mv Norfolk to Munich in which case the marks will be as follows:

T.S. Ltd.,
1783
Munich
via
Hamburg
679

The top line identifies the consignee or receiver. However for reasons of security and to eliminate pilferage, a simple identity code mark is often used — which is varied from time to time — which is neutral without any specific reference to the consignee. This is usually adopted by consignees who receive regular substantial shipments. Below this entry is the ultimate destination together with the sea port or airport of entry and packaging number.

In some trades, it is the practice to give the dimensions of the package in metres which may be used in assessing the freight. Moreover, it is preferable for the gross and net weights to be likewise shown. Overall, it is desirable that the foregoing markings should be portrayed on three faces of the package — preferably side, end/or ends and top — with all markings clearly shown using large clear lettering. All the foregoing criteria of cargo marking applies to other international transportation distribution modes such as air freight, road haulage, train ferry, and containerization, but it must be borne in mind they vary by individual trade and circumstance. It is also important to mention that the cargo markings are recorded on the bill of lading or other consignment note, such as CMR, CIM, air waybill used according to transport mode.

To facilitate handling and overcome differing language problems a recognized international marking symbol code is used, such as, *this way up, keep dry*, etc. These are printed on the exterior of the packing and a selection of them which have been accepted by the International Standards Organization is given in DIAGRAM IV.

Finally, it must be mentioned that the consignment must be adequately labelled giving the delivery address details. Nevertheless, it is relevant to note the export shipping mark forms the principal identification for the movement of the goods.

DANGEROUS CARGO

The movement internationally of dangerous cargo is very much on the increase and a strict code of acceptance is laid down for all forms of transport relative to the acceptance of this cargo particularly packing, documentation and marking specification. To the exporter who is unfamiliar with the situation and wishes to have adequate advice on a consignment, it is wise to consult a freight forwarder, container operator, airline or shipowner depending on the transport mode involved. Failure to comply with such regulations, particularly in documentation declaration and stowage, can lead to severe penalties and likewise endanger the transport mode involved together with other merchandise carried and crew.

The regulations relating to the movement of dangerous cargo by sea are defined in the UK by the Department of Trade and Industry. They conform to the Inter Governmental Maritime Consultative Organization Code. Details of the classification are given below:

Class I: Explosives.

Class II: Gases — compressed, liquified or dissolved under pressure.

Class III: Inflammable liquids.

Class IV: Inflammable solids and substances spontaneously combustable, or substances emitting inflammable gases when wet.

Class V: Oxidizing substances and organic peroxides.

(a) Oxidising substances.

(b) Organic peroxides.

Class VI: Poisonous (toxic) and infectious substances.

(a) Poisons.

Class VII: Radioactive substances.

Class VIII: Corrosives.

Class IX: Miscellaneous dangerous substances.

The shipowner like the airline will only handle such dangerous cargo by prior written arrangement and in the express condition the shipper provides a very full and adequate description of the cargo. If accepted a special stowage order will be issued which will indicate to the Master the cargo conforms to the prescribed code of acceptance laid down by the shipowner. It cannot be stressed too strongly that shipment will not take place until a special stowage order has been issued by the shipowner, which is the authority to shipment. Moreover, the shipper must fully describe the cargo and ensure it is correctly packed, marked and labelled. This he can do through a freight forwarder, which is often the practice.

To amplify the code of procedure regarding the movement of dangerous cargo internationally, it would be appropriate to examine shipment in ISO maritime covered containers which now follows.

In the main, the container is ideal for the shipment of dangerous cargo particularly as it avoids multiple handling, protects the goods from interference by unauthorized persons and eliminates the risk of damage from the use of inappropriate methods of slinging. The following information is required at the time of booking the container:

(1) Name of vessel.

(2) Port of loading.

(3) Port of discharge.

(4) Correct technical name of the substance.

(5) Quantity — gross and net weight in kilos.

(6) Description of packing (with inner if valid).

(7) Classification of substance (IMCO code).

(8) Properties of substance.

(9) Flash point, if any.

With 'tween deck or bulk cargo shipments the loading of the ship is undertaken by stevedores, but with containerization this is done by container packers which are usually container operators or freight forwarders. Accordingly, with regard to the latter, a 'packing certificate' must be completed which certifies the following:

(1) The container was clean, dry and fit to receive the cargo.

(2) No cargo known to be incompatible has been stowed therein.

(3) All packages have been inspected for damage, and only dry and sound packages loaded.

(4) All packages have been properly stowed and secured and suitable materials used.

(5) The container and goods have been properly labelled.

(6) A dangerous goods declaration has been received/completed for each dangerous consignment packed in the container.

Basically the code of 'one class — one container' must be observed unless the container operator has expressly agreed to a relaxation. Substances which fall into the same class but are incompatible must also be stowed in different containers, for example, peroxides and permanganates (both oxidizing substances).

Dangerous goods may be incompatible with certain non-dangerous substances. Examples are poisons and foodstuffs, or those which react in contact with harmless organic materials such as nitrates, chlorates, etc.

A container in transit is subjected to acceleration and deceleration factors in a longitudinal and to some degree, a lateral direction when travelling overland, and in a vertical and lateral direction at sea. At all times it is subjected to some degree of vibration. Hence, the contents must be firmly stowed and secured against movement and chafing. Particular care with dangerous cargoes must be taken to ensure that the contents will not fall outwards when the doors are opened. Dangerous cargoes forming only part of the load must be stowed in the door area of the container for ease of access and inspection. In the case of non-dangerous goods, damage arising from poor stowage is usually confined to the container concerned, but in the case of dangerous goods the effects could be widespread.

It is relevant to note that obnoxious/irritant substances are classified as non-hazardous, but must be stowed and treated as dangerous cargo. Hence, any cargo having such substances must be clearly labelled prior to shipment and the carrier notified.

All dangerous cargo offered for shipment must be correctly labelled with the appropriate IMCO dangerous goods label(s) of 10 x 10 cm minimum size. It should indicate the principal hazard, and where one or more secondary hazards exist, additional labels indicating that hazard, but with the numeral on the label deleted, must be affixed. The label should be affixed at a height of approximately

1.70 m (5 ft 7 in) from the base of the container and currently are sited one on left side near the closed end, a second on the right side near the door end, and a third label on the left-hand door. The right-hand label should be positioned so that it will not become obscured by the door when fully opened.

The universal adoption of the International Maritime Dangerous Goods Code (IMCO) has greatly facilitated the movement of dangerous goods between countries. Accordingly, a dangerous goods labelling code for maritime consignments exists and some codes are given in DIAGRAM VI.

With regard to dangerous classified cargo conveyed by air, the code of regulations are defined by the International Air Transport Association (IATA). They are more severe than maritime transport. Some substances are entirely prohibited, others may only travel in all cargo aircraft, whilst some are permitted to be conveyed in passenger aircraft. All those which may travel by air require special packaging, labelling and documentation. Moreover, quantity restrictions are also applied per flight in the interest of safety. Details of the IATA classification are given below:

Combustible liquids.
Compressed gases (flammable and non-flammable).
Corrosive materials.
Etiologic agents (highly infectious cultures and material).
Explosives.
Flammable liquids and solids.
Magnetized materials.
Other restricted articles (ORA), groups A, B and C.
Oxidizing materials.
Poisons.
Radioactive materials.

As an aircraft climbs the atmospheric pressure outside decreases. Hence depending on the type (and angle) of the aircraft involved the hold and cabin pressure will rise in varying degrees. Temperatures in the holds of aircraft drop considerably depending on the direction and altitude of the flight. On some occasions, temperatures may fall below freezing point, yet on the ground, particularly in tropical areas, very high temperatures may be experienced. Such temperature changes affect substances in varying ways. Liquids, especially

VI IMCO dangerous goods labels

volatile ones, are susceptable to changes in temperature and most of them expand as the temperature rises. Containers of liquids must not be entirely filled, but provided with adequate ullage (outage) space to allow for their expansion. Flammable and other volatile liquids with a high co-efficient of expansion require a minimum ullage (outage) of 2% at 54.4°C (130°F). As a broad guide, the extremes of temperature which could be encountered in air transportation including ground handling range from —40°C to 54.4°C (—40°F to 130°F).

Packaging of restricted substances are given in Sections IV and VI of the IATA regulations and the exporter should obtain and study them closely. Alternatively, consult the airline or freight forwarder. The general packaging principles are given in Section V of the IATA regulations. The following principles should be applied both to dangerous classified and ordinary air freight cargo:

(1) The container must be tested to ensure it will withstand a first ascent-descent pressure change, but not subsequent ones encountered on a multi-sector journey. Special attention to be given to closures, gaskets, can seams, and soldered joints.

(2) Plastic bags to be checked as pressure alteration may cause ballooning and bursting.

(3) Low temperatures can affect some materials, particularly some plastics. These should not be used as, for example, low temperature shrinkage of necks or shoulders in spray or syphon containers fitted with screw caps.

(4) Containers of liquid restricted substances must be capable of withstanding a minimum internal gauge pressure of 11 lb/in^2 (7.5 x 10^3 kg/m^2) without leakage when filled to the appropriate ullage. Certain specific containers, such as drums and barrels must withstand a higher pressure.

(5) Breakable or puncturable containers such as glass, earthenware, plastic, must be well cushioned in absorbent material and packed in strong outside containers.

(6) Absorbent materials must be selected carefully. Some articles require non-combustible and/or non-reactive absorbents.

(7) All packaging must be resistant to its contents. The shipper must ensure the packaging contains nothing which could be eroded by its contents or form a hazardous compound with them. For example, certain types of plastic are unsuitable for some ethers, mineral oils and acids.

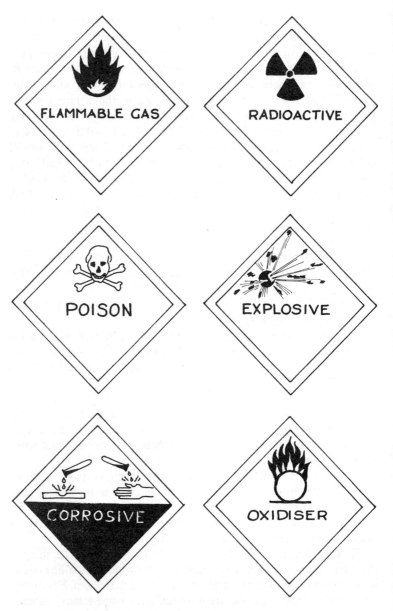

VII   IATA dangerous goods labels

(8) All different restricted articles must be packed individually. Outside containers must not enclose inside containers of substances which when mixed would cause a dangerous evolution of heat or gas, or produce corrosive substances.

(9) Friction-type lids on metal containers of paints and other products must be fitted with retaining clips or other suitable locking devices.

(10) Sacks, when permitted, must be water resistant and made tight to prevent sifting of contents.

(11) Dangerous classified cargo is not permitted to be carried in unit load devices.

Documentation relative to restricted air cargo is most important and must be strictly adhered to. The air waybill must adequately describe the cargo and quantity in accord with the following:

(1) The proper shipping name of the restricted article. The proper shipping name for 'not otherwise specified' items will be followed by the name or composition of the article in brackets.

(2) Its article number and class are given in Section IV of the regulations.

(3) The type of label, if any, required.

If the shipment is only acceptable on all-cargo aircraft, it should be marked 'cargo aircraft only'. Likewise restricted articles should be identified separately if they form only part of a consignment. Goods which are not covered by the restricted articles rules, which are named in a way which could indicate that they are restricted, for example, chemical, toiletries, should be marked, 'not restricted' by IATA regulations.

The shippers certificate must be completed by the shipper in duplicate for all restricted cargoes. This gives the fullest details of the consignment and signed by the shipper, and not by the IATA cargo agent, consolidator, or freight forwarder. It accompanies the air waybill throughout the transit.

The correct label to each individual restricted article package must be provided and the relevant class label found in Section III of IATA regulations. A selection is found in DIAGRAM VII.

Dangerous cargo now forms an important part of international trade. The exporter should seek advice if in doubt before preparing for any shipment.

Finally, in regard to the movement of dangerous goods by road within Europe, the relevant conditions are found in the European Agreement concerning the international carriage of dangerous goods by road (ADR). This came into force on 29th July 1968 in the territories of those countries which had notified or acceded to the Agreement. At present these countries are Austria, Belgium, France, Federal Republic of Germany, German Democratic Republic, Italy, Luxemburg, the Netherlands, Portugal, Spain, Sweden, Switzerland, Yugoslavia and the United Kingdom. The purpose of ADR is to ensure that dangerous goods being conveyed by road are able to cross international frontiers without hindrance, provided such goods are packed and labelled in accordance with Annex A to the agreement, and that vehicles comply with the provisions of Annex B.

An important feature of ADR is that tank vehicles and certain other vehicles carrying explosives are subject to technical inspection and a certificate procedure in their country of registration to ensure that they conform with ADR requirements and with the normal safety regulations in force in the country of origin governing brakes, lighting, steering etc.

UK road hauliers intending to carry dangerous goods to or through these countries will require an ADR certificate. Vehicles are inspected for this certificate at certain Department of the Environment Goods Vehicle Testing Stations by the Department's vehicle examiners, and application forms for this test may be obtained from Traffic Area Office. Before this test is carried out the tanks vehicles must be examined and tested by an inspecting authority approved for the purpose by the Home Office. Copies of the ADR are available from HM Stationery Office.

Operators wishing to take vehicles by sea to Continental ports should bear in mind that the carriage of dangerous goods by sea in the UK is governed by the Merchant Shipping (Dangerous Goods) Rules, 1978. Advice on the suitability of the design of road tankers to be used for the carriage of dangerous goods in ships may be obtained from the Department of Trade and Industry, Sunley House, 90/93 High Holborn, London, WC1. Basically, Department of Trade and Industry (DTI) recommendations are in some respects more stringent than ADR and it is, therefore, advisable for operators to clear any proposals for the shipment of vehicles containing dangerous goods with the DTI.

CHAPTER 7

Export Customs Practice

*Organization and workings of the HM Customs and Excise Department.
Bonds, deposits and guarantees. Brussels Nomenclature. Export controls.
Export documentation and procedures. Outward clearance of a vessel.
Inward processing relief. Outward processing relief. The European Economic Community documentation. Common agricultural policy. ATA carnets. TIR carnets. The international road haulage consignment operation.*

ORGANIZATION AND WORKINGS OF THE HM CUSTOMS AND EXCISE DEPARTMENT

Over the past ten years there has been a gradual change in the pattern of control exercised by the Customs and Excise Department with relaxations being introduced where appropriate to facilitate the clearance of imported goods, especially those from the EEC and a tightening of some aspects in the control of exported goods.

It must be borne in mind that 'Customs' have to cope with various requirements both at export and at import. These are as follows:

(1) The provision of a record of exports and imports which will provide the HM Government with sufficient information to assess, and in turn, control the 'balance of trade'.

(2) To ensure that no goods liable to duty or levy enter or leave the country without that duty or levy being brought to account.

(3) To ensure that temporarily imported goods which have been relieved of duty are re-exported within the time allowed for relief or, if not exported, that the appropriate duty is paid on them.

(4) By collecting revenues due and to provide a valuable source of income for the Government working under the general control of the Treasury, the Customs and Excise Department is responsible for collecting revenue from three sources detailed as under:

(i) Customs duties. Under UK and EEC regulations these duties are levied on various classes of imported goods.

(ii) Excise duties. Levied on certain classes of goods manufactured, and on transactions taking place in the UK.

(iii) Value added tax. Charged on a wide range of goods and services originating in the UK and on most imported goods.

In addition to its main functions of assessing, collecting and safeguarding the revenue, the Customs and Excise Department is often called upon to perform non-revenue functions for other HM Government departments. Consequently, at all ports and airports of any appreciable size the Customs and Excise Department exercises control over goods and persons entering or leaving the country.

These non-revenue functions include such items as: the control of goods entering or leaving the country requiring a licence from the Department of Trade or other Government departments (for example, Ministry of Agriculture, Fisheries and Food, Home Office etc.); exchange control; the collection of statistical information for the Department of Trade; work for the Ministry of Defence (Admiralty) and Environment (Transport and Civil Aviation); health control of passengers and crews (in conjunction with the Ministry of Health); and the collection of light dues for Trinity House.

At the head of the Customs and Excise Department is a Board consisting of a chairman, two deputy chairmen and nine commissioners each having a functional responsibility in the organization and running of the Department. The Board operates through headquarters offices situated mainly in London and Southend-on-Sea. For ease of control, the country is divided into twenty-nine geographic areas called 'collections', each in the charge of a senior Customs Officer with the rank of Collector. Depending on the size and work load of his collections, a Collector may be aided in his administration by a Deputy and Assistant Collectors. Within each collection there are smaller areas called 'districts' consisting of one or more 'stations'. Stations may be specialized, for example, dealing with the work of a particular wharf, warehouse or distillery, or may be general, dealing with all forms of Customs and Excise work in the locality. In cities and large ports, a station may have a dozen or more officers, while in other places there may be only one officer. A district usually consists of several stations and is under the control of a surveyor.

Officers working within a collection may be called upon to perform a wide variety of jobs and could be used in one or more of the following areas of work:

(1) Landing and shipping.
(2) Warehousing.
(3) Excise.

(4) Value added tax.
(5) Preventive duties.

(1) Landing and shipping officers are the people who directly control the importation and exportation of goods. They are responsible for ensuring that correct documentation is produced to cover the transaction, that all Governmental requirements are fulfilled and that all revenues due are collected.

(2) The lodgement of goods into a 'bonded warehouse' is a method by which traders may defer payment of duty, or at times, reclaim duty already paid. The term bonded warehouse indicates accommodation for which the owner has given his written promise under bond to comply with certain conditions laid down when the Commissioners approved the premises for 'Customs' business. Bonds may be given as security for a number of different transactions and will be described fully later in the chapter. The warehouse officer is responsible for the control of all receipts into warehouse, operations within warehouse, for example, bottling of wines, and deliveries of goods from warehouse. He is also required to ensure that duty is paid on all goods delivered from warehouse to a dutiable use.

There are two main types of warehouse:

(i) Crown locked. In which typed stock records are maintained by a resident officer and the premises may only be opened in his presence. At other times the warehouse door is secured by both a trader's and a 'crown' lock.

(ii) An open warehouse. Here the officer is not resident and the warehouse keeper is allowed free access to his premises and maintains his own stock account. The main stipulation here is that the officer must give his permission for all receipts, operations and deliveries, and must be allowed free access to both premises and stock records at all reasonable times.

The conditions of approval of a warehouse are rather complicated and do not form part of this section. If the reader is interested an explanation of Customs requirements is given in HM Customs Notice Number 186 available from their office address found in Appendix B. This applies to all such HM Customs Notices mentioned in this chapter.

(3) Excise. As mentioned earlier, the Excise Officer is responsible for collecting the revenue on certain classes of goods manufactured

and transactions taking place within the UK.

There is quite a large difference between Excise duties which are levied to raise money and Customs duties which are for the main part imposed to protect home industries. The goods listed below are liable to excise duty when produced in the UK but to both excise and customs duties if imported from abroad.

Beer   Hydrocarbon Oils
Wine   Matches
Spirits   Mechanical Lighters
Tobacco

The transactions mentioned above are largely involved with the production and sale of the goods listed but may also cover such items as pool and betting duties, gaming machines and bingo, distillers and rectifiers premises and various other facets.

(4) Value added tax. This tax was introduced into the UK on 1st April 1973, as one of the conditions of membership of the EEC. It replaced two existing taxes viz: (i) Purchase tax — considered by the original six members of the EEC to be too selective, and (ii) Selective employment tax — a rather unfair tax for labour intensive trades.

Value added tax is a consumer tax which is levied on goods and services supplied in the UK and on goods imported from abroad. All supplies must be either exempt or liable but if liable may fall under any one of three headings: (a) Zero rated (b) Positive standard rates and (c) Positive higher rated.

Currently (January 1979), the standard rate is set at 8% and the higher rate at 12½%. When endeavouring to decide which rate (if any) applies to goods and services, it is best to work by a process of elimination. First ascertain whether they are listed as exempt, if not then turn to the list of zero rated items, and failing this turn to the list of higher rated items. If they do not appear on any of these lists then they must be standard rated. The lists are contained within HM Customs Notice number 701, 'Scope and Coverage of VAT'. In addition to the lists, they provide further notes relating to specific headings within the particular lists and give details of the proper liability where there are borderline cases.

A trader who is registered for VAT is entitled to reclaim input tax on those goods which he exports. In order to be able to make a claim, the trader must keep adequate records of all export transactions which must be in sufficient detail for Customs to be able to identify the goods against proof of exportation. The type of proof required will differ according to the way in which the goods are exported.

Any trader whose annual turnover exceeds £7500 is required to apply to his local VAT Office (address can be found in the local telephone book) for registration. Once registered, the trader is given a unique nine digit number and is required to make a quarterly return on form VAT 100. On this return he shows the total of all purchases on which he has paid VAT, together with the amount paid. He also gives all suppliers to which he has charged VAT together with amount collected. By deducting VAT paid from VAT collected he can see how much VAT must be paid to Customs. At times the tax paid may exceed the tax collected in which case the trader makes a claim upon Customs. With regard to imported goods, most traders simply quote their registered number on the import document (called an import entry) and account for tax payable on their quarterly return. Should the importer not be registered, or be using the goods for a purpose for which he may not use his registered number, tax must be paid at the same time as import duty and before the goods are released. Value for VAT is defined as 'value for duty, plus duty, plus any other dutiable charges, for example, CAP levy.'

(5) Preventive duties. Though numerically small, the preventive staff or waterguard, as they are often called, are probably the best known members of the Customs and Excise Department. These are the people seen manning the ports and airports, and whose main task is the prevention of smuggling and the apprehension of smugglers. Besides these purely Customs tasks, they are involved in the control of imported and exported goods, and are employed both for Customs purposes and for local and central government purposes where they have an agency function. We normally think of goods and people entering the UK through ports and airports, but there is a third entry point. This is by land over the land boundary between Northern and Southern Ireland. Here too Preventive Officers are stationed to carry out checks on both persons and vehicles to prevent the importation or exportation or prohibited items and to assess and collect any revenues due.

BONDS, DEPOSITS AND GUARANTEES

Mention has already been made of the fact that a bond is required in certain circumstances as security for unpaid duty. Customs insist on various types of security to cover the situations where duty has not been paid outright, although the goods involved are liable. Depending on the circumstances, three basic types of security are used as follows:

(1) Bonds.
(2) Deposits.
(3) Guarantees.

(1) Bonds. These fall into three categories: (i) Ordinary. (ii) General. (iii) Premises.

(i) An ordinary bond serves as security for one transaction — examples are: (a) Temporary importation. (b) Transhipment. (c) Removal of goods from one Customs controlled point to another.

(ii) General bonds are similar to ordinary bonds except they cover a series of transactions the nature of which is detailed in the wording of the bond.

(iii) The premises bond, as the name implies, is entered into to cover the duty liability of any goods within those premises, which could be such places as wharves, transit sheds, warehouses, inland clearance depots, hydrocarbon oil installations and excise factories, that is, a place where goods liable to excise duty are produced, possibly from goods not liable to duty. In fact, a premises bond can cover any place in which goods are stored on which any duty or tax or levy is liable to be paid but has not been paid.

In Customs parlance, a bond is called 'An Instrument Under Seal', wherein the signatories bind themselves to pay to the crown any monies due should any of the conditions of the bond not be fulfilled. No matter what type of bond is used, four key words also pertain as follows:

Principal. The person who undertakes to comply with the conditions of the bond and to pay the Crown any monies due should any of these conditions not be fulfilled.

Surety. The person or firm acting as guarantor for the principal and who will be called upon to pay any monies due should the Principal fail or be unable to do so.

The Crown. In the person of a member of the Customs and Excise Department who allows goods to be released, stored or acted upon without payment of duty.

Penalty. This is a sum of money based on the duty liability of the goods released or in the case of premises, the anticipated maximum liability of dutiable goods within those premises at any one time.

The status of Principal and Surety will differ according to the Penalty involved. Up to £5000 it may be two members of the firm involved but over that amount the surety must be a guarantee society approved by Customs for that purpose.

(2) Deposits. Again deposits fall into three categories: (i) GO 12/30 deposits. (ii) Miscellaneous cash deposit. (iii) Standing deposits.

(i) GO 12/30: This was originally named after Customs General Order Number 12 of 1930 and, although the order no longer exists, the terminology has been retained because of its familiarity and ease of use. Its use is covered by Sections 255/255(a) of the Customs and Excise Act 1952 and deals with the release of imported goods when there is insufficient evidence to take duty outright or where evidence of origin is needed to authenticate a claim to a preferential rate of duty. Examples are as follows:

(a) Basis of value. At times, it is not evident whether imported goods are being entered at a value which is acceptable to Customs for duty purposes, in which case release is offered on deposit pending an investigation into the offered basis of value.

(b) Out-turn — where goods are imported in bulk final assessment of duty liability is deferred until the actual quantities out-turned from the vessel are known. Deposit being based on the invoiced quantity.

(c) Account sales. Similar to (b) except that in this case imported goods are fresh fruit and vegetables and the deposit is based on an average market for similar goods and final duty is calculated on actual prices realized.

(d) Evidence of origin. Before imported goods can be released at a preferential rate of duty acceptable, evidence of the origin of the goods must be produced. If this evidence is not forthcoming or is unacceptable, Customs will allow release on deposit at the full rate of duty pending production of satisfactory evidence of origin.

(ii) Miscellaneous cash deposit. Usually referred to by initials, the MCD is used in two basic circumstances:

(a) As security for temporary importations.

(b) Where release of goods is required before documentation can be finalized. For example, bill of sight, pending result of test, incorrect tariff code.

The most usual use of the standing deposits is in the rapid clearance of perishable goods. The importer/agent lodges a sum of money with the Collector of Customs who then allows release of the goods upon presentation of import documentation to the Customs Officer at the actual place of importation.

Release of the goods is allowed against and up to the total of the sum deposited. When the documentation is complete and duty paid, the figure on deposit will be increased by the sum paid.

Although very useful for quick release of goods, the deposit system has its disadvantages insofar that it ties up money which could possibly be used to advantage elsewhere.

(3) Guarantees. Guarantees are similar to bonds and deposits in that they are used as a safeguard for unpaid duty but are less formal than either. They are required for three types of transaction as under: (i) Deferred duty payments. (ii) Agricultural levy. (iii) Movements under full community transit procedure.

(i) Deferred duty payments. This is a very useful system whereby imports (and agents) are allowed to defer payment of duty for up to about 45 days, with an average of 30 days. Duty payable under this system is called for on the fifteenth day of the month following that in which the transaction took place. The guarantee must be sufficient to cover the potential liability for a complete months trading; it must be given by a bank approved by the Commissioners of Customs and Excise; and fulfil the following conditions:

(a) The guarantee must be lodged with the Collector where deferment is claimed.

(b) The guarantee must cover all the duties etc. deferred throughout the Collection in any one month.

(c) The total guarantee may be divided and portions allocated to sub offices only on written application to the collector. Importers and agents may also be allowed to lodge guarantees with specified allocations to meet requirements in more than one Collection. The guarantee is given on Customs form C 1201 with the guarantor being held responsible for seeing that the monthly limits are not exceeded.

(ii) Agricultural levy. Under the Common Agricultural Policy, guarantees are required to cover various transactions involving Intervention Board licences, pre-fixing certificates, and pre-financing of exports. The full details will be given later in a section on Common Agricultural Policy.

(iii) Movements under full community transit procedure. With a few exceptions, which will be mentioned in a section on community transit (CT), all movements under full CT procedure requires to be guaranteed. There are three types of guarantee used for full CT procedure, which are as follows:

(a) Individual (forms C1145 and C1147). This covers a single movement and bears a list of the goods involved but does not show the duty liability. The guarantee is accepted at the Office of Departure and is retained there together with copy one of the relevant 'T' form.

(b) Comprehensive (form C1144 or C1146). This guarantee is used to cover a number of transactions and specifies a sum of money which the guarantor is liable to pay. The guarantee may only be accepted at Customs offices which have been designated as guarantee offices. The collector decides the liability to be specified which is usually calculated as one quarter of the total duty, levy etc. at risk during any 28 day period. The collector's office retains the comprehensive guarantee and issues to the guarantor one or more guarantee certificates on form C1141 for him to produce in support of any 'T' forms presented.

(c) Flat rate. A flat rate guarantee is an undertaking by the guarantor to pay on demand any amount up to a maximum of 5000 units of account in respect of any guarantee voucher (on form C1142) issued by him. The acceptance of a flat rate guarantee by the Commissioners of Customs allows the guarantor to issue guarantee vouchers to any person he choses. These vouchers are retained by the office of departure. Normally only one voucher is required to cover one operation regardless of the liability involved, but in certain circumstances more vouchers can be called for.

BRUSSELS NOMENCLATURE

The Brussels Nomenclature Tariff was first introduced into the UK on 1st January 1958 as a result of a conference of the Customs Co-operation Council who agreed to use a common Customs tariff. The idea of a common tariff was first mooted just after the First World War, the basic idea being that if there was an internationally agreed way of describing goods this would help to avoid ambiguities and make the fixing of duty rates between nations easier. The advent of the Second World War caused the idea to be shelved although quite a good deal of work had been done on a decimally based system of identifying goods. In the early 1950s the idea was again considered. Interested parties worked together in Brussels to formulate a workable nomenclature so that anybody describing goods in one country could be sure that somebody in another country would be able to identify those goods within prescribed limits by consulting their own copy of the nomenclature. The Brussels Nomenclature was completed by 1957 and was accepted by all members of the Customs Co-operation Council (and also by most non-members) as being an ideal system of internationally identifying goods for tariff purposes.

The UK Customs and Excise tariff, besides being a complete nomenclature, is also a very useful book of reference. It contains a great deal of information, useful to importers, exporters and their agents, relating to basic procedures and also contains information relating to reliefs from duties, preferential rates of duty, suspensions from duty etc. In many cases, where information given in the tariff is not fully comprehensive, it gives sources for further reading, for example, the numbers of relative HM Customs Public Notices. Because of its importance and the vast amount of information contained within it, one cannot emphasize too strongly the need for all those involved in importing or exporting to familiarize themselves with its contents. Incorrect tariff description is one of the most frequent causes for rejection of documentation by Customs.

Many years ago Conan Doyle made his best known character, Sherlock Holmes say, 'If you first eliminate the impossible, whatever is left, however improbable, must be the answer.' The identification of the appropriate tariff number works very much on this principle — by first eliminating what the goods are not, we are eventually, with care, left with the correct identifying number.

The Brussels Nomenclature is divided into 21 Sections which is subdivided into 99 Chapters and 1905 main headings. By glancing through the list of chapters, it is possible to see that each chapter covers a particular type of commodity, for example,

Chapter 01 — Live animals	Chapter 73 — Iron
39 — Plastics	84 — Machinery
44 — Wood	94 — Furniture
48 — Paper	97 — Toys and Games

It is not an easy task to correctly identify goods against a particular tariff number even with this information. The best method is to set about it in a systematic fashion by first identifying the approximate position of the goods and then using the process of elimination to arrive at the final answer.

Stage 1. Consult the pink index at the back of Section 8 of the tariff. In most cases, this will identify the first four digits of the eight digit number. In some cases, you may have to use a little imagination, for example, seawater is water containing salt so it is shown under that heading in Chapter 25. Having identified the first two or possibly four digits, turn to the front of the relative chapter and read the notes to the chapter. These are very useful for explaining definitions and also for indicating items not covered by the chapter. These exclusions are usually because the item has its own chapter heading, for example, (i) a wooden box does not fall under Chapter 44 as wood but under Chapter 42 as a box, (ii) a plastic toy does not fall under Chapter 39 as plastic but as a toy under Chapter 97. It is very important to check these notes and also the notes which head most of the sections before deciding on a tariff heading.

Stage 2. Having decided that the goods are proper to a chapter we must then work on the process of elimination making sure of the first four digits before attempting to identify the second four. If you examine any page within the tariff, you will see that some figures and letters are in heavy type while others are in a lighter type. The heavy type indicates the tariff description and, incidentally, the appropriate rate of duty, while the lighter type simply indicates a trade description. This is why it is essential to find the first four digits because it is possible to have the same trade description for goods falling within a different tariff heading, for example, garments containing varying amounts of man made fibre (mmf).

Stage 3. Having decided on the first four digits and, where appropriate, the rate of duty, now is the time to arrive at the second four digits. This is where Conan Doyle's words come into their own — we have eliminated the impossible and are often left with the improbable, for example, a description which may read: 'other articles of iron or steel, other, other, other.' This type of description tends to be rather irreconcilable until one realizes that this is a catchment phrase to identify goods other than those already described.

One aspect must be emphasized. When completing Customs documents, it is not sufficient merely to copy a description exactly as it appears in the tariff. In the words of the tariff itself 'goods must be described in sufficient detail for them to be identified both for tariff and for trade code purposes,' that is, if you are importing ammonium sulphate, do not describe it as 'other nitrogenous fertilizers'.

At times, it may be difficult to readily identify the appropriate CT Code because of similarity of description, so we must take our attempt at classification a stage further and invoke what are called 'the interpretive rules.' These are to be found at the beginning of Part 8 of the tariff and explain the stages for correctly classifying goods which cannot be classified by the three stages shown above.

As this portion of the book is basically concerned with Customs organization and functions in general and export control and procedures in particular, it is now appropriate to consider the export controls which exist and show how they are achieved.

EXPORT CONTROLS

There are three main reasons for controlling the exportation of goods and persons from the UK. These are as follows:

(1) Revenue interests.
(2) Prohibitions and restrictions.
(3) Trade statistics.

(1) *Revenue interests.* These interests (and the economy) may suffer if the following types of transaction are not controlled:

(i) Transhipment goods — should these goods not be transhipped, there is the possibility of loss of revenue.

(ii) Goods for re-exportation after temporary importation.

(iii) Goods exported from a bonded warehouse.

(iv) Goods exported from an excise factory.

(v) Goods exported on drawback.

(vi) Car supplied free of VAT to overseas residents.

(vii) Goods exported for process and subsequent re-importation.

Should these types of transaction not be controlled, there is a strong possibility of loss of revenue through dishonest people claiming that goods had been exported etc. when in fact they had found their way onto the home market. The insistence on proper documentation of these transactions ensures that the revenue is safeguarded.

(2) *Prohibitions and restrictions.* The regulations regarding prohibitions and restrictions change periodically but the latest

information can always be found in Part 2 (ii) of the tariff but can include such items as a need for an export licence from the Department of Trade or the Intervention Board for Agricultural Produce (IBAP) and prohibitions on the exportation of certain animals and drugs.

(3) Trade statistics. For many years the gathering of trade statistics on exported goods was hampered by the laxness of exporters and their agents in supplying the necessary Customs documentation. This led to incorrect balance of trade figures, so much so that on 25th October 1971 new regulations regarding the documentation of exports were brought into force. Very broadly, the new regulations require all goods to be pre-entered unless the person exporting the goods is a 'registered' exporter.

EXPORT DOCUMENTATION AND PROCEDURES

Having mentioned the 'registered exporter' let us now look at the registration procedure and how it affects export documentation.

All regular exporters and agents are encouraged to apply for registration and, if approved, they will be issued with a Customs assigned number (CAN) which should be shown on all their export documents. The Commissioners of Customs and Excise will register an exporter or agent and assign to him a number in respect of each address in the UK at which he keeps a record of export transactions provided that he will comply with certain conditions.

Briefly these are as follows:

(1) That he will deliver to Customs full and accurate details of exported goods within a prescribed period.

(2) That he will maintain a business address within the UK.

(3) That he will maintain at that address a record of export transactions for a period of 12 months from the date of exportation, and make such records available for inspection by an officer of Customs and Excise at any reasonable time.

(4) That he will inform the Commissioners of any change of address or of trading name.

Exporters who always use forwarding agents need not themselves be registered if their agent is registered. A person's registration will remain in force for as long as they comply with the conditions stated above, but the Commissioners of Customs and Excise reserve the right to cancel a registration and withdraw the facility for using an assigned number if at any time the conditions for its use are not fulfilled.

Persons wishing to apply for registration should do so by completing a Customs and Excise form C275 in respect of each trading address and by forwarding the completed form(s) to their local officer of Customs and Excise. In due course, details of the number assigned and of the records required to be kept will be returned to the applicant. The Customs assigned number will consist of the letters CAN and five digits.

It is possible for one trader to use another's CAN for the exportation of goods, but to do so without the written permission of the holder renders the user liable to a fine of £100.

With the following exceptions, all goods for exportation require Customs documentation:

(1) Goods exported by post.

(2) Goods shipped as stores for use on a voyage.

(3) The accompanied effects of crew and passengers.

(4) Touring vehicles.

(5) Road and rail vehicles and freight containers, whether full or empty, used for the carriage of goods; that is, unless the vehicle or container itself is being exported or sold to a purchaser abroad.

(6) Certain goods or through waybills for which special arrangements exist.

(7) Diplomatic mail.

(8) Commercial samples in baggage.

It was mentioned earlier that all goods for exportation must be pre-entered unless the exporter is a registered person. There are, however, some types of export transactions which must always be pre-entered whether the exporter is registered or not.

These are as follows:

(i) Goods exported from a bonded warehouse.

(ii) Goods in transit.

(iii) Goods on which drawback or any other form of relief is claimed.

(iv) Goods being exported temporarily for subsequent re-importation.

(v) Any goods liable to duty or any other charges where these have not been paid, for example, temporary importations.

(vi) Goods on which there is an export restriction, for example, when export licences are required.

(vii) Merchandise in baggage.

For goods in the above categories the appropriate shipping bill must be presented in duplicate to Customs before the goods are loaded. Customs will number and stamp the duplicate for presentation to the shipping company or airline.

Part 3B (iv) of the Customs and Excise Tariff gives a good explanation of Customs requirements at exportation and Notice 276 gives a box by box guide to the completion of Customs forms in the C273 and C63A series. Full details are not given here as both forms and requirements change periodically and one is best advised to consult sources currently appropriate.

Those goods which do not require to be pre-entered, (that is, Customs entry is presented before the goods are loaded for export) are entered on a form C273 (specification) which form may be lodged with Customs any time up to 14 days after the exporting ship leaves, where a specification or 'spec', as it is usually called, is sufficient. The person actually delivering the goods for export merely quotes his CAN to the shipping company whereupon it is entered against the appropriate bill of lading on the manifest, a copy of which is given to Customs for verification, again within 14 days of the vessel's departure. Before goods can be exported aboard a vessel, Customs documentation for the vessel itself must be completed. This is referred to as outward clearance and forms an integral part of the Customs control procedures.

OUTWARD CLEARANCE OF A VESSEL

Prior to the departure of a vessel the Master (or his agent) is required to attend before the Collector, or some other designated Customs officer, to complete the necessary forms and deal with all questions relevant to the vessels departure. The Master is not normally required to attend in person but may give written authority to an agent to clear the vessel on his behalf.

The following documents are required to be completed or presented when application is being made for outward clearance:

(1) Form C13 in duplicate. A general declaration of ship's depar-

ture must include details of any goods remaining on board for exportation.

(2) Ship's certificate of Registry.

(3) Light dues certificate. These dues are monies collected by Customs on behalf of Trinity House and are for the maintenance of lighthouses, light vessels, bouys, etc. on the coast of the UK.

(4) Load line certificate. This certificate is issued by the Department of Trade in accordance with various international safety authorities. It gives details of the ship and its gross tonnage and details of the distance there must be between the load line of the ship and its free-board dependant on its various situations throughout the world.

(5) Wireless certificate. All ocean going passenger ships and cargo ships exceeding 500 gross registered tons must be equipped with a wireless, which must be surveyed annually.

(6) Safety equipment certificate. This indicates that the applicable Merchant Shipping Acts have been observed.

(7) Passenger certificate. This is only found on passenger ships authorized to carry 12 or more passengers. It gives details of the maximum total number of passengers which may be carried and confirms that the legal requirements in respect of safety equipment have been complied with.

(8) Form C15. Clearance outwards. This gives details of particulars of stores on land at time of clearance.

(9) Inward clearance bill. Until a ship has been cleared inwards, that is, all goods, stores, passengers and crew properly accounted for as far as Customs are concerned, an inland clearance bill will not be issued and without it outward clearance cannot be effected.

When all these formalities are completed to the satisfaction of the Customs Officer the ship will be allowed to leave port and proceed on her voyage. Within 14 days of clearance, the shipping company must present to Customs a copy of the ships manifest giving full details of cargo (including nature of goods, marks, shippers and consignees) and passengers names.

At times, the vessel clearing may have already cleared from another port and has carried goods from that port to the one where clearance is now being effected. In this case, clearance documents must include documents from the first port and, instead of an inward clearance bill, a transire.

INWARD PROCESSING RELIEF

Formerly known as Section 7 relief, inward processing relief is a system of relief granted on goods imported from a third country, that is, from a country which is not a member of the EEC, processed and re-exported to a destination outside of the community. Relief can be granted on the following:

(1) Import duties shown in the Common Customs Tariff of the EEC.

(2) Common Agricultural Policy (CAP) levies.

(3) Anti-dumping Duty.

The conditions governing the process and re-exportation are considered to have taken place if the compensating products are merely placed in a bonded warehouse for subsequent exportation from the Community.

Certain processes are covered by a general Customs authority (see Appendix D of Customs Notice 221). However, should this not be the case, the trader must apply for relief, on form C & E 990, to his local Customs officer before the goods are actually imported.

In his application, the trader must give sufficient details to satisfy Customs of his firm intention to re-export the goods; that the importation of the goods for processing and re-export would not be harmful to community producers; and that it is necessary to import the goods for processing rather than to obtain them from within the Community. Relief may only be granted to individuals and businesses established within the Community.

Except in the case of CAP goods, which must be exported within six months of importation, goods are normally allowed at least six months before exportation must take place, but this limit can be extended by the local Customs Officer should he agree that there is a need to do so. Any requests for an extension of time must be made before the time limit expires.

No special records have to be kept provided that the normal commercial records are adequate to trace all movements of goods on which relief is being claimed.

There are two methods by which relief is given as follows:

(1) Duty suspension under which customs duties are not paid at the time of importation but are secured by either a bond or cash deposit.

(2) Reimbursement. Where the duty is paid outright at importation and reimbursed when the goods are exported and a satisfactory claim for relief made. This second method cannot be used for relief on CAP goods.

Customs entry is made on form C10 quoting the appropriate Customs transaction code in box 7, giving details of the relief claimed in box 57 and for duty suspension details of the security offered in box 43. For relief by reimbursement, an extra copy of the entry form is required.

On occasions, goods arrive between the times application has been made and relief granted. Should this occur, release of the goods may be obtained by entering the letters AC (application under consideration) and security offered by means of a miscellaneous cash deposit. Should the value of the goods to be processed exceed £750, an AC entry must be supported by a declaration of value on C105. When the letter granting relief is received it will usually give the option of converting security by deposit to security by bond and will cover any similar importations for a period of one year from the date of issue.

Relief goods may pass from one trader to another provided that each trader is authorized, the goods remain in Customs Control and that the receipt and disposal of the goods can be traced through each trader's records.

In certain circumstances, the local officer of Customs and Excise may require the trader to give prior notice of his intention to pack relief goods for export. Should this happen, the goods must not be despatched until permission is given or the date notified for completion of packing has passed. The normal documentary procedures for exportation are to be followed but in addition the figure 78 is to be inserted in the first of the three positions in box 23 of C273 or 63A. To substantiate the right to relief, proof of exportation must be retained for production on request to an officer of Customs and Excise. The proof of exportation required is the same as that already detailed in respect of claims made when goods liable to VAT are zero rated at exportation.

Completion of transaction
(1) Remission. Agreement must be reached between importer and local Customs Officer as to the way in which relief goods are to be reconciled against exportations of compensating products. For receipts

and exports reconciled against individual consignments, a balanced account must be prepared in duplicate on form CTE 986 and submitted to the local officer as soon as the compensating products are exported or on the expiry of the relief period. If receipts and exports cannot be reconciled against individual consignments, stock records must be kept and balanced monthly and a balanced account forwarded to the local officer on form C & E 986 within 14 days of the end of the agreed period. These accounts must give details of the total relief goods received, those exported, any wasted or scrap and any diversions to Community use (free circulation). In the case of goods diverted to community use and to waste and scrap in excess of an agreed amount, import duty must be paid. The rate at which this duty is charged is that which was in effect when the goods first entered the country.

(2) Reimbursement. The procedure at exportation is exactly the same as for remission goods, the only difference being the way in which claims for reimbursements are made. Claims for reimbursement of duty are to be made on form C & E 987 and sent to the local Officer of Customs and Excise at regular intervals. The frequency with which claims are made will be on a basis agreed with this officer but are normally between one and three months. Claims which cannot be verified may be disallowed. Hence a copy of the import entry and proof of exportation must be kept until such time as the claim has been allowed and reimbursement made.

Returned goods relief EEC 1977

The procedure for making Customs entry for re-imported British goods was drastically changed with effect from 1st January 1977. Prior to this date, provided that it was reasonably certain the imported goods had been exported from the UK, that all duties had been paid and not repaid before re-importation, and that the goods had not been processed or repaired abroad, importation was allowed free of duty on completion of a simple declaration on form C179 and entry on form XS141 without any restrictions as to how long the goods had been out of the country or whether the person importing was the same as the one who exported the goods.

For goods known to be the subject of a temporary exportation (other than for a process on repair) a declaration to this effect is given on form C1310 for goods to be exported by sea or on form

C1311 for exports by air. Certification of exportation may be achieved in three ways:

(1) Examination at exporter's premises. Goods for temporary exportation may be examined during packing at the exporters premises by the local Customs Officer who will certify the shipping bill to this effect and return the original copy of the bill to the exporter for production at ships side to the Customs Officer responsible for the exporting vessel.

(2) Examination at agent's premises. As (1) above with the addition that the exporter must give written authority for the agent to act on his behalf. In both (1) and (2), sufficient notice of 'intent to pack' must be given to the local Officer, such notice to arrive at the Customs and Excise Office at least 24 hours prior to the time of packing specified in the shipping bill. The final closure of the packages must not take place until after the time stated on the shipping bill unless the Customs Officer has already examined the goods and given his permission for closure to take place. Should the Officer not attend, the packing goods must be produced to the Export Office. In most cases examined goods need not be produced to the Export Officer unless he specifically requests their production.

(3) If the exporter has decided not to have goods examined at his or his agents premises, then they *must* be made available for the Customs Officer's examination at the place of shipment. In this third case the 'notice to pack' portion of the shipping bill must be deleted and the bill boldly endorsed 'goods to be examined at the place of shipment'. Each package is to be clearly marked 'to be produced to the Customs Officer for examination before shipment'.

Re-importation
Goods which were exported under the conditions shown above are entered at re-importation on form C10 supported by the duplicate shipping note and providing no process or repair has taken place while they were abroad will be admitted into the country free of duty. In all other cases, entry is still made on form C10 but this form must be accompanied by a declaration on form C1314 and supported by any additional evidence of exportation that may be available, for example, export invoices, copies of shipping notes etc.

It is possible to obtain relief from the following import charges provided that certain conditions can be met.

(1) Import duty.

(2) CAP charges.

(3) Value added tax.

(4) Excise duty.

Let us consider each of these in turn:

(1) Import duty. Import duty is normally relieved if:

(i) The goods are entered for free circulation (home use) within three years of exportation.

(ii) The goods were previously exported to a 'third country' from a member state.

(iii) The goods are being imported by the original exporter.

(iv) The goods were in free circulation when exported.

(v) The goods were not exported to undergo a process or repair.

With reference to condition (v), having undergone process or repair does not necessarily debar goods from receiving some form of relief on re-importation if it can be proved to the satisfaction of Customs that it was unforeseen and merely returned such goods to their original condition without enhancing their value.

Goods intentionally exported for a process or repair may qualify for some form of relief under 'outward processing relief'. This will be dealt with later.

(2) Common agricultural policy (CAP) charges. All those conditions given in relation to import duty apply to CAP charges with the exception of clause 1(i). CAP goods *must* be re-imported within six months of exportation to be eligible for relief. There are additional conditions to be met should any monies have been claimed at exportation. These conditions are fully covered in Part III of Customs Notice 236 which should be carefully read should such circumstances pertain. One special point to note is that it is unlikely that any goods exported under the provisions of an IBAP licence or pre-fixing certificate will be afforded relief.

(3) Excise duty. Again the basic conditions for import duty apply. Any excise duty unpaid at exportation must be paid before duty free importation can be allowed. Any processing of excise goods renders them ineligible for relief.

(4) Value added tax. A person registered for VAT will account for VAT on returned goods in the same manner as for any other importation. For exempt traders, VAT will not be chargeable where it can be proved to the satisfaction of the commissioners of Customs and Excise that:

(i) The importer is not a taxable person or, if he is, the goods are being imported other than in the course of business.

(ii) Either (a) The goods were exported from tax paid stock or (b) The importer is the person who made the goods.

(iii) The goods were not zero rated at export.

(iv) The goods were not the subject of a process or repair.

(v) The goods were last exported by the importer, or on his behalf.

(vi) The goods were either (a) intended to be re-imported at the time of exportation; or (b) have been returned for repair or replacement after rejection by an overseas customer; or (c) were in private use and possession in the UK before they were exported.

Procedure on re-importation. Box 57 of the form C10 is to be endorsed 'relief claimed under returned goods regulation EEC 754/76' and the entry accompanied by either a certified copy of the shipping bill or a declaration on form C1314. Any additional evidence of exportation should be attached in support of the claim for relief. Before completing the declaration on C1314 it is suggested careful study be made of the notes on completion shown on the form. These will help avoid possible errors and subsequent rejection by Customs.

Simplified entry procedure

A simplified entry procedure is in force for goods of the following kinds:

(1) Professional effects (for example, tools, film and radio equipment, theatrical effects etc.) exported for a specific use and return.

(2) Goods and works of art exported for exhibition, display or demonstration and subsequent return.

(3) Trade samples exported for use abroad and subsequent return.

Normally, in these circumstances it is sufficient to give a general description of the goods and their value without detailing individual items for tariff/trade code purposes. As conditions for simplified entry procedure vary from time to time, it is advisable to make enquiries from your local Customs Officer for current requirements before making entry.

Regular importers. Those traders who regularly re-import goods may, in certain circumstances, be allowed to use a simple 'general declaration' instead of making individual declarations on form C1314. This procedure can only be used by those traders who re-import more than 100 consignments exceeding £100 in value per year. The goods concerned must be eligible for re-importation without payment or refund of any duties on agricultural levies. Traders wishing to take advantage of this concession should make application to their local Customs Officer. Further information concerning this relief can be found in Customs Notice 236.

OUTWARD PROCESSING RELIEF

Outward processing relief, which came into operation on 28th June 1976, permits certain goods which are in free circulation to be exported from the Community for processing in a third country. On their return in the form of compensating products, these goods may be admitted either wholly or partly free of any import charges. Before going further into documentation and procedures it is appropriate to give explanations of some of the terminology used in connection with this form of relief:

Import charges. Any Customs protective duties under EEC legislation and CAP. N.B. Relief will not be allowed on Excise duty or VAT.

Process. (a) Working of goods including fitting, assembling or adjusting them to other goods. (b) Processing the goods, that is, doing something with the goods themselves. (c) Repair. This includes restoring goods to their original condition and putting them in order.

Compensating products. These are the goods resulting from a process carried out upon goods exported under the terms of outward processing relief.

Intermediate products. These are goods resulting from a process not fully carried out to the extent provided for.

Unaltered state. This refers to goods being returned without a process having been carried out.

Member state. One of the nine member states of the EEC.

Documentation. C & E 1152. Authorization for relief and confirmation of shipment. C & E 1153 — Shipping or postal bill. C & E 1154 — Declaration in support of C10 when goods are re-imported.

Conditions for relief
These are detailed as under:

(1) The goods must be exported from the Community and the compensating products returned to a member state.

(2) The exported goods must be in free circulation and no refund of duty claimed on exportation.

(3) The exportation must not give rise to any remission or repayment of CAP charges.

(4) Prior to exportation:

(i) An authorization for relief must be obtained on form C & E 1152.

(ii) The goods must be entered on the appropriate export form.

(iii) The exported goods must be capable of being recognized in the compensating products.

(iv) An acceptable rate of yield of the compensating products is declared.

(5) The compensating products are to be imported by the original applicant or by someone holding his written consent to do so.

(6) The compensating products are imported as soon as processed, but within 12 months of exportation. (Given a valid reason for so doing Customs are at times prepared to allow an extension of time for re-importation).

(7) Any further documentary evidence of the transaction is produced to Customs if requested.

(8) Customs are satisfied that the conditions for relief have been fulfilled. Should goods be returned without having undergone a process or if the process is incomplete; conditions for re-importation may be partly waived or relaxed should the circumstances warrant it.

At times it is possible to have goods undergoing a combination of both inward and outward processing relief. For example, certain goods are imported under inward processing relief but it is found that some further processing is necessary abroad before the processing in this country can be finalized. Application is made and the goods exported under outward processing relief for this further process to be carried out. The processed goods are then returned and the original inward processing relief finalized. Should this intermediate process have increased the value of the goods, it is a stipulation that the security originally offered to cover the inward processing relief be increased to cover the extra duty liability.

VAT. Relief from duty does not extend to VAT which is payable on the full value of the goods after process plus any duty or levy which may be payable on the cost of processing.

Authorization. There is no provision for relief to be granted retro-actively, therefore, in order to benefit, traders must apply for relief *before* the goods are exported. Relief will only be granted where it is possible to recognize the goods exported in the compensating pro-ducts and the method of this identification must be noted on the application form C & E 1152.

Rate of yield. It is a requirement for relief that the rate of yield be determined at the time the authorization is given. This is usually expressed in terms of units of compensating products per unit of goods exported. For example, x dozen handkerchiefs per kilo of material exported. Once a rate of yield has been accepted by Cus-toms on the C & E 1152, no change in this rate will normally be allowed. Should the yield be in excess of that authorized, no addi-tional relief will be given nor conversely, will the amount of relief be proportionally bigger should the yield be less than agreed.

Preference rates. If goods can definitely be imported free under a preferential tariff or are shown as free in the full duty column of the tariff there will be no need to apply for relief. However, if there is any doubt, or if the goods have only a partial reduction of duty, it is advis-able to go through the full procedure for claiming relief.

Records. Customs require that adequate records be kept of all transactions where there is to be a claim for relief and such records must be kept available and in a form whereby verification is made easy, should the need arise. The form C & E 1152 authorizing relief should be kept carefully until all compensating products have been imported. It should then be surrendered to Customs.

Re-importation procedure

Compensating products imported under these arrangements should be entered on form C10 supported by the following docu-ments:

(1) Form C & E 1154.

(2) Original C & E 1152 and duplicate C & E 1153.

(3) Documentary evidence of identity where required.

(4) The processor's invoices showing charges made in respect of the compensating products.

(5) Form C105 should be suitably amended and produced if the value of the compensating products exceeds £750.

(6) If the compensating products are imported by a person other than the applicant, the latters written consent to transfer the authority should be obtained and attached to the entry.

Calculation of duty payable

Provided that the procedure set out above has been followed the duty normally due on the compensating products may be reduced by a sum equal to the duty which would have been chargeable on the exported goods had they been imported at the same time as the compensating products. This principle will also apply should the imported goods qualify for a reduced or preferential rate of duty, that is, duty is calculated on both exported and imported goods at the reduced rate. All necessary particulars and reduced duty calculations are to be set out on form C & E 1154 under the appropriate printed headings.

Valuation

The values to be used in calculating the duty payable are as follows:

(1) The value for duty of the compensating products is the open market value of the imported goods at the time of entry. In the absence of better evidence this may be calculated on a built-up basis including the following items:

(i) The value at the time of exportation of the exported goods as shown on form C & E 1153 including any material lost or wasted before, during or after the process.

(ii) Packing, freight, insurance and all other charges outwards to the processor's premises (including any foreign Customs duties or levies).

(iii) Purchase price or free delivered value to the processor's premises of other materials, separately charged, and used in the processing.

(iv) Cost of process as charged to the importer.

(v) Agent's commission, if any.

(vi) Packing, freight, insurance etc. charges inwards.

(2) For the purpose of calculation of the deduction in respect of the exported goods, the export value as shown on the form C & E 1153 plus actual charges for freight etc. outwards and a notional amount in respect of freight inwards (for convenience this can be the equivalent as that shown for freight etc. outwards).

Value for VAT
Where VAT is actually being paid at importation for example, importation by an exempt trader, and goods were exported from tax paid stock, VAT payable can be calculated on the value arrived at by deducting (2) above from (1) plus any duty payable. For tax free stock, the full built-up value is taken, adding any duty payable and calculating VAT on this total figure.

THE EUROPEAN ECONOMIC COMMUNITY (EEC) DOCUMENTATION

Community transit (CT)
The EEC was formed as a Customs Union so that certain goods could pass freely through the member states without having to pay protective duties at each country border. This free passage was achieved by a system known as Community transit. In order to use the full Community transit procedure it is necessary for the status of the goods to be shown, that is, an indication given as to whether the goods qualify for 'free circulation' or not. In order to qualify for free circulation, the goods must be either wholly the produce of a member state or, if imported from outside of the community, have had all protective import duties paid.

The status of goods in full Community transit is indicated by the issue of a transit form ('T' form) with a T1 form issued to show that goods are *not* in free circulation and a form T2 to indicate that they are. When goods are only required to cross one border during their travels a simpler form is used — T2L. As from 1st January 1978, the same form is used for both T1 and T2, the appropriate number being inserted. Both the T form and the T2L have continuation sheets available usually indicated by the word 'BIS' after the number.

The full Community transit procedure was designed to protect Community funds and the internal duties and taxes of the member states through which the goods are to pass. The form which this protection takes is a guarantee. A person undertakes to transport goods from one member state to another and lodges a cash deposit or guarantee to cover Community charges and any internal tax or duties which become due in a member state should the goods become lost or any other irregularity occur during the course of the movement.

There are several 'Customs' public notices applicable to Community transit procedures. These are listed below:

750   Community transit
750A List of Community transit offices
751   Completion of T forms
753   Rail simplified procedure
755   Special control procedures

Procedure. 'T' forms are supplied in packs of four (a fifth copy is required for goods exported under special control procedures) and must be presented intact to the Customs Officer at the office of departure (see notice 750A) together with guarantee documents and the export entry, and also a transit advice note (TAN) for each office of transit to be passed during the journey.

After checking, copy 1 of the T form is retained in the office of departure and copies 2, 3 and 4, together with other supporting documents and TANs, are returned to accompany the goods on their movement through the Community.

During the movement, the goods must enter each state at a Community transit office. If this is not the office of destination it must be an approved office of transit. Should goods leave and re-enter the EEC during the course of a movement they must pass through an office of transit at the points of exit and re-entry.

A completed TAN giving details of the means of transport and T form used must be lodged at each office of transit, and the goods and T forms produced for inspection if required. Upon arrival at the office of destination, goods and T forms must be presented without delay, ensuring that the arrival is within the time limit set by the office of departure. In their own interest, principals are advised to obtain a receipt for T forms produced to an office of arrival. This receipt can be on form C1129 or on a privately printed form with the same format.

Disposal of Copies 2, 3 and 4 of T form. Once the importing member state has accepted and dealt with the imported goods and T forms, the latter are disposed as follows:

Copy 2   Retained with import entry.
Copy 3   Returned to office of departure
         so that guarantee may be discharged.
Copy 4   Used for statistical purposes in
         the country of arrival.

It is important to remember that, although goods may be shown as free of protective duty in the country of arrival, they may be liable to some internal duty in the other country or countries crossed during the transit movement. If copy 3 is not produced at the office of arrival it cannot be forwarded to the office of departure and therefore the guarantee will not be discharged, thus possibly involving the principal in the payment of charges.

In addition to the forms already covered, there are other forms used to cover the movement of goods through the Community. As these transactions are usually allowed without the need for full Community transit guarantees, the form used is referred to as a movement certificate. Although the forms are simpler than the full CT forms they are sufficient to grant 'free circulation' status to the goods covered.

T2L. This form may only be used for movements of Community goods transported directly from one member state to another, for example, crossing only one border, or by a direct sea or air crossing. In this context, member state may be taken to include Austria and Switzerland.

Form T2L cannot be used for goods:

(1) Intended for export outside the Community, or Austria or Switzerland.

(2) Subject to special Community controls.

(3) In packing which does not, itself, also qualify as Community goods.

DD3. This form is used for Community goods consigned to a non-Community country and expected to be reconsigned to a Community country within six months of consignment and in the same state as when consigned out of the Community. Form DD3 may not be used for goods subject to the common agricultural policy.

At times, the DD3 may be used in conjunction with a 'T' form if the goods are to travel under full CT procedure to the point of exit from the Community.

Form DD5. This form covers fish caught by a Community fisheries vessel and landed in a member state. Should the fish have been landed in a non-member state and then brought on to a member state, the DD5 must be supported by a certificate given by the Customs authority of that country stating that the fish had not been subjected to any processing or handling in the non-Community country and that they had remained in Customs control for the period of their stay.

For fish landed into one member state and then consigned to another, form DD5 is not acceptable and should be replaced with a form T2 or T2L as appropriate.

Rail simplified procedure

The rail transit procedure is a simplified version of the full CT procedure. It uses the existing railway consignment notes both for Customs control purposes and to indicate the status of the goods. The rail simplified procedure differs from the full CT procedure in two ways as follows:

(a) Special Community T forms are not required — status is shown on the railway forms.

(b) As the railway authorities assume responsibility for the transit operation, the principal does not need to enter into a separate guarantee.

COMMON AGRICULTURAL POLICY (CAP)

The need for a common agricultural policy is one of the few areas in which agreement has been reached by all member states, although its implementation is often criticized as leading to high prices and costly surpluses.

When the common agricultural policy was written into the Treaty of Rome it laid down four main objectives:

(1) The increasing of agricultural productivity.

(2) The stabilizing of markets within the Community.

(3) Ensuring supplies of agricultural products to Community members at reasonable prices.

(4) Ensuring a fair standard of living for those engaged in agricultural production.

The goods covered by the CAP are products of the soil, stock farming and fisheries, and the first stage processing of any of these products.

The EEC as a whole produces about 80% of its requirement of foodstuffs so there is still a need to import large quantities of these goods from countries outside the EEC. Unfortunately, the Community farms are not as productive as their counterparts in temperate countries outside EEC and so, to fulfil the objectives of CAP, require some form of protection from the lower prices of goods available in places like the USA, Canada, Argentina and Australia. The system in the UK was one of allowing foodstuffs into the country free of duty at world prices and then subsidizing the farmer out of the tax-payers money. This was an unrealistic situation and one which would have been impossible in the original EEC where (in 1972) approximately 13% of the population, compared with less than 3% in the UK, was engaged in agricultural production. In consequence, the Community plan to maintain stability of prices was to agree an artificial price somewhat higher than the prevailing world price and require goods imported from countries outside EEC to attract a levy payment. This levy figure represents the difference between the world price and the artificial price agreed by the CAP organization in Brussels.

In addition to this method of maintaining stability, wide ranging structural reforms were advocated so that by 1980 the farming popu-lation would be reduced to about six million and the farming acreage reduced by about 12½ million acres. This was to be achieved on a voluntary basis with financial incentives for withdrawal, amalgama-tion of farms, early retirement and re-employment in other areas of work.

The aims of the structural reforms are as follows:

(1) To encourage farmers and landworkers to leave the land.

(2) For those who remain — to give help from appropriate develop-ment schemes.

(3) To set up information and training services.

(4) To improve marketing methods.

(5) To prevent new land from being brought into agriculture.

The CAP is controlled by a group of commissioners in Brussels who operate under a complex system of regulations which are bind-ing on every member state. Periodically, these commissioners, together with representatives of each member state, meet and agree a 'fair market price' for all commodities in the CAP field. These prices are then used as a datum line in comparison with world prices to decide on the rate of levy to be imposed. These levy figures are then notified to an organization within each member state who in turn pass the information to those responsible for collecting the levies. In the UK, this organization is called The Intervention Board for Agricultural Produce and they are located at Reading. The levies are collected on their behalf by Customs and it is to Customs that one has to apply for the current rate of levy. One might ask why it is necessary to apply to Customs for the current rate; why cannot it be published as a book or perhaps even included in the Customs tariff? The main reason for this is that for certain commodities the world prices fluctuate so rapidly that it would be impossible to do so. In fact, the levy rates could change with frequencies varying from daily to quarterly depending on the commodity. Rate charges are notified to Customs by the Intervention Board by means of a daily telex message. By telephoning Customs it is possible to ascertain the current rate. Customs will also give details of the formula to be used when calculating the amount of levy payable.

Goods which may be liable to a levy payment are indicated in the tariff by a letter 'L' in the right hand column of pages dealing with (mainly) the first 24 chapters. Non-liability is shown by a dash. Processed foodstuffs are usually liable to a special type of levy called a variable charge (VC) which may be increased by an additional duty on sugar or flour (ads or adf) or limited by a maximum percentage, for example, VC max 13% + adf. This means either the variable charge or 13%, whichever is the less, plus the additional duty on flour.

All home produced and imported CAP goods, if exported, will possibly qualify for a payment from the Intervention Board. This is called for export refund. For eligible goods, a claim is made on Customs form C1220.

In order to provide information to the commissioners in Brussels, certain CAP items require a licence issued by the Intervention Board. Details of the particular goods and the licencing arrangements are given in Intervention Board Leaflet No. LRI.

Intervention board licenses both authorize and require the importation of the goods licenced. As the information gathered is used when deciding levy rates, it is important to remember that when a licence is applied for, the importer must honour it by importing all the goods licensed. In order to ensure that importers do honour their obligations, they are required to take out a guarantee, which will not be discharged until all the goods named therein, within a small tolerance, (7% cereals, 5% other goods), have been imported. Licences issued in one member state may be used to cover importations into any of the other member states. It is important to retrieve the licence from Customs after each importation and, when exhausted, send it to Reading for discharge of the guarantee. Should the licence not be fully exhausted, the guarantee cannot be discharged until a sum of money, roughly equal to the missing levy, is paid.

The form used as an IBAP licence has a second function, that of acting as an advance fixing certificate. In order to be able to maintain a stable price to their customs, certain importers apply to the Intervention Board for a certificate which will fix the amount of levy to be paid on a commodity for a stated period of time. This price represents the average expected levy rate over the period named and, once issued, must be the price used by the importer no matter what the actual levy figure is.

Two terms which may be mentioned by Customs when the levy rate is supplied are:

(a) Co-efficient.

(b) Monetary compensatory amount (MCA).

These are used to protect the common price system in the member states against changes in the relative currencies of the individual member. The MCA will be used to abate the import charges. Should there be a balance of MCA after the charges have been abated this amount may be claimed from the Intervention Board. In order to do so, it is necesary to obtain from Customs a certified copy of the import entry.

Certain reliefs from and reductions in protective duty charges may be extended to include CAP charges, for example, process inwards, end use relief samples etc.

ATA CARNETS

ATA carnets are international Customs documents issued by Chambers of Commerce in most major countries throughout the world. The carnets facilitate Customs clearance of certain classes of temporary importation and exportation by replacing the following:

(a) Normal Customs documentation in the country of temporary exportation.

(b) Normal Customs documentation and security, for example, by bond or deposit in the country of temporary importation.

Carnets do not however, confer immunity from other conditions of temporary exportation or temporary importation. Further details of the ATA carnets are found in Customs notice No. 104 available from HM Customs and Excise whose address is found in Appendix B.

TIR CARNETS

The UK is a party to the Customs Convention on the International Transport of Goods under cover of TIR carnets (TIR Convention) 1959 which is designed to facilitate the international transport of goods on road vehicles by simplifying Customs requirements. It covers road vehicles, trailers, semi-trailers and containers — road or rail borne, including those of demountable body type.

The guaranteeing association which issues the TIR carnet, guarantees the duty payable on the goods carried under cover of the carnet. The TIR carnets in the UK are issued by the Freight Transport Association and the Road Haulage Association on behalf of their members. Road vehicles and containers must be approved by a competent authority before they may be used for the transport of goods under cover of a TIR carnet. The competent authority must be satisfied that the vehicles or containers comply with the technical annexes to the Convention before such approval will be granted. On all TIR journeys, approved vehicles must have with them a valid certificate of approval issued by a competent authority, such as, Department of Environment, Bureau Veritas, American Bureau of Shipping etc.

A TIR carnet gives no right to operate; it is purely a Customs facility which enables goods in Customs sealed vehicles and Customs sealed containers to transit intermediate countries with the minimum of Customs formalities. TIR cannot be used for journeys wholly within the territory of the EEC, where the Community transit system applies as explained in page 122. TIR can, however, continue to be used for journeys which start and finish outside the EEC.

Countries which are party to the Convention include Afghanistan, Albania, Australia, Belgium, Bulgaria, Canada, Czechoslovakia, Denmark, Finland, France, German Democratic Republic, German Federal Republic, Greece, Hungary, Iran, Ireland (Republic of), Israel, Italy, Japan, Jordan, Liechtenstein, Luxembourg, Morocco, Netherlands, Norway, Poland, Portugal, Romania, Spain, Sweden,

Switzerland, Turkey, Union of Soviet Socialist Republics, United States of America and Yugoslavia.

THE INTERNATIONAL ROAD HAULAGE CONSIGNMENT OPERATION

Our study of Customs would not be complete without examining the international road haulage consignment operation which now follows.

The movement of international consignments solely by road is very much on the increase, particularly within the UK/Continental trade and beyond, including the Middle East. Overall the regulations relating to such British goods vehicle operations are extensive and the following is an attempt to identify the more salient factors involved, the majority of which are obligatory.

Road operators must ensure that before leaving the UK, their drivers must be in possession of all the necessary documents and are familiar with the traffic rules/highway code of the countries in which they will travel. In all countries British operators must comply with national laws and regulations in force concerning, for example, such matters as third party insurance; the construction, use and fitness of good vehicles; traffic regulations; drivers' hours and the keeping of drivers' records. Any infringement of national laws or of the provisions of bilateral agreements may result in a permit being withdrawn and/or applications for future permits being refused indefinitely or for a limited period.

International road haulage permits are required by British hauliers involved in hire and reward operations, but not usually by those having an 'own account' operation to carry goods through certain countries in Europe. Permits for the former are issued by the Department of Transport on an equitable basis, as far as practicable, bearing in mind that applications tend to exceed supply. The Road Haulage Association works in close liaison with the Department of Transport to help achieve such an equitable allocation.

The UK has negotiated bilateral road agreements with a large number of countries for British goods vehicle operators making journeys to or through them. In the main, the agreement permits the conveyance of goods to, from and in transit through the country concerned. This involves, for example, the acceptance of a return load. The vehicles may enter or leave the country, for example, Austria, in a loaded or empty condition. Additionally, it permits the movement of road haulage merchandise between Austria and a third country, in either direction, provided this is allowed by the law of the third country and by the terms of any agreement between that country and the UK or Austria. British operators may not engage in cabotage within Austria, that is, pick up goods at one point in Austria for delivery to any other point in that country.

Insofar as the 'own account' road operator is concerned, the haulier should carry a document embracing certain information and which is in lieu of the road haulage permit. Such details include: the name of the operator; his trade or business; the goods being carried; the individual transit loading and unloading points; the vehicle being used; and the route. This data is required to substantiate the transit operation and is for the operators 'own account'.

Permits for Austria are issued under an annual quota basis. Each permit is normally valid for a period of six months from the date of departure except when issued in conjunction with Federal German road/rail permits. In this case, they are normally valid for only three months. It must be stressed that the foregoing only applies to Austria and the situation/conditions vary in each individual country. For example, in Italy a circulation tax is payable by British operators with the amount varying according to the carrying capacity of the vehicle. Moreover, it is necessary to obtain prior permission for the movement on Italian roads of extra-long and extra-wide loads, and for procuring police escorts for such loads. In the Netherlands and Luxembourg, together with many other countries, no vehicle or transport taxes are payable by British operators. Quota permits are operative in Spain both for own account, and hire or reward operations. Each permit is valid for two months and special permits are required for vehicles of 16 tons and over. For journeys to the Middle East, the UK has no bilateral agreements with the countries concerned and conditions vary regarding permit applications. In particular, operators going overland to the Middle East will pass through a number of European countries and it is essential they have the appropriate, necessary transit documentation. An international certificate of vaccination against smallpox is required on entry to most Middle East countries.

The UK has concluded bilateral road haulage agreements with the following countries: Austria, Belgium, Bulgaria, Czechoslovakia, Denmark, Finland, France, German Democratic Republic, German Federal Republic, Greece, Hungary, Italy, Luxembourg, Netherlands, Norway, Poland, Romania, Spain, Sweden, Switzerland and Yugoslavia. Special conditions are applicable to British operators in such countries. Negotiations with other European countries are proceeding with the aim being to secure liberal conditions of operation by road on a reciprocal basis.

With regard to the road haulage permit, these are required under agreements and arrangements with some countries. Such bilateral permits may be on a general quota basis as obtains for France, West Germany and Italy together with many other countries. Each permit is valid for one return journey; transit journeys — outward and return — through a country count as one complete journey. Period permits, for example, are issued annually for both general quota and non-quota to France. General quota period permits count as 50 journey permits against the quota but they may be used for a indefinite number of journeys. Use of a permit is restricted to the operator named thereon, that is, a haulier may not use a permit in the name of another operator or transfer a permit directly to another operator. Firms misusing permits in this manner will be penalized. Permits may only be used for vehicles currently authorized on an operator's licence and excise licence, unless exempted in either case, at the appropriate rate of duty. Permits must be returned properly completed within 15 days of the completion of the journey, or if the permit is unused, within 15 days of its expiry. Statutory fees are raised both for the journey and period permits.

The UK has been allocated a small number of EEC permits which enable operators to make journeys between any of the nine member countries (Belgium, Denmark, France, Western Germany, Irish Republic, Italy, Luxembourg, Netherlands and UK). Thus tramping operations using empty or laden vehicles are possible, including third country traffic which is not permissible under certain bilateral agreements. Cabotage is prohibited. Such EEC permits are allocated prior to the beginning of the year and are not available during the course of the year. Such permits are for hire or reward operations only and may not be used for any unaccompanied trailer or semi-trailer. Each permit is valid for one calendar year and can be used with only one vehicle at a time. There is no limit on the number of journeys which may be made within the Community under each permit. Basically, EEC permits cannot be used to transit EEC countries in order to deliver or pick up loads in countries which are not members of EEC. Such permits are intended primarily for multi-lateral journeys, for example, UK — France — Belgium — UK, UK — Netherlands — Western Germany — Netherlands — UK, or for bilateral journeys which do not involve UK, such as, France — Western Germany — France. Bilateral journeys between the UK and another EEC country are not, however, entirely excluded. An administrative fee is charged for each permit issued. All permits, including those dealt with in the preceding paragraph, are issued to UK operators by the International Road Freight Office, Department of the Environment whose address is found in Appendix B.

On all journeys abroad, as in the UK, a valid vehicle excise licence disc should be displayed on the vehicle. Likewise, such good vehicles are subject to the normal vehicle taxation system of any country through which they pass. The amount of taxation payable varies from time to time and from country to country. Moreover some countries, either additionally or alternatively, levy other taxes often based on ton-mileage or length of stay. Exemptions from the foregoing exist, insofar as the following countries are concerned, on the basis that the vehicle will not be charged the equivalent vehicle excise whilst in Austria, Belgium, Bulgaria, Czchoslovakia, Denmark, Finland, France, Hungary, Irish Republic, Luxembourg, Netherlands, Norway, Poland, Portugal (50% reduction only), Romania, Sweden, Switzerland, Turkey, Western Germany and Yugoslavia. Motor fuel is generally taxed with the duty being included in the sale price. Some countries do not permit commercial vehicles to use the roads at weekends and/or public holidays.

For all international journeys, the UK operator must take the following documents:

(1) Operator's licences relevant to the vehicle issued in the country in which it is licenced.

(2) Third party insurance. This is compulsory in most countries and in some countries extends to case of liabilities for damage to the property of third parties as well as coverage for liabilities for death or personal injury. An international motor insurance card (green card) issued by an insurance bureau will provide evidence of insurance against compulsory insurable liabilities in those countries in which

the card is shown to be valid. Green cards are not essential in EEC countries and certain other countries, but it is advisable to carry them, or a British Insurance certificate, to counter the situation of a routine check following an accident. In some countries, insurance cover of goods must be provided and failure to do so or proof thereof results in a premium being payable.

(3) Registration documents. Drivers of goods vehicles must be in possession of the vehicle registration book.

(4) Nationality sign. All vehicles must display the British international registration letters which is for the British operator GB.

(5) Passport. The driver and any other crew member must carry a valid standard (blue) passport together with visas as required. A visitor's passport is not acceptable for road haulage work.

(6) Driving licences. Most European countries accept a current British driving licence valid for the category of vehicle being driven. An International Driving Permit issued to their members by the Automobile Association, the Royal Automobile Club or the Royal Scottish Automobile Club (in accordance with the provisions of the International Convention relating to Motor Traffic, 1926, or the Convention on Road Traffic, 1949) and covering the category of vehicle being driven is also generally accepted. Additionally, drivers are recommended to carry an authority from the operator to drive the vehicle in question. For Hungary, Poland, Spain and Turkey, an International Driving Permit should be carried as a British licence is unacceptable. International Driving Permits are required in USSR and Italy, but a British valid driving licence is valid if accompanied by translations from the appropriate language.

Drivers must be at least 21 years old to drive vehicles of over 7.5 metric tonnes maximum and at least 18 years old to drive vehicles of over 3.5 metric tonnes.

Most European countries now permit the temporary importation of foreign goods vehicles (including trailers accompanied by the prime mover) free of duty or deposit and without guaranteed Customs documents. However, a 'Carnet de passages en douane' which can be issued to their members by the Automobile Association, the Royal Automobile Club or the Royal Scottish Automobile Club is still required for vehicles entering Gibraltar, Greece, Portugal (for visas of more than one month duration) and Turkey. The carnet is also required by France, Spain and Yugoslavia for all trailers, and by

Italy for vehicles which remain there for more than three months. Trailers entering Belgium or Luxembourg must be covered by a carnet if they are towed by a vehicle registered in one of the aforementioned countries; otherwise, trailers entering the Benelux countries (Belgium, Luxembourg and the Netherlands) do not require carnets provided they show signs of use and are towed by a vehicle which itself does not require a carnet. Trailers, not accompanied by a prime mover, must be covered by a deposit of duty when temporarily imported into Norway, and by a deposit of duty or carnet when temporarily imported into Denmark.

Most European countries readily permit temporary importation of a container free of Customs duty under the Container Convention, 1956. Overseas Customs formalities required for goods in transit when not covered by a 'T' form or when carried in vehicles not covered by a TIR carnet.

When neither a TIR carnet nor a 'T' form is used, it will be necessary to comply with the Customs requirements of each country through which the goods pass. Deposit or guarantee in lieu of import duty is normally required before the goods are allowed entry.

The Freight Transport Association or Road Haulage Association offer an advisory service to their members on taking a lorry overseas. Likewise, the Department of Environment International Freight Office will provide details whose address is found in Appendix B.

It must be mentioned that for dangerous cargo conveyed by road, the appropriate ADR regulations must be strictly observed. These are defined in Chapter 6, pages 86-94.

To conclude, it is important each Ro/Ro journey is adequately planned/routed and the crew are issued with the appropriate instructions, particularly in regard to check points on the route where messages can be accepted and despatched. Special attention needs to be given to documentaion and observance of the various regulations viz. driver hours, periods of operation, vehicle construction etc.

CHAPTER 8

Cargo Insurance

Cargo insurance market. Fundamental principles and process of effecting cargo insurance. Cargo insurance policy form, clauses and premium. Cargo insurance claims. CMR liability.

Marine insurance is defined in the Marine Insurance Act of 1906 as 'a contract of insurance as a contract whereby the insurer undertakes to indemnify the assured in a manner and to the extent thereby agreed, against marine losses, that is to say, the losses incidental to marine adventure.' Hence this includes cargo insurance involving the maritime conveyance of merchandise from one country to another.

Cargo insurance is an extensive subject and it would be wrong not to include a chapter on it in a book of this nature. Nevertheless, in so doing the reader must be reconciled to the fact that it is only possible to deal briefly with the salient parts of the subject. For further study the student is recommended to read one of the excellent cargo insurance textbooks available on the market.

This chapter deals with the practical considerations which affect export interest in terms of financial protection of goods in transit to overseas destinations. It is not an in-depth study of marine insurance as such; insurance and exporting can and do exist independently of each other. Furthermore, it is by no means coincidental that the insurance of ships and goods is the oldest form of insurance protection. Moreover, the advantages which accrue from a proper appreciation of the role cargo insurance plays in the transference to others of those risks to which goods consigned by sea and air are exposed, must be thoroughly understood by the exporter/shipper.

In its proper context, cargo insurance must be seen as an indispensable adjunct to overseas trade. Adequate insurance is vital to protect the interest of those with goods in transit. Accordingly, the student of the subject is well advised to obtain a copy of the Marine Insurance Acts of 1906 and 1909 available from the HMSO and study them closely. The 1906 Act contains the basis of all cargo insurance affecting export consignments, whilst the 1909 Act deals with the prohibition of gambling in maritime perils.

It is appropriate to mention that this chapter will not be dealing with credit insurance as this will be found in Chapter 10 on Export Credits Guarantee Department.

It is important to indicate in examining cargo insurance one must reconcile it with ship insurance insofar as maritime transits are concerned. The reason being that the voyage is still regarded as an 'adventure' which involves both ship and cargo being at risk to maritime perils. This joint cargo/ship interest emerges when, for example, a general average contribution arises including jettison of cargo to preserve the general safety of the vessel.

CARGO INSURANCE MARKET

There are no fixed rates in marine insurance and the actual premium for a particular ship or cargo is assessed on the incidence of losses in that trade and the risks that the ship conveying the cargo is likely to undergo. This process of assessing the premium is known as underwriting and the marine insurance contract is embodied in a document called a policy. Marine insurance is undertaken by insurance companies or by Lloyd's underwriters — primarily the latter through a broker.

Lloyds of London is an association of insurers specializing in the insurance of marine and similar risks. It had its origin in the seventeenth century when shipowners and merchants meeting at Lloyd's Coffee House in London began to underwrite risks among themselves. Lloyd's was incorporated by Act of Parliament in 1871 and is governed by an elected committee.

The Corporation of Lloyds, which incidentally has no connection with Lloyd's Register of Shipping, does not accept insurance or issue policies. All the underwriting business is transacted by members of Lloyd's trading as individuals. Briefly, the Corporation provides the facilities and the members transact the business. Lloyd's underwriters which total in excess of 6000 are individually liable under Lloyd's policies and their liability is absolutely unlimited. Although Lloyd's underwriters transact their business as individuals, it is usually found that they associate with one another in groups of varying size, known as syndicates, with an underwriter acting for each group.

The Corporation of Lloyd's owns the premises and provides the various departments necessary for the conduct of such a large organization. Separate departments are maintained for the signing of policies, the settlement of claims, the collection of general average refunds, salvage and recoveries from third parties, and for the payment of claims abroad. The Corporation is also responsible for the chain of signal stations on the trade routes of the world, and the maintenance of a Lloyd's agent in every port of importance. Other important activities include the publication of Lloyds List, a daily shipping paper and many other technical publications.

The part played by the broker in the process of underwriting is a leading one. The public have no direct access to the underwriter. Business is brought to him by the broker who, having learnt the needs of his client, prepares the 'slip' which is the basis of the policy to be, presents it to likely underwriters and secures the best terms for insurance, collecting the initials of various underwriters until the 'item' is completely insured. When the item is completely insured, the broker informs his client and subsequently a policy is issued on behalf of the underwriters involved.

Overall in brief terms as defined by Lloyds Act of 1911, Lloyd's objectives are as follows:

(1) The carrying on by members of the Society of the business of insurance of every description, including guarantee business.

(2) The advancement and protection of the interests of members of the Society in connection with the business carried on by them as members of the Society, and in respect of shipping and cargoes, and freight and other insurable property or insurable interest or otherwise.

(3) The collection, publication, and diffusion of intelligence and information.

(4) The performing of all things incidental or conducive to the fulfilment of the object of the Society.

Associated with the Corporation of Lloyds are Lloyds' agents which are established at almost every port in the world. Details of their salient duties are given below:

(1) Protecting the interests of underwriters (Lloyds or otherwise) according to instructions which may be sent to them, for example, by endeavouring to avoid fraudulent claims.

(2) Rendering advice and assistance to masters of shipwrecked vessels.

(3) Reporting to Lloyds information regarding all casualties

which may occur in their district and information as to arrivals and departures.

(4) Appointing surveyors to inspect damaged vessels and granting certification of seaworthiness when called upon to do so by masters of vessels which have suffered damage.

(5) Notifying London headquarters of all information of relevant interest which may come to their notice.

(6) Surveying or appointing surveyors when called upon by consignees of cargo or by underwriters to survey damage and issuing reports stating the cause, nature and extent of all damage. Lloyd's agents will survey and issue reports in connection with damaged goods at the request of any interested party on the payment of a fee, quite apart from any question of insurance. All reports issued by Lloyd's agents are made 'without prejudice' and subject to the terms, conditions and amount of any policy of insurance.

Whilst it is true to say that the bulk of marine insurance is effected through the Corporation of Lloyds, a significant proportion of cover is provided by insurance companies specializing in marine insurance. Overall, there are about one hundred such companies with the bulk of them situated in London and Liverpool. The premium rates can vary significantly between the Lloyds underwriter and the insurance company reflecting their experience and assessment of the risks involved. However, there is no doubt that the Corporation of Lloyds has an immense reputation throughout the world and over half its business is transacted from abroad.

FUNDAMENTAL PRINCIPLES AND PROCESS OF EFFECTING CARGO INSURANCE

The three fundamental principles of insurance are insurable interest, good faith and indemnity. This applies to all aspects of marine insurance but, in the case of cargo, there is a distinct variation in the application of the principle of insurable interest. The assured must be interested in the subject matter insured at the time of the loss even though he may not be interested when the insurance is effected.

Basically, a person has an insurable interest in a marine adventure when he stands in any legal or equitable relation to the adventure or to any insurable property at risk therein in consequence of which he may:

(a) benefit by the safety or due arrival of the insurable property or,

(b) be prejudiced by its loss or by damage thereto or by the detention thereof or

(c) incur liability in respect thereof.

The subject matter insured in connection with insurable interest is usually either ship, goods or freight, although it may sometimes be an interest arising from one of these, for example, profit, wages or disbursements.

A good example of insurable interest is absolute ownership of the subject matter insured but there are a number of other circumstances in which a person may possess an insurable interest. For instance, persons responsible for goods whilst in their charge have an insurable interest in respect of their legal liability for such goods, even if the owner himself has effected a full insurance. Of course, the owner could not recover from his insurers and also from the third party. If he recovers from his insurers he must subrogate them — his rights — against third parties. Again, if goods are consigned to an agent for sale on commission, the agent has an insurable interest because, if the goods are lost, he will be precluded from earning his commission in their sale.

Various other forms of insurable interest exist which are detailed below:

(1) A defeasible or contingent interest. A defeasible interest is one which ceases during the currency of the risk by the exercise of an option or election, such as when the commodity ownership changes hands during the course of the transit. A contingent interest is one which may be acquired during the currency of a risk through the operation of some contingency. An example is a buyer acquiring an interest in the merchandise during the course of the transit.

(2) Bottomry and respondentia bonds. Bottomry is the transaction of advancing money in time of necessity to the Master on the security of a vessel and freight being earned, or on a vessel, freight and cargo. Money advanced in bottomry bonds is only repayable in the event of the safe arrival of the vessel. Hence the rate of interest is comparatively high. Moreover, the bond is void at law if it agrees to repay the money, in the event of the vessel not completing the adventure. Respondentia is the similar advance of money in the security of cargo alone but such a loan is repayable even if the vessel be lost, provided the cargo is saved. Such loans are now rarely necessary.

(3) Charges of insurance. The assured has an insurable interest in the charges of any insurance he may effect. In cargo insurance, the premiums paid form part of the value of the goods themselves. Insurance on premiums as such is normally only taken out in connection with hull risks. Where the subject matter is insured 'lost or not lost', the assured may recover although he may not have acquired his interest until after the loss unless, at the time of effecting the contract of insurance, the assured was aware of the loss and the insurer was not.

In the formation of a contract of cargo insurance the utmost good faith (*uberrima fides*) must be observed by both the assured and insured. If either party fails to observe good faith, the other may avoid the contract. Breach of good faith may be either positive or negative in character. It may consist of either material misrepresentation, or of non-disclosure of a material fact. Such a breach does not make the contract void, but it may be avoided by the injured party. Hence the assured must disclose to the insurer, before the contract is concluded, all material circumstances which are known to the assured. A material circumstance is one which will influence the judgement of a prudent underwriter to decide whether or not to accept the risk and under what terms.

A cargo insurance policy is basically a contract of indemnity, thereby indemnifying or compensating the assured against the loss. The fundamental indemnity principle governing contract of marine insurance is found in the judgement Castellain v. Preston 1883, which indicated 'the replacing of the assured, after a loss, in as nearly as may be the same relative pecuniary position as if a loss had not occurred'. However, the contract of cargo insurance is not a contract of perfect indemnity, as an arbitrary valuation of the subject matter insured is almost invariably inserted in the policy as a basis of indemnity. This arbitrary valuation, in the absence of fraud, is the amount recovered by the assured if there is a total loss, though it may be more or less than perfect indemnity. In other words, the basis of indemnity under a marine policy remains constant throughout the risk.

The only practical way of conducting marine insurance is on the basis of agreed values. In the case of fire insurance it is usually an easy matter to arrive at the value of goods at the time and place of the fire, but it would be a much more difficult matter to arrive at the value of goods at the time and place where they are lost or damaged at sea. Again, bankers when financing shipments of goods require the shippers to provide cargo insurance policies fully covering them for the amount of their advance.

Whilst such agreed values must of necessity be arrived at in a somewhat arbitrary fashion, they do, however, represent a figure which in most circumstances will more or less provide an indemnity for the assured. The normal basis of valuation is cif, cost plus an agreed percentage, usually between say 10% or 25%, to cover a measure of anticipated profit for the buyer as well as landing charges, carriage cost etc. Thus, if a loss occurs at the very end of the transit when all cost and charges have already been paid, the insured value does not normally provide a near profit indemnity, but if on the other hand it occurs at an earlier stage when some of these costs and charges have not been insured, for instance, through the sinking of the carrying vessel, it would provide more than a perfect indemnity. Market fluctuations also affect this consideration.

It is possible for the market value of goods, especially basic commodities, to rise or fall considerably during the course of a long transit. In the event of a rise, it could be quite possible for the insured value to represent less than the actual value of the goods at the time of a loss. The assured is then out of pocket to the extent of the higher profit than he would otherwise have made. If the cargo is undervalued, the assured is his own insurer in respect of the balance. As regards overvaluation, the use of valued policies does not enable the assured to grossly overvalue the subject matter of the insurance. The value must be fixed in such a manner as to indicate that the assured only desired an indemnity.

Additional to the three main principles of cargo insurance, it is appropriate to mention briefly the proximate cause and principle of subrogation.

The proximate cause is concerned solely with establishing the actual cause of loss or damage of the cargo as, in many circumstances, there may be more than one cause. This involves determining only the proximate or nearest cause of the loss or damage thereby eliminating remote causes. In turn, this reduces the underwriter's liability to within tolerable limits.

When the underwriter has paid a loss under his policy, he is entitled to place himself in the position of the assured and to take over all rights of the assured in respect of the loss he has paid. The principle is called subrogation. For example, if goods are jettisoned for the common safety, on paying for a total loss of the jettisoned goods, the underwriter stands in the place of the assured and is entitled to general average compensation for the jettison. The principle of subrogation is inherent in every contract of marine insurance and is linked to the principle of indemnity. Its application renders it impossible for the assured to defeat the principle of indemnity by receiving from two or more parties sums exceeding a trade indemnity.

To conclude, one cannot stress too strongly the need for the exporter to adhere to the foregoing principles when effecting cargo insurance for overseas shipments.

CARGO INSURANCE POLICY FORM, CLAUSES AND PREMIUM

The exporter will be influenced by two salient factors in deciding the nature of the cargo insurance required viz. the actual insurable interest, and the terms of sale and type of contract. These factors must be borne in mind in considering the cargo insurance arrangements.

Before examining the content of the policy, it is appropriate first of all to consider the three main categories of general cargo insurance available:

(1) All risk. In theory, this provides cover against all risk or loss or damage but, in reality, much depends on the type of merchandise involved. It does not extend, as recorded in the clause paramount of the Institute cargo clauses, to cover loss, damage, or expense proximately caused by delay or inherent vice or nature of the subject matter insured.

(2) With average (WA). This type of policy provides extensive cover against all loss or damage due to marine perils throughout the duration of the policy. It is subject, however, to any specific franchise which may be introduced into the policy, such as those below a certain specified percentage value and non-recoverable. However, when the specified amount is reached the claim is honoured in full.

(3) Free of particular average (FPA). Basically, this is a limited form of cargo insurance cover inasmuch that no partial loss or damage is recoverable from the insurers unless the actual vessel or craft is stranded, sunk or burnt. Under the latter circumstances, the FPA cargo policy holder can recover any losses of the insured merchandise which was on the vessel at the time as would obtain under the

more extensive WA policy. Basically, the FPA policy provides coverage for total losses and general average emerging from actual 'marine perils'. For example, the total loss of an insured consignment during discharge, loading or transhipment.

It is important the reader has a proper comprehension of the more commonly used delivery terms particularly within the context of cargo insurance. These are detailed below:

(1) Cost, insurance and freight (CIF). Under such terms the seller is responsible for all expenses including the cargo insurance premium.

(2) Ex Works. Under such terms the buyer makes all the distribution arrangements relative to the consignment including financing the cargo insurance premium.

(3) Free on board (FOB). The buyer meets all the transportation cost including cargo insurance premium from the time the goods pass over the ships rail.

(4) Goods sold cost and freight (C & F). Under such terms the buyer arranges the cargo insurance.

One must bear in mind these can be varied to meet individual circumstances.

There is one form of marine policy which is frequently used for cargo insurance. This is the old Lloyds form which has been in use for hundreds of years and is still issued by both Lloyds and insurance companies. It is called Lloyds SG Policy (Ship and Goods Policy). The wording is old-fashioned and today is invariably modified by the attachment of clauses and typed wordings which may restrict or extend the standard cover as required.

The particular advantage gained by retaining the old policy is that almost every word has acquired a precise legal definition. This policy is not a comprehensive form to cover all requirements by suitable reference or endorsement but provides rather a simple basic framework for both cargo and hull insurance risks, the detailed conditions for the particular insurance being contained in the attachment clauses or typed wording. It may appear unorthodox that cargo in transit by air or land is covered by the standard marine policy but it should be remembered that the clauses which are attached thereto or typed therein give a precise description of the cover and the form is retained because of its flexibility.

It is appropriate to mention that the word average features in the policy and it means loss in marine insurance, whereas in non-marine insurance it concerns the actual values to the sum assured.

The standard policy covers the following perils:

(1) Perils of the seas. These include all navigational hazards to be met on the sea, such as stranding, sinking, collision (with other vessels or other objects), heavy weather or sea water, but not wear and tear and natural deterioration.

(2) Fire.

(3) Thieves. This does not include petty pilferage nor theft by the crew. However, this definition should not cause confusion because the risks of theft, pilferage and non-delivery may be covered under a special clause.

(4) Jettison. Throwing the cargo overboard.

(5) Barratry. Wrongful acts of the Master or crew of the vessel to the prejudice of the owner.

The standard policy covers all 'losses' caused by the foregoing perils as under:

(1) Total loss including constructive total loss. A constructive total loss arises when the cargo is so damaged that to repair it would cost more than its original value.

(2) Partial loss including particular average and general average sacrifice.

(3) Various charges and expenses incurred to avert a loss covered by the policy, for example, general average contributions, salvage charges, sue and labour charges.

The standard policy also contains a footnote, known as the memorandum, which excludes particular average in certain circumstances for some cargoes and provides franchises for particular average for various types of cargo and the ship. These provisions are in most cases overruled by special clauses or typed wording.

The standard policy specifically excludes the following:

(a) All war risks, capture, seizure etc. and piracy. This is known as the FC & S clause.

(b) Strikes, riots, and civil commotions.

When cover against war, strikes etc. is needed, these exclusions are deleted and special clauses are attached to the policy.

There is an important point concerning the standard marine policy; the cover attaches in respect of goods from time of loading on board the vessel but in most instances cover is required from commencement of transit ex store. Under the Institute of Cargo clauses, the cover attaches from the time the goods leave the warehouse at the place named in the policy and continues until the goods are delivered to the consignees at the final store as named in the policy, subject to a limit of 60 days after completion of discharge from an overseas vessel.

While all Lloyds' policies are issued in a standard form, many companies use their own wording. Such policies are, in the main, similar to Lloyds' marine policy, but there are a number of differences, especially in the printed marginal clauses.

The following clauses are only printed in the marine insurance company issued policy.

(1) Memorandum.
(2) Institute dangerous drugs clause.
(3) FC & S (free of capture and seizure) clause.
(4) FSR & CC (free of strikes, riots and civil commotions)
(5) Frustration clause.
(6) Waiver clause.

Any additional clauses which the company may wish to include must be agreed upon at the time the insurance is placed and such clauses will then be gummed or typed on the policy when issued, but the brokers know that the actual printed policy wording of each company is identical in essentials.

The standard policy form is the backbone of every cargo insurance contract, but, in order to express it in up-to-date terms, it is essential to modify the policy by the attachment of suitable clauses.

The majority of clauses are promulgated by the Institute of London underwriters and are known as the 'Institute clauses.' In addition there are clauses which are approved by certain trade and underwriters' associations such as the timber load clauses, the frozen meat clauses and many others.

The most common Institute clauses are given below:

(1) Institute cargo clauses (all risks) — explained above.
(2) Institute cargo clauses (with average) — explained above.
(3) Institute transit clauses — explained above.
(4) Institute cargo clauses (free from particular average) — explained above.
(5) Institute war clauses.
(6) Institute strike clauses.

(7) Institute air cargo clauses. Insofar as air freight is concerned, Institute air cargo clauses (all risks) were introduced in 1965 and these are briefly detailed below:

No. 1. Transit clause. This provides 30 days coverage as distinct from 60 days for marine clauses.

No. 2. Termination of adventure clause. Again 30 days limit applies.

No. 3. Change of transit clause.

No. 4. All risk clause.

No. 5. Constructive total loss clause.

No. 6. Bailee clause.

No. 7. Not to insure clause.

No. 8. FC & S clause.

No. 9. Frustration and confiscation clause.

No. 10. Free of strikes, riots and civil commotion clause or

No. 11. Strikes, riots and civil commotions clause.

No. 12. Institute war clause.

Postal consignments are excluded from the clauses and, in the main, the terms follow closely the standard marine cargo clauses adequately amended for air freight transits.

Endorsements are not numerous in cargo insurance. Cargo policies issued to cover specific consignments are invariably assignable by the seller to the buyer. It is seldom necessary to interrupt or intercept the normal transfer of documents from seller to buyer in order to alter the conditions of cover. One exception is the endorsement to extend the policy to include further storage at destination pending withdrawal from the customs or in forwarding to final destination.

Premium rates are determined by numerous factors which are detailed below:

(1) Nature of the packing used. This has to be related to the mode of transport and its adequacy as a form of protection to the cargo. Air freight and maritime container shipments tend to require less packing.

(2) Type of merchandise involved. Some commodities are more vulnerable to damage than others. Additionally, one must relate this to the cover provided and experience, if any, of conveying such cargo.

(3) Nature of transit and related warehouse accommodation. Generally, the shorter the transit time, the less vulnerable the cargo to

damage/pilferage. Again the mode(s) of transport involved influence premium determination. Maritime containerization has tended in many trades/cargoes to reduce risk of pilferage, but the cargo still remains susceptible to damage.

(4) Previous experience. If the cargo involved has been subject to significant damage or pilferage the premiums are likely to be high. In the main, the shipper and broker tend to work well together in devising methods to minimize damage/pilferage and overcome inadequate packing.

(5) The type of cover needed. This is a critical area and obviously the more extensive cover required, the higher the premium rate. Again the broker will advise the shipper the extent of cover required, but much depends on terms of delivery.

(6) The volume of cargo involved. A substantial quantity shipment of export cargo may obtain a more favourable premium, but much depends on the circumstances, particularly transport mode and type of packing, if any.

Normally, alternative rates are available for different covers. For example, glassware may be insured at a high rate against all risks including breakage, or at a much lower rate excluding breakage, cracking or chipping. The degree of fragility is not the same for all commodities and obviously there cannot be a universal rate for breakage. To the exporter fresh to the business, it is wise to shop around to obtain the most favourable rates or seek advice from the freight forwarder.

CARGO INSURANCE CLAIMS

Most insurance company policies require that immediate notice be given to the nearest branch or agency in the event of damage giving rise to a claim under a policy on goods. Lloyds' policies stipulate that a Lloyds' agent shall be called in should damage occur.

When notified of damage, the company's agent or Lloyds' agent proceeds to appoint a suitable surveyor to inspect the goods and to report on the nature and extent of the damage. A common practice is for a report or certificate of loss incorporating the surveyors findings to be issued to the consignees, the latter paying the fee. This is the usual procedure relative to the Lloyds' agent. This certificate of loss is included with the claim papers and, if the loss is recoverable under the insurance cover, the fee is refunded to the claimants.

In some circumstances, the claim papers are returned to the place where the insurance was effected and subsequently presented to the underwriters. However, especially where goods are sold on CIF terms and the policy is assigned to the consignees, arrangements are made for any claims to be paid at destination. In such cases, the consignees approach the agents named in the policy for payment of their claims. Lloyds' agents undertake this service. The policy must be produced by the claimant when a marine claim is put forward because of the freedom with which the marine policy may be assigned. In circumstances where the policy or certificate of insurance has been lost or destroyed, underwriters are generally willing to settle the claim, provided that the claimant completes a letter of indemnity.

The presentation of claims is by negotiation on documents supporting the assured's case. It is very difficult to state with any degree of legal precision exactly on whom the onus of proof falls in every case, but generally speaking, the assured must be able to prove a loss by a peril against which he was insured. Once the assured has presented a prima facie case of loss by a peril insured against, the onus is on the insurers to disprove liability.

The following documents are required when making an insurance claim:

(1) The export invoice issued to the customer together with shipping specificiation and/or weight notes.

(2) The original bill of lading, charter party, air waybill, or CMR or CIM consignment note.

(3) The original policy or certificate of insurance.

(4) The survey report or other documentary evidence detailing the loss or damage occurred.

(5) Extended protest or extract from ships logs for salvage loss, particular average in goods, or total loss of goods for maritime consignments.

(6) Letters of subrogation for total loss or particular average on goods.

(7) Any exchange of correspondence with the carriers and other parties regarding their liability for the loss or damage.

(8) Any landing account or weight notes at final destination.

It is important to bear in mind that clean receipts for imported cargo acceptance should never be given when the goods are in a doubtful condition, but the receipt should be suitably endorsed and witnessed if possible, for example, if one package is missing. Furthermore, if the loss or damage incurred was not readily apparent at the time of taking delivery, written notice must be given to the carriers or other bailees within three days of delivery acceptance.

It is desirable the claim be progressed as quickly as practicable.

It is desirable the exporter has a good comprehension of the term general average (GA) which features in any standard maritime policy. It is defined as a 'loss arising in consequences of extraordinary and intentional sacrifices made or expenses incurred, for the common safety of the ship and cargo.' Examples of general average include jettison of cargo, damage to cargo, etc.

In the event of a shipowner declaring a general average loss occurring, each party benefiting from the voyage must contribute proportionate to their interest in the maritime venture. This, of course, involves shippers who may not have suffered any damage or loss to their cargo. The cargo is only released in such a situation when the shipper/importer has given either a cash deposit or signed a general average guarantee provided by the insurers. Overall, this involves signing a general average bond which confirms the importer will pay his general average contribution following the average adjuster's assessment.

CMR LIABILITY

The Carriage of Goods by Road Act, 1965, which came into force in 1967 notified and enacted the provisions of the Convention on the International Carriage of Goods by Road (CMR). The Convention represents an attempt by the principal European nations to regulate the responsibilities and liabilities of carriers engaged in the international distribution of goods by road. Consequently, the Convention applies throughout the entire duration of the carriage, even if certain sections of the transit may be by sea, rail or air (although in the event of loss, liability would be determined according to the particular requirements of the law relating to the actual form of transportation involved, for example, Hague rules in respect of shipments by sea.)

Broadly speaking, the Convention applies to contracts for the carriage of goods in vehicles for reward between termini situated in two different countries of which at least one is a signatory to the Convention. At the present time signatories include the United Kingdom, France, West Germany, Belgium, Holland, Luxembourg, Italy, Austria, Sweden, Poland and Yugoslavia. The Convention does not govern carriage between the UK and Eire, or to internal sendings within the UK, neither does it apply to postal sendings, funeral consignments or furniture removals.

The contract of carriage is evidenced by a CMR consignment note, containing a description of the goods, carriage charges and any special provisions such as agreed values, special interests, delivery instructions etc. The consignment note states that the Convention is to apply, although it should be understood that the Convention would operate even if no document at all was issued.

Briefly the CMR Convention provides that the carrier shall be liable for the total or partial loss of the goods from time of receipt to time of delivery. In particular, the carrier is conclusively liable for loss if the goods have not been delivered within 30 days from the expiry of any agreed time limit, or 60 days after taking over the goods in the absence of such limit. Moreover, the carrier is responsible for the acts of employees and agents, including sub-contracts and sub-bailees.

The carrier may be relieved from all liability if the loss is due to the wrongful act of the claimant, inherent vice of the goods or through circumstances the carrier could not avoid or prevent but the onus of proof is on the carrier.

On the other hand, the carrier discharges the onus of proof if it can be shown that the loss can be attributed to:

(1) Permitted use of open unsheeted vehicles.
(2) Improper packing, marking and numbering.
(3) Handling operations undertaken by the cargo owner.
(4) Nature of the goods (ordinary breakage, leakage, wastage).
(5) Carriage of livestock.

In the event of loss or damage, the carriers liability is related to the market price of the goods at the place and time at which they were accepted for carriage, but not exceeding 25 gold francs/kg of gross weight plus carriage charges, customs duties, and other charges incurred in respect of the carriage of goods, which are totally lost, or in proportion of partly lost or damaged. By arrangement between the carriers and consignor, a higher amount may be substituted for the convention limit if a special interest or higher value has been agreed between the parties. Should the consignee be able to prove that loss or damage has resulted from delay the carrier is required to pay compensation not exceeding the carriage charges (unless specially agreed).

Notwithstanding the above limitations and immunities, the carrier is liable to pay full compensation if the loss, damage, or delay is caused by the wilful misconduct or default of the carrier or his servants or agents acting within the scope of their employment.

The Convention regulates the procedures to be followed concerning claims against the carrier. The consignee must reserve the right to claim for any apparent damage not later than the time of delivery. If the damage is not apparent, the consignee must give written notice of damage within seven days. Claims for delay must be notified in writing within 21 days from the time the goods were placed at the disposal of the consignee. Legal action must be brought within a year but, in the case of wilful misconduct, the period of limitation is extended to three years.

Normally, the carrier in whose custody the damage occurred is liable to indemnify the claimant but frequently responsibility for loss or damage is difficult to determine. Furthermore, action may be brought only against the first carrier, the last carrier or the carrier in whose portion of carriage the loss occurred. The Convention, therefore, provides that the carrier who has paid compensation is entitled to recover from other carriers who may be primarily responsible, or alternatively, if liability cannot be determined accurately, responsibility may be apportioned according to each carriers proportion of the total carriage charges and recovery made accordingly. If a carrier becomes insolvent, the other carriers bear his proportion of any outstanding claims.

From the exporters point of view, it will be noted that the opportunities for recovery of losses sustained while goods are in road hauliers possession are quite extensive. The UK's accession to the EEC has produced a dramatic increase in the volume and value of goods consigned to the Continent. Sellers in this country who utilize the through transit facilities now provided by hauliers should be fully aware both of their own and the carrier's legal position if rights of recourse are to be successfully pursued.

CHAPTER 9

Export Finance

Introduction. Export and import prices. Payments for imports and exports. Documentary credits and allied documents. Transferable credits. Back to back credits. Revolving credits. Red clause credits. Acceptance credits. Bank finance for export and factoring. Factoring. Medium and long term finance. Less common methods of trade. Methods of payment.

INTRODUCTION

In what some would still call the 'good old days', the selling of goods abroad did not present the same problems as those encountered today. There was no balance of payments problem and we had extensive overseas investments and were suppliers to the world. Consequently, there was no pressing need to export and it was undertaken only by those who had the facilities and expertise to handle it successfully. All transactions were conducted in sterling and so there arose no exchange problems. In a seller's market we could dictate our terms and grant credit only when we so desired.

Today, the picture is entirely different. We have a serious balance of payments problem, our overseas investments have been dispersed to pay for two wars, our products have now to compete with equally, and sometimes more, efficient producers in a buyer's market. Sterling is no longer the dominant currency and exchange rates tend to fluctuate quite widely. These are the circumstances in which we have to expand our export trade.

Whereas at one time the ability to sell our goods abroad depended on quality, delivery and price, there has now entered a new factor which tends to play an increasingly important part — the ability and willingness to give credit. The granting of credit terms, which are growing longer as buyer pressure increases, mean that the exporter is out of his money for longer periods of time. This automatically reduces cash flow and creates a finance problem for the exporter who, sooner or later, has to seek assistance from his bank. The financial aspect of selling goods abroad, which once was just one normal step in the export procedure, has now assumed such importance as to become a problem in its own right.

The exporter, after consideration of all the usual marketing requirements such as suitability for the market, delivery dates, price etc. and coping with carriage and freight problems, has to consider whether he can offer the credit terms provided by his competitors and find the finance to do so. This element is further complicated by the credit and political risks inherent in overseas trade, not to mention exchange risks where the buyer is asking for prices and invoices in his own currency.

EXPORT AND IMPORT PRICES

In the uncertain situation of today, price policy has become much more important but at the same time more difficult. When rates of exchange remained stable for many years prices found their own proper level. Such price policy as we had was probably not the outcome of serious research and careful consideration but it just 'happened'. Because it could be followed for a long while, few traders were equipped to deal with frequent changes. In November 1967, they were faced with stark reality; few had any contingency plans to deal with devaluation and over a weekend had to decide what to do about export prices.

Some held their sterling prices level and passed on to their overseas dealers and customers the 'full benefit of devaluation'. In consequence, they were flooded with orders which they were unable to manufacture, finance or deliver on time and so lost many orders and customers. Some in similar business held their overseas prices level by raising their sterling export prices and in consequence upset their customers who thought they were being cheated out of a lower price to which they were entitled.

International trade was first conducted by merchant adventurers who travelled with their goods from place to place. At each place they sold what they had bought and purchased what was available locally and, for this purpose, they used either barter or what passed for currency in that place. Then they moved on to another country and repeated the process. This is basically the principal on which many multinational companies operate.

As a matter of policy, the first decision to make as regards pricing is whether to charge in each market 'what it will bear', or whether to charge a price that covers costs and gives a reasonable return on the capital employed. If one does not charge what the market will bear, somebody in that market will add the difference and make an easy profit. The final consumer is not likely to be charged any less. If on the other hand, a price based on cost is more than the market will bear, then orders will be lost.

When considering what policy adjustments to make in the wake of devaluation, it should be borne in mind that a 10% devaluation does not mean a 10% change in the local price. The sterling price is only a part of the final cost to the consumer. Customs duty, import and distribution costs and local mark-ups are expressed in local currency and are not affected. Duty, if *ad valorem*, may vary with the price but the rest are more or less constant and, in many cases, double the export price by the time the goods are finally sold. So, a 10% devaluation corresponds to about a 5% change in local price.

The whole question of pricing then will revolve around:

(1) How far minimum costs and return on capital can be related to that which the market will pay. This will involve a close study of the market, its extent and potential, the strength of competitors and the elasticity of demand for the profit.

(2) To what extent the fluctuation in exchange rates can be used to advantage.

(3) What credit terms are usual in the market and whether the cost of the credit is borne by the buyer.

(4) Sources of raw material and possible price changes.

As a basic principal of price policy there is much to recommend selling in the customer's currency and using the forward exchange market. It is a good marketing ploy and a courtesy to the buyer. He knows exactly how much the goods will cost in his own currency and has no pre-occupation with exchange rates. By selling in foreign currency, the exporter has assumed the exchange risk himself but he can protect himself against any exchange rate fluctuations by selling the currency in the forward exchange market. This is a simple operation through one's bank and means that one is now quoted a rate of exchange at which one's currency will be exchanged when received. Moreover, with currencies such as the deutschmark, which are at a premium forward, the forward rate of exchange will be more favourable and more sterling will be received in exchange for the currency received.

It is apparent then that export prices must be established in the market place always bearing in mind the cost. There are many instances of goods being sold abroad at prices far below that which the market would be prepared to pay and, on the other hand, many cases of markets lost because the calculation of cost was too high. Marginal selling is not a sound policy, every sale should show some return.

As far as import prices are concerned it is 'what the market will pay' which is all important. Consumer goods have to be retailed at a price which the consumer will pay. Raw materials must be at a price which will enable the end product to sell at a profit. Many of the bulk raw materials are sold through specialized commodity markets as explained in Chapter 1.

Goods purchased at prices expressed in foreign currency will, of course, be subject to exchange rate fluctuations but, as in the case of exports, the exchange risk can be covered in the forward exchange market by buying the currency forward.

PAYMENTS FOR IMPORTS AND EXPORTS

Credit terms and the method by which payment will be effected are agreed at the time the sales contract is concluded. If the relationship between the buyer and seller are good, then it may have been agreed to trade on 'open account' terms. This means simply that the seller will despatch the goods directly to the buyer, send him an invoice and await the remittance of payment from the buyer, as in domestic trading.

There are several methods by which the debtor may remit payment to his supplier:

(1) Debtor's own cheque. This is not a very satisfactory method from the creditor's point of view. Apart from the usual risk that the cheque may be unpaid, it has to be sent back through banking channels to the buyer's country for collection, thus incurring additional expenses.

(2) Banker's draft. This would be a draft drawn by the buyer's bank on its correspondent bank in the exporter's country. As such it is good payment but there is always the danger that the draft may be lost in the post and a bank draft cannot be 'stopped'. A new draft could only be issued against indemnity.

(3) Mail transfer (MT). This is the most common method of payment. The debtor instructs his bank to request its correspondent

bank in the exporter's country to pay the specific amount to the exporter. The whole procedure is done by entries over banking accounts; the buyer's bank debits his account and credits the account of the correspondent bank which, on receipt of the payment instructions, passes a reciprocal entry over its account with the remitting bank and pays the money over to the exporter. The instructions between the banks may be by ordinary mail or air mail.

(4) Telegraphic transfer (TT). The procedure is similar to that of MT except that the instructions are sent by cable. This means that the payment is effected more quickly.

Where 'open account' terms have not been agreed, then it is for the exporter to arrange for payment to be collected from the buyer. The usual way in which this is done is by the use of bills of exchange. This is the traditional method of claiming that which is due from the debtor, and has been used as a basis for international trade throughout its history.

Instead of merely sending the documents to the debtor with only the covering invoice, the exporter draws a bill of exchange on the debtor for the sum due and attaches the documents to the bill. This is then sent through banking channels for presentation to the buyer. There are several advantages in the employment of bills:

(1) The bill of exchange is an instrument long recognized by trade custom and by the law; there is in consequence an established code of practice in relation to bills.

(2) The bill is a specific demand on the debtor and if it is drawn in proper form in respect of a debt justly due the debtor refuses it at his peril.

(3) The bill is a useful instrument of finance (see Chapter 12).

(4) The bill provides a useful mechanism for the granting to an overseas buyer of a pre-arranged period of credit. Thus if an exporter has, for some reason, to offer his buyer a period of credit, say 90 days, then the bill can be drawn at 90 days sight. At the same time, the exporter can maintain a degree of control over the shipping documents by authorizing release of the documents on payment, or acceptance of the bill. The bill does provide an instrument on which action can be taken at law.

It should be noted that the drawing of a bill of exchange on the buyer does not guarantee payment and the seller has lost control of the goods to some extent as they are out of his country. Moreover, he may have to arrange for storage and insurance or even re-shipment.

The procedure for the exporter, having obtained the shipping documents, is to draw the bill and lodge it with his bank together with the documents for collection. When lodging the bill, the exporter must give to his bank very precise and complete instructions as to what action to take in certain circumstances: whether to forward the bill by air mail etc. and ask for proceeds to be remitted by cable or air mail; whether the documents are to be released against payment or acceptance of the Bill; whether the Bill is to be 'protested' if dishonoured; whether the goods should be stored and insured if not taken up by the buyer; whether rebate may be given for early payment, who is the Case of Need (usually the exporter's agent) to whom the collecting bank may refer in case of dispute.

The exporter's bank will forward the bill and documents to its correspondent bank in the buyer's country passing on exactly the instructions received from the exporter. The correspondent bank (collecting bank) will present the bill and documents to the buyer, and release the documents to the buyer in accordance with the instructions received. If the arrangement was for payment to be made immediately then the bill of exchange will be drawn at 'sight' and the instructions will be to release documents against payment (D/P). If a period of credit has been agreed, then the bill will be drawn at say '90 days sight' and the instructions will be for the documents to be released against acceptance by the buyer of the bill (D/A). In this case, the buyer signs his acceptance across the face of the bill, which now becomes due for payment in 90 days time and the buyer obtains the documents of title to the goods. The collecting bank will advise the remitting bank of the date of acceptance, and hold the bill until maturity, when the collecting bank will present it to the buyer for payment. In case of dishonour, and if so instructed, the collecting bank will arrange 'protest' by a notary. This procedure provides legal proof that the bill was presented to the drawee and was dishonoured, and enables action to be taken in the courts without further preliminaries.

The procedures and responsibilities of the banks and other parties are laid down in the 'Uniform Rules for the Collection of Commercial Paper' issued by the International Chamber of Commerce and subscribed to by the major banks throughout the world.

The method of collecting payment described above is based on the documentary bill, but in certain circumstances use may be made of a 'clean' bill, that is, a bill to which no documents are attached. Such bills may be drawn for the collection of monies due for services etc. or for any debt which is not a payment for goods. A clean bill may also be used to obtain payment for goods sent on 'open account', especially where payment is overdue.

   Because they are a traditional and accepted means of obtaining payment in international trade, bills of exchange can be used, with one of two exceptions, throughout the world. In the case of some markets, it would be unwise to operate without the protection a bill can provide.

DOCUMENTARY CREDITS AND ALLIED DOCUMENTS

Apart from 'cash with order', the documentary credit provides the most satisfactory method of obtaining payment. It provides security of payment to the exporter, and enables the buyer to ensure that he receives the goods as ordered and delivered in the way he requires. It is an arrangement whereby the buyer instructs his bank to establish a credit in favour of the seller. The buyer's bank (issuing bank) undertakes, or authorizes its correspondent bank in the exporter's country, to pay the exporter a sum of money (normally the invoice price of the goods) against presentation of shipping documents which are specified in the credit. It is a mandatory contract and completely independent of the sales contract. It is concerned only with documents and not the goods to which the documents refer. Liability for payment now rests with the issuing bank and not the buyer. The usual form of these credits is the 'irrevocable' credit, which means that it cannot be cancelled or amended without the agreement of the beneficiary (the exporter) and all other parties. Such a credit, opened by a reputable bank in a sound country, means that the exporter can rely on payment being made as soon as he has shipped the goods and produced the documents called for in accordance with the terms of the credit. The security provided by an irrevocable credit may be further enhanced if the bank in the exporter's country (advising bank) is requested by the issuing bank to add its 'confirmation'. The exporter then has a 'confirmed irrevocable credit' and he need look no further than his own local bank for payment. With a credit which is not 'confirmed', however, the point of payment is the issuing bank (abroad), although the advising bank would usually be prepared to negotiate with recourse.

The credit will set out in detail a description of the goods: price per unit and packing; name and address of the beneficiary; the voyage, that is, port of shipment and port of destination; whether the price is FOB, C & F or CIF; and whether part shipments and transhipment are allowed. In some cases, the ship will be nominated. Details of insurance (if CIF) and the risks to be covered will also be shown. The credit will specify a latest date for shipment and an expiry date which is the latest date for presentation of documents.

The basic documents which are usually called for are:

(1) *Invoice*. The amount must not exceed the credit amount. If terms such as 'about' or '*circa*' are used, a tolerance of 10% is allowed (in respect of quantity the tolerance is 3%). The description of the goods on the invoice and the packing must be exact and agree with the credit. An essential part of the description is the marks and numbers on the packages. These must appear on the invoice. The invoice should be in the name of the buyer.

(2) *Bills of lading*. This is the document of title to the goods, without which the buyer will not be able to obtain delivery from the shipping company. The credit will call for a full set (they are usually issued in a set of three). They must be clean, that is, bearing no superimposed clauses derogatory to the condition of the goods such as 'inadequate packing', 'used drums', 'on deck', etc. Unless the credit has specifically permitted the circumstances contained in the clause, the negotiating bank will call for an indemnity. The bills of lading must show the goods to be 'on board' — 'received for shipment' bills are not acceptable. They may, however, have a subsequent notation, dated and signed, which states the goods to be 'on board' and they are then acceptable. Under the new regulations set out in the 'Uniform Customs and Practice for Documentary Credits' the following bills of lading will be accepted:

(a) Through bills issued by shipping companies or their agents even though they cover several modes of transport.

(b) Short form bills of lading which indicate some or all of the conditions of carriage by reference to a source or document other than the bill of lading.

(c) Bills covering unitized cargoes such as those on pallets or in containers.

Unless specifically authorized in the credit, bills of the following type will not be accepted:

(a) Bills of lading issued by forwarding agents.

(b) Bills which are issued under and are subject to a charter party.

(c) Bills covering shipments by sailing vessels.

The Bills must be made out to the order of the shipper and endorsed in blank. If the sales contract is CIF or C & F, then the bills must be marked 'freight paid'. The general description of the goods including marks and numbers must match the invoice. The voyage and ship, if named, must be as stated in the credit. Unless tranship-ment is expressly prohibited in the credit, bills indicating tranship-ment will be accepted provided the entire voyage is covered by the same bill. Part shipments are permitted unless the credit states other-wise. Besides stating an expiry date for presentation of documents, credits should also stipulate a specified period of time after the issu-ance of the Bills during which the documents must be presented for payment. If no such period is stipulated in the credit, banks will refuse documents presented to them later than 21 days after the issu-ance of the bills of lading.

(3) *Insurance*. The document must be as stated in the credit (policy or certificate) and issued by an insurance company or its agent. Cover notes issued by brokers are not acceptable.

The details on the policy must match those on the bills of lading — voyage, ship, marks and numbers etc. It must also be in the same cur-rency as the credit and endorsed in blank. The amount covered should be at least the invoice amount — credits usually call for invoice value plus 10%. The policy must be dated not later than the date of shipment as evidenced by the bill of lading. The risks covered should be those detailed in the credit, usually Institute cargo clauses W & SRCC. If cover against 'all risks' is called for (which is unobtain-able) a policy which states that it covers all insurable risks will be acceptable.

According to circumstances, the credit may call for other docu-ments such as consular certificate, certificate of origin, quality, analy-sis or health certificate (ensures to buyer that the goods are as ordered), air waybill, railway (CIM) or road (CMR) consignment notes or Post Office receipt.

The credit may stipulate a last shipment date and the bill of lading must show shipment by that date. Extension of the shipment date automatically extends the expiry date but not vice versa.

It is very important that exporters, when they receive advice of a credit established in their favour, check the details immediately to see that the goods and terms agree with the sales contract, and they can comply with all the terms and provide all the documents required. If any amendment is required, they can then take it up with the advising bank in good time for action to be taken before expiry.

Besides the basic irrevocable credit (confirmed or not), there are revocable credits which, as the name implies, can be cancelled or amended at any time without notice to the beneficiary. They do not constitute a legally binding undertaking by the banks concerned. Once transmitted and made available at the advising bank, however, its cancellation or modification is only effective when that bank has received notice thereof and any payment made before the receipt of such notice is reimbursable by the issuing bank. The value of these credits as security for payment is plainly doubtful. They are used mainly for parents and subsidiaries companies, where a continuing series of shipments is concerned or as an indication of good intent.

Where a buyer wishes to provide his supplier with the security of payment by documentary credit, but at the same time requires a period of credit, he may instruct his bank to issue a credit calling for a bill of exchange drawn at so many days after sight instead of the usual sight draft — this would, of course, be an irrevocable credit. In this case, the beneficiary, when presenting the documents, would not receive immediate cash as under a sight credit but his term bill would be accepted by the bank. It could then be discounted in the money market at the finest rates. Thus the beneficiary would still receive payment, but the buyer would not be called upon to pay until the bill matured.

TRANSFERABLE CREDITS

These arise where the exporter seller is obtaining the goods from a third party, say the actual manufacturer, and as a middleman does not have the resources to buy outright and await payment from his overseas buyer. The credit is established in favour of the middleman seller (prime beneficiary), and authorizes the advising bank to accept instructions from the prime beneficiary to make the credit available, in whole or in part, to one or more third parties (second beneficia-

ries). The credit is then advised to the second beneficiary in the terms
and conditions of the original, except that the amount and unit price
are reduced and the shipment and expiry dates shortened. The original credit is for the price the buyer is paying to the prime beneficiary,
but the latter will be obtaining the goods at a lower price and so the
credit is transferred for a smaller amount. When the second beneficiary presents shipping documents, he obtains payment for his
invoice price, and the prime beneficiary is called upon to substitute
his own invoice and receive the difference (his profit). The negotiating bank then has documents in accordance with the original credit.

Where there is more than one second beneficiary the credit must
permit part shipments. If the prime beneficiary does not wish his
buyer and supplier to be aware of each other, he may request that his
name be substituted for that of the opener on the transfer credit, and
that shipping documents be in the name of a third party blank
endorsed.

BACK TO BACK CREDITS

Back to back credits arise in circumstances similar to those of the
transferable credit and particularly where the supplier as well as the
buyer is overseas. In this case, the middleman receives a credit in his
favour from the buyer and asks his bank to establish a credit in
favour of his supplier against the security of the credit in his own
favour. There are two separate credits, not one as in the case of a
transferable credit, and this can create problems in the matching of
documents and credit terms.

REVOLVING CREDITS

Revolving credits are used where there are shipments in a series at
intervals and the parties wish the programme to proceed without
interruption. A credit is established for a certain sum and quantity of
goods with a provision that, when a shipment has been made and documents presented and paid, the credit automatically becomes re-
available in its original form and another shipment can be made and
so on.

RED CLAUSE CREDITS

Red clause credits are sometimes called packing credits. These are mainly encountered in connection with shipments of wool from Australia, New Zealand or South Africa. A clause (in red) inserted into the credit authorizes the negotiating bank to make an advance by way of loan or overdraft to the beneficiary to enable him to purchase the wool, collect and warehouse it and prepare it for shipment. When the shipping documents are presented under the credit the loan is repaid out of the payment due under the credit.

ACCEPTANCE CREDITS

Acceptance credits are a facility provided originally by the merchant banks but now available although through the clearing banks. The bank establishes its own credit in favour of the exporter. This credit provides for bills to be drawn by the exporter on the bank which are accepted by the latter and can then be discounted in the money market at the finest rates. It is usual for such credits to run parallel with the bills drawn by the exporter on his overseas buyer and which he lodges with the bank for collection. The bills under the credit will be drawn at the same term as those on the buyers and, in due course, the payment received for the commercial bills will meet the amount due to the bank on its acceptances. This facility is a means of obtaining export finance and can on occasion be cheaper than ordinary bank accommodation.

BANK FINANCE FOR EXPORTS AND FACTORING

Theoretically, a company should be able to finance all its operations from the resources available to it, that is, its capital plus whatever it is able to borrow from the bank. Its capital will depend on how much the members of the company are prepared to invest in the enterprise, and its borrowing from the bank will depend on such factors as the balance sheet figures, profit and loss, turnover etc. or on the security it can offer by way of mortgages, life policies and stocks. Both these sources are subject to strict limitations and, for reasons already mentioned above, they are bound to prove inadequate for a company expanding its export trade. To meet the cash flow problems engendered by long credit terms, extra sources of finance must be tapped over and above the basic sources of capital and bank lending. This finance can best be found through channels relative to the export transactions themselves and, in particular, to the method of payment. Let us examine the various methods by which payment is made and what type of finance which is linked thereto:

(1) Sales on open account. Here the exporter is entirely dependent on the goodwill of the buyer to remit payment when due. Admittedly, the outstanding debts will increase the debtor item on the company's balance sheet and may, therefore, enable it to obtain additional overdraft facilities from the bank. The best answer to the problem of finance in this case would be by the use of the services of a factoring company (see latter part of chapter).

(2) Collection by means of bill of exchange drawn on the buyer. Extra finance may be obtained by discounting the bills with the bank or obtaining loan accommodation against the bills outstanding for collection. The bank has some element of security in the documents, covering the goods, which are attached to the bills. The possibility of obtaining bank finance in this way is enhanced if the export sale is covered by an Export Credits Guarantee Department (ECGD) policy. The rights under the policy may be assigned to the bank.

(3) Documentary credits. Under an irrevocable credit, the exporter is assured of payment immediately he has shipped the goods and presents correct documents to the bank and so his need for finance is reduced. He may, however, be able to obtain some extra help from his bank to produce and ship the goods on the strength of the payment assured under the credit.

As outlined above export finance is also available from merchant banks by means of an acceptance credit facility.

The services of a confirming house, which acts for the buyer, will provide payment promptly on shipment as the confirming house arranges the credit terms required by the buyer. Exporting through an export merchant will also provide ready cash as the merchant will buy the goods (making it a home sale) and handle the sale to the overseas buyer himself.

Because all the sources of export finance mentioned above were proving insufficient or were not always readily available and, moreover, were too costly special arrangements were made between the banks and ECGD. This is known as the short term finance arrangement and is designed to provide finance for exporters of consumer or consumer durable goods where the credit terms will not normally exceed two years. There are two separate schemes:

(a) Bills and notes. Where there is an instrument, that is, where the exporter draws a bill of exchange on the buyer or receives from him a promissory note, the bank will advance 100% of the face amount of the bills. In the case of sight bills and unaccepted term bills, the bank retains recourse to the exporter if the bills are not met. Once the bills are accepted the bank's recourse is to ECGD only. In the case of non-payment of an accepted bill, the bank recovers from ECGD but ECGD retains recourse to the customer for the difference between that which is paid to the bank and that which is due to the customer under his ECGD policy. It is required that original shipping documents be attached to the bill.

(b) Open account scheme. Where there is no instrument such as bill of exchange and the sales terms do not exceed 180 days from receipt of goods or cash against documents. Under this scheme, the exporter issues his promissory note to the bank for the invoice value of the goods exporter and falling due for payment in any one month. The due date of the promissory note will be the last day of the month when settlement is due. The bank advances the face value of the promissory note at once and the note must be paid at maturity whether or not the proceeds of the invoice have been received. The bank only has recourse to ECGD if the customer fails to honour his note. Copy shipping documents are required.

The interest rate charged under both these schemes is ⅝% over the bank's base rate.

FACTORING

Although 'factoring' as we know it today had its origins in the representatives set out to North America by the textile manufacturers of the North of England to conduct the sales and collect payment, it is now looked upon as an American idea which has been introduced to this country in recent years. The underlying function of the factoring service is the maintenance of the supplier's sales ledger. It provides an administration service based on the copy invoices received from the supplier. It does not make sales or even raise invoices at the time of delivery of the goods. These functions are performed by the supplier against the background of the factor's credit approval. The factoring of export sales is still relatively in its infancy but provides a comprehensive package of export services to short term exporters.

The collection of exporters' invoices is handled in overseas markets either by the British factor's own offices or through correspondent factors. This network provides the factors with a broad knowledge of payment patterns for credit control purposes, enables them to deal with overseas buyers in their own language and handle sales expressed in foreign currency. Credit cover of 100% is provided for approved buyers. Suppliers cash flow is increased by the factors being prepared to make advance payments in anticipation of the collection of outstanding receivables. This advance is usually about 70% of outstanding debtors and can be taken either immediately on passing copies of invoices to the factor or at any time and up to any amount within the agreed ceiling.

MEDIUM AND LONG TERM FINANCE

Whereas the short term finance arrangement is to assist the exporter of consumer durable goods with relatively short terms of credit the medium term arrangement is designed to assist the exporter or producer of capital goods where credit terms may be up to five years. In this field, the exporter is faced not only with the longer wait for payment but also the extra cost of financing the credit period and the greater possibility of changes in interest rates. To meet these problems, the arrangement between the banks and ECGD is as follows.

The bank provides post-shipment finance to the exporter selling on credit terms of from 2-5 years from date of shipment against a specific unconditional guarantee from ECGD. Finance is at a fixed rate of 7% up to five years and 7½% for longer periods and is available only to the extent of the guaranteed amount. It should be noted that the ECGD guarantees are normally effective from date of shipment and any finance required before that stage must be taken within the customer's normal banking arrangements.

ECGD has laid down certain conditions:

(1) The goods must be deemed to be capital goods or of a category acceptable to the Department.

(2) The period of credit is limited to five years but in certain cases six or even seven years have been agreed exceptionally.

(3) ECGD usually requires the buyer to put up a deposit on the order being confirmed and a further percentage when shipment is made — a fair average is 10% in each case.

(4) The cover provided under the guarantee is 100%.

(5) The exporter will be expected to arrange to draw bills of exchange for acceptance or obtain from the buyer promissory notes covering the instalments of principal and interest spread over the period of credit. These are usually drawn in series, payable at six-monthly intervals and bear an interest clause. When negotiations have taken place between the exporter, the bank and ECGD, the bank draws up a facility letter addressed to the exporter setting out the terms and conditions under which it will make funds available to him on a non-recourse basis. Agreement in principle for finance under this scheme is usually given for three months to enable the customer to complete his negotiations with the buyer. If at the expiry of this period the negotiations are incomplete, a new approach by the customer must be made.

For exports of heavy capital equipment and ships which call for even longer terms of credit than the medium term five years, ECGD introduced the 'financial guarantee'. This is to provide buyer finance as opposed to supplier finance as under the short and medium term arrangements.

The guarantee covers direct loans made by a bank to the overseas buyer and so enables him to pay the exporter on cash terms. The buyer is expected, as a rule, to put up from his own resources 20% of the purchase price, the remaining 80% being paid to the exporter out of the loan made to the buyer. The loan is guaranteed by ECGD up to 100% of capital and interest thereon.

The pattern is for the bank to purchase the buyer's promissory notes covering repayment and claused to cover interest. The exporter is paid irrevocably out of the proceeds of the purchase of the notes after presentation to the bank of the documents set out in the supply contract and the financial agreement. The buyer has full responsibility for repayment of the finance irrespective of the supply contract. Preliminary discussions with ECGD and the bank must be commenced by the supplier as soon as he starts negotiations with a buyer.

These guarantees are designed for capital projects and there is a normal minimum amount for consideration of £250 000. The interest rates are the same as those for the medium term arrangement.

This procedure is ideally suited to cases where there are several suppliers to the one contract. Where the amount involved is considerable and the credit terms correspondingly long, the loan may be put up by a consortium of banks often with a merchant bank acting as manager. Where the buyer is also seeking means to finance the 20% which he has to provide himself it is sometimes possible for one of the banks or merchant banks to arrange a Europe-currency loan which would be outside the guarantee arrangement.

Within the buyer credit context the ECGD provides cover for the financing of contracts under lines of credit. This financing is in the form of loans made available by British banks to overseas borrowers to facilitate the purchase of a wide range of capital goods from diverse British suppliers under an overall financing scheme. Contract values may be down to £5000. Some of the lines are allocated to particular projects, in which case the borrowers are often governments or government agencies. Other lines are 'general purpose', in which case the borrower is usually a bank and the line may be used by any buyer approved by this bank. The interest rate applicable is the same as for other buyer credit. ECGD actively encourages the financing of buyer credits in foreign currency.

LESS COMMON METHODS OF TRADE

(1) Consignment trade — goods sent by an exporter to a nominal importer in another country, that nominal importer being, in fact, a nominee or agent of the exporter. The intention is that the merchandise shall come into the physical possession of the agent whose duty it is to sell the merchandise on the exporter's behalf and remit to his principal the proceeds of sale, less all expenses of handling, storing and transport, customs duties and fees and his commission.

(2) Participation — joint venture where the British manufacturer takes a share with a local concern in either marketing the exporter's product, local assembly or local manufacture.

(3) Licensing — where a licence is granted to an overseas company to manufacture the products on a royalty basis using either the UK manufacturer's brand name or the name of the licensee.

(4) Barter or compensation trade — arising from the restrictive effects of exchange control and the shortage in some countries of for-

eign exchange. This would occur if the buyer is unable to obtain an allocation of sterling or some acceptable alternative currency and so he offers goods in payment of those he wishes to buy. This has been quite a common practice with some of the Eastern Bloc countries, South American countries and underdeveloped countries in Africa. This type of trade presents many problems: whether the goods offered are required by the seller or whether they can be disposed of easily; it is difficult to get the amounts to co-incide; and the supplier finds himself involved in trades with which he is not acquainted. Some of the merchants and merchant banks in London have set up a type of 'clearing'. They will undertake the exchange of goods and find outlets for the goods received in settlement.

METHODS OF PAYMENT

Other parts of the book have described the methods by which and the channels through which payments in international trade are effected. There has naturally been a constant demand from traders for these payments to be expedited, and over the years the banks have evolved systems whereby delays could be reduced.

A recent development is the introduction of a procedure known as 'swift'. This is a highly sophisticated, computerized, financial communication network. It is aimed to provide its members with a means of sending automatically authenticated messages which would be expressed in standardized formats to one another. The messages, cheaper than telex, may be assigned two levels of priority — normal or urgent. The time for transmitting a normal message is expected to be ten minutes and for an urgent message one minute.

The system is designed to cater for inward and outward payment instructions in sterling and currency, funding advices, sterling account statements, debit and credit confirmations and a variety of foreign exchange work.

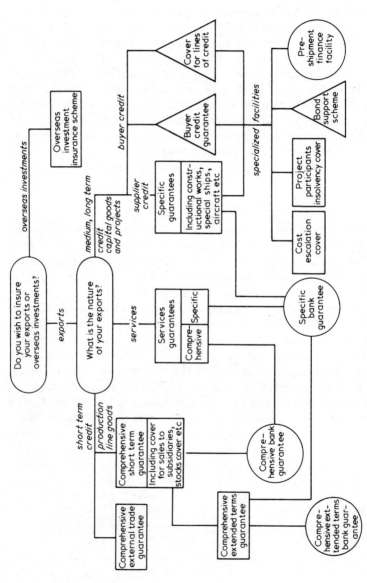

VIII ECGD facilities 'at a glance' chart

CHAPTER 10

The Export Credits Guarantee Department (ECGD)

Overall role of ECGD. ECGD credit insurance. The role of ECGD in export finance. ECGD cover. More recent 'new' ECGD facilities. Berne Union.

OVERALL ROLE OF ECGD

Our study of export practice would not be complete without adequate consideration of the function of the Export Credits Guarantee Department (ECGD) which is playing an increasing decisive role in the development of UK exports.

Basically, ECGD was established in 1919 with powers to grant credit and undertake insurance 'for the purpose of re-establishing overseas trade'. The Department's powers are still 'to encourage trade', but there have been many changes in the range and quality of facilities provided. The changing pattern of international trade and the varying needs of British exporters have involved a constant reappraisal and adjustment of ECGD facilities. The Department's activities are affected by international obligations, for example, in the GATT, EEC and OECD, but it remains HM Government policy that, taken as a whole, the package of facilities available from ECGD should stand fair comparison with that available to exporters in the major competing countries. The ECGD still remains an organization run by HM Government, currently under the aegis of the Secretary of State for Trade. Basically, there are three main elements in ECGD's current operation which are detailed below:

(a) Credit insurance for exporters.

(b) Guarantees and refinancing facilities to banks financing credit.

(c) Facilities introduced in 1975-1976 to meet the special needs of exporters of major capital goods.

Details of the ECGD facilities are also found in DIAGRAM VIII.

When considering ECGD's operations the following points are relevant:

(1) Some 90% of British exports are sold on cash or short credit terms, and this is reflected in 80% of ECGD's business being on credit terms of six months or less.

(2) In the post-war period, the proportion of British exports insured by ECGD has risen from 8-35%.

(3) ECGD potential liabilities have grown from £370 million in 1956 to £1643 million in 1966, and stood at £20 billion in 1978.

(4) During the past 20 years, there has been a changing pattern of British exports. Over this period there has tended to be a move from known buyers in traditional export markets towards new lesser known buyers and to markets where the risk of non-payment may be thought to be greater.

(5) Importers now make greater use of export credits as a means of financing purchases of capital goods.

(6) Increased competition for markets for capital goods exports has resulted in an international tendency towards lengthening credit terms and subsidy of rates of interest as a means of getting business.

(7) As ECGD's business has expanded, so has the amount paid out in claims: in 1977-1978 ECGD paid £94.2 million in claims compared with about £63.1 million in the previous year.

(8) Premium rates for credit insurance and bank guarantees were increased in 1978 for only the third time since the war (the first time ever for buyer credits and bank guarantees). Premiums for comprehensive short term business — some 80% of ECGD's total business — still costs no more than 32p per £100. The need for premium increases arose from increased claims and potential claims against the background of ECGD's financial objective in order to operate its credit insurance operators at no net cost to public funds.

ECGD CREDITS INSURANCE

Basically, ECGD's main function continues to be the provision of export credit insurance against the major risks in overseas trading. Although changing world conditions may have brought in their wake new problems and risks for some exporters, many continue to require insurance against the risks that, having made a sale and satisfactorily delivered the goods, they failed to receive payment from the buyer.

ECGD applies the principle of comprehensive insurance to all goods (and services) where the business is of a continuous, repetitive miums to be kept as low as possible, while maintaining a flexible nature. In this way, ECGD obtains a broader spread of risk and a continuous and solid base of premium income. This enables premiums to be kept as low as possible, while maintaining a flexible underwriting approach to buyer and country risks. An exporter is, therefore, expected to insure all (or a reasonable spread) of his routine business over an agreed period. This comprehensive insurance constitutes by far the majority of ECGD's total business, accounting for 87% of turnover in 1977-1978 and is still growing rapidly. Ten years ago, comprehensive business insured amounted to £1600 million per annum. In 1976-1977, comprehensive insurance covered exports worth more than £10 000 million and in 1977-1978 exceeded £11 000 million. Of the business underwritten in 1977-1978, over £10 500 million was on short payment terms (anything from cash to six months credit).

The growth in business insured with ECGD has brought with it a growth in day to day enquiries. Applications for limits on individual buyers are now running at almost 1000 per week and information on some 150 000 foreign buyers is already held by the Department. In order to simplify procedures and improve the service, work has been decentralized to the ten major regional offices. In addition, a new computer unit is being installed at Cardiff to undertake not merely the routine matters already computerized but to provide an on-line service to ECGD's regional offices. This service will enable speedier decisions to be given on credit limits, where the buyers are known to ECGD, and will lead to a reduction in ECGD's costs in operating the credit limit service. Part of the streamlining to enable the Department to continue to efficiently handle this increase in growth in business has been the extension of the discretionary provisions under which exporters may determine for themselves their credit limits on individual buyers. Furthermore, ECGD usually undertakes for applications of up to £15 000 and, where it has no information on a buyer, to underwrite on information from a bank or credit information agency supplied by the exporter. Nevertheless, the credit limit service has for many years represented an important part of ECGD facilities. Many exporters tend to rely on it exclusively for credit control and others who have the capacity and the ability to form their own judgements place great value on the ECGD view.

Increased competition for export business has resulted in lengthening credit terms and official intervention to reduce rates of interest as a means of getting business. The British Government's policy has always been to remain competitive without leading a credit race. This policy recognizes the self-defeating nature of a credit race and the need to bring credit competition under greater control has long been recognized by the governments of the major trading nations, who in 1976 established a 'consensus' determining the maximum credit terms and minimum interest rates for officially supported credit.

Despite the continuing efforts to simplify and standardize the more routine aspects of cover, the Department still attempts to adapt the basic facilities to meet the special needs of particular exporters, particular trades, and particular methods of doing business. Many of the problems which face exporters whether they relate to a particular market, to particular goods, to methods of distribution, or the financing of exports etc. can be solved by making the fullest use of ECGD's credit insurance scheme and the financing facilities (described later) which are associated with it. These problems can be dealt with not so much by writing new forms of cover but in arranging business in such a way that the best possible use can be made of the facilities available. Although the type of problems encountered may fall into general broad categories, ECGD experience shows that the best solution is a full discussion of the individual exporter's problem between ECGD and that exporter. Solutions which may be suitable for one exporter may be unsuitable or unacceptable to others for a variety of reasons, even where the basic problem appears to be the same.

The consensus lays down guidelines for maximum credit periods and minimum interest rates, related to the relative wealth of importing countries. Countries are classified as 'rich', 'intermediate', or 'poor'. The guidelines are:

	Rich	Inter-mediate	Poor
(a) *Minimum* payments by delivery	15%	15%	15%
(b) *Minimum* interest rates for credits between 2 and 5 years inclusive	7¾%	7¼%	7¼%
(c) *Minimum* interest rates for credits over 5 years	8%	7¾%	7½%
(d) *Maximum* credit periods	5-8½ years	8½ years	10 years

THE ROLE OF ECGD IN EXPORT FINANCE

ECGD is not an export bank and does not itself provide finance direct to exporters. Traditionally, the Department has not sought to intervene in the provision of export finance but the basic credit insurance cover to exporters has always been useful collateral security in raising finance. But over the past 10-20 years, ECGD has been brought more directly into the raising of finance particularly for medium term credit. This involvement can be considered from the point of view of the three areas of concern to the banks as follows:

(a) Security for lending.
(b) Liquidity of the banks assets.
(c) The rate of return to the banks on their lending.

A package of facilities has been devised which ensures that business which ECGD is prepared to underwrite will not be lost through lack of finance and, at the same time, meets the banks' requirements on all three points. Unconditional guarantees to the banks on their lending (to the exporter or, under Buyer Credit facilities, to the overseas borrower) dispose of the problem of security. For the extended and medium term sterling credits of two or more years from date of shipment, Government refinancing facilities, operated through ECGD against a formula agreed with the banks, deal with the problem of banking liquidity on lending for export credit, while an interest make-up facility from the Government also enables the banks to obtain a commercial rate of return on their own lending, whilst charging an internationally competitive fixed interest rate to the exporter or buyer.

From the exporter's point of view, these facilities to the banks ensure his access to export finance — for the most part after goods have been shipped — at the keenest commercial rate ($\frac{5}{8}\%$ over base rate) for routine business on short credit terms of less than two years, and at fixed rates of interest in line with international competition for longer credit periods. With limited exceptions, these facilities do not directly affect the availability of working capital for production, nor does the Department have any influence over banks' policy towards total overdraft finance including finance for export credit. Nevertheless, the facilities do serve the purpose of ensuring a degree of preferential access to finance for exports. They ensure that more finance is available than might otherwise be the case and that finance is made available earlier than would be the case if the supplier had to provide credit from his own resources.

The facilities to the banks for the benefit of exporters and their buyers do, however, involve a considerable burden on public funds.

By the end of March 1978, the total amount of fixed rate export finance outstanding was £4279 million of which £1871 million was refinanced by ECGD. On an annual basis, the increase in public expenditure by way of refinancing loans through ECGD to the banks rose from £294 million in 1972-1973 to £505 million in 1976-1977. There was a net decrease in 1977-1978 of £263 million. In addition, the annual cost of the grant to bridge the gap in interest rates on such finance rose from £20 million in 1972-1973 to £220 million in 1976-1977 but fell to £116 million in 1977-1978. It was in an attempt to reduce this Exchequer cost and, at the same time, to assist the capital amount of the balance of payments which led to the Chancellor's announcement of a new policy in 1976 to encourage a switch in the medium term financing of British exports from sterling to foreign currencies, initially dollars and deutschemarks, for which the Department has devised new documentation and taken additional statutory powers, to act as a lender of last resort.

ECGD COVER

In addition to the credit risks, that is, insolvency of the buyer, the buyer's failure to pay within six months of the date due for goods accepted or his failure to take up the goods, ECGD also covers the transfer and political risks. Examples of these are: general moratorium on external debt decreed by the government of the buyer's country; any action by the government of the buyer's country which prevents performance of the contract in whole or in part; political events; economic difficulties; legislative or administrative measures arising outside the UK which prevent or delay the transfer of payments or deposits made in respect of the contract; war; and certain other events preventing performance of the contract, provided that the event is not one normally insured with commercial insurers, cancellation or non-renewal of a UK export licence etc.

MORE RECENT 'NEW' ECGD FACILITIES

Through what is now 60 years of active life ECGD has tried to adjust its policies and technique to meet the changing needs of exporters. The early 1970s brought a series of more sudden changes than in the past and witnessed the introduction of a number of new ECGD facilities. The impetus for this development came largely from the effects of the increased oil prices and the growth of opportunities for large project business. These events coincided with inflation in the United Kingdom (and in some other industralized countries) at an unprecedented rate. These new conditions, and in particular the growing scale of overseas projects, particularly in the oil producing countries, coupled with the onerous contractual terms which some of these buyers sought, posed new and serious problems for exporters.

Many buyers now insist on their suppliers providing 'performance bonds' and other guarantees, for example, bid and tender bonds and advance payment guarantees. Where exporters find it difficult to arrange such bonds, ECGD can provide support, in the form of a guarantee to a bank or surety company who will then issue the bond. In the event of a call under a guaranteed bond, ECGD has recourse to the exporter for the amount of any call, but in the event that satisfactory evidence can be produced that the call was an unfair one not resulting from any failure of the exporter to fulfil his contractual obligations, ECGD will refund any monies paid to it by the exporter by way of recourse. If a number of firms are jointly contracting for a project and the acceptance of joint and several recourse in respect of the bond facility would pose difficulty, ECGD is prepared to consider taking recourse to each firm only to the extent of its individual share of the contract. The guidelines of this scheme have been relaxed since its introduction and it is now available for export contracts on cash or near cash terms with a contract value of £½ million or more, which are acceptable for basic credit insurance cover. It is no longer necessary for the firm to prove exhaustion of commercial bond raising facilities before ECGD support is available. Where full ECGD support is not necessary to obtain bonds, firms may, as an extension of their normal credit insurance cover, seek ECGD protection against the unfair calling of a bond.

If, due to the special problems of large value projects with long manufacturing periods, firms have cash flow difficulties and are unable to obtain production finance from normal sources, ECGD will consider issuing guarantees to banks to facilitate the provision of pre-shipment finance. This scheme is limited to contracts with a manufacturing period of at least one year and a contract value of £1 million or more. The overall cost of the finance provided by banks against these guarantees, including ECGD's premium, is slightly higher than exporters normal overdraft rates.

Under the Project Participants Insolvency Cover Scheme, ECGD will cover main contractors against 90% of any loss arising from the insolvency of a sub-contractor or consortium member, to the extent that the insolvent party is contractually liable for such losses. Thus, any exporter wishing to avail himself needs to be clear about the extent to which his sub-contracts or joint venture agreements impose liability on a 'defaulting participant' for any additional costs incurred in completing an insured contract. The cover is available in respect of acceptable UK and overseas sub-contractors for projects with values of around £20 million or more.

The Cost Escalation Scheme was introduced to provide partial protection against some of the effects of high and unpredictable rates of inflation. It applies to export contracts of £2 million or more (with a minimum unit value of £¼ million) and a minimum manufacturing period of two years. The Department covers a proportion of annual cost increases above our agreed threshold within a fixed band of cover. Exporters can choose their threshold, subject to a minimum of 7% a year. The higher the threshold, the wider the band of cover, with wider bands and higher percentages of cover applying to contracts on cash terms or financed in foreign currency. This scheme is subject to renewal by Parliament annually.

There has been a growing interest in recent years in UK exports being financed in foreign currencies. The most recent figures show that some 30% of UK trade is now invoiced in foreign currency. ECGD has developed, and is still in the process of developing, new techniques to deal with problems of contracting in foreign currencies. New support has been introduced which is designed to remove what some exporters have seen as obstacles to contracting in foreign currencies. Hitherto, ECGD cover had been available for contracts expressed in currencies other than sterling, but the Department's maximum liability has been fixed at the outset according to the rate of exchange ruling on the date of commencement of risk (date of contract or shipment). Thus exporters invoicing in foreign currencies by selling forward or borrowing externally might, in the event of not receiving payment under the contract, have had to pay more to purchase foreign currency to meet such forward commitments than they would have received under ECGD's guarantee. The new provisions are designed to close this 'gap'. In the project field, the intention is to give guarantees expressed in foreign currencies which, in the event of an insured loss arising, will provide full cover against the effects of exchange rate changes, thus helping to make the invoicing and financing of exports in acceptable foreign currencies a viable option for exporters and financing banks.

To meet the risks involved for a UK company participating with other companies in very large projects, the ECGD has introduced a 'joint and several facility'. This is available selectively for such projects with a minimum contract value of £50 million where they are judged to be of exceptional national interest. It will enable estimated sums in the tender price to cover such risks to be reduced to the level of the ECGD premiums and thereby make the bid more competitive. The facility can be used to advantage by main contractors in relation to UK sub-contractors amounting to 5% or more of the total project value, or it can be adapted to cover UK members of consortia or joint ventures. ECGD will indemnify the insured contractor against cost over-runs which are judged by ECGD to be unavoidable and irrecoverable, incurred for reasons outside the insured's control in connection with sub-contracts. The amount of ECGD's cover will be 80% of the admissible losses with a maximum liability of 20% of the total UK value of the project contract.

To conclude, there is no doubt the ECGD will continue to make an outstanding contribution to the facilitation of UK export development. Further information relative to ECGD activities can be obtained from their office P.O. Box 272, Aldermanbury House, Aldermanbury, London, EC2P 2EL.

BERNE UNION

The International Union of Credit and Investment Insurers was established in 1934 with ECGD as a founder member. It now acts as a forum for international consultation on overseas investment insurance but its main object is to work for the international acceptance of sound principles of export credits and investment insurance and the establishment and maintainance of discipline in the terms of credit for international trade. This is achieved partly by *ad hoc* meetings between members and partly by regular meetings and, in the case of export credits insurance, the circulation through secretariat of information about defaulting buyers and claims experience. Day to day contacts have been developed with the object of restraining competition on credit. To an appreciable degree, these arrangements act as a brake upon the tendency of export credit terms to lengthen. The exchange of information on contracts in negotiation helps to curb the worst excesses of international credit competition.

CHAPTER 11

Transport Distribution Analysis

The relative importance of speed, frequency, reliability and cost of transport. Evaluating the suitability of transport modes of an international consignment. Transport distribution analysis.

Transport distribution analysis is featuring increasingly in the exporter's or shipper's evaluation of the technique of processing an export order. Undoubtedly this is due to much increased competition in world markets and the desirability of attaining the best method of distribution considering all the circumstances, Moreover, an increasing number of export companies now have their own shipping department, which is building up an expertise of international distribution techniques designed to secure the best method of distribution for their company products. The result is that these shipping departments are doing more than earning their keep and are thereby helping to keep their companies' products competitive in very competitive overseas markets.

Transport features very much in such an analysis and it is, therefore, appropriate that an examination first be made of the salient points that influence a transport service.

THE RELATIVE IMPORTANCE OF SPEED, FREQUENCY, RELIABILITY AND COST OF TRANSPORT

Basically, there are four factors which influence the nature of a transport service: speed, frequency, reliability and cost.

Speed is important to the shipper who wants to market his goods by an accurate arrival date and to eliminate banking charges for opening credits. This can be achieved by selecting the fastest service available and thereby obtain the minimum interval between the time the goods are ordered and the date of delivery at their destination. Speed is particularly important to manufacturers of consumer goods as it avoids expense and the risk of obsolescence to the retailer carrying large stocks. This is particularly so in the case of ladies clothes which are influenced by fashion, and retail in a very sensitive market. Reduced stocks results in less warehouse accommodation needs; less working capital by which the company operates; and overall, a better cash flow situation as the turnover is quicker. These factors strongly favour air freight which features very prominently in the distribution of fashionable ladies clothes on certain routes, particularly the North Atlantic.

In the case of commodities such as, fresh fruit and semi-frozen products, a regular and fast delivery is vital to successful trading. These aspects act as a constraint on their trade development and confine such products to selective overseas markets within a defined transit time band. These factors are very relevant to the large volume of fruit imported from European countries by sea transport involving train ferry wagons, TIR road vehicles and sometimes containers. For products requiring chilled or frozen conditions, one must acknowledge that in recent years the enormous advancement in the techniques of despatching food products in such conditions involving refrigerated containers, road vehicle units and train ferry wagons.

The need for speed is perhaps most felt in the long distance trades where transit times may be appreciably reduced and the shipper given the benefit of an early delivery. This is particularly relevant in air freight which has opened up new markets simply through fast transit times when related to sea transport. Nevertheless, deep-sea container schedules have revolutionized liner services transit times in recent years and become more competitive with air freight in certain trades. Indeed the liner operator, to whom speed is expensive both in terms of initial expenditure on the marine engines and the actual fuel cost, aims to provide a vessel with the maximum speed at the maximum cost at optimium expense, thereby meeting the shippers need. Overall, those aspects have partially precipitated the development of container services in liner cargo trades offering faster transits. Speed is likewise very costly to the air freight operator — indeed economically more so bearing in mind the limited capacity of the aircraft of up to 30 cargo tonnes compared with the container vessel with 2500 containers (with a total of 40 000 tonnes of cargo). On the North Atlantic service, air freighters have a capacity of up to 93 tonnes. The question can be rightly posed whether speed will continue to rise. Evidence suggest it will tend to become stabilized.

Improvements will be sought in overall transit time through quicker transhipments and the development of the through transport service concept offering door to door transit probably using unitized cargo consignments.

Speed is not so important where generally low value cargos are being carried as in the world tramp trades and where many trades are moving under programmed stockpiled arrangements. In this category are included coal, minerals, ores, etc. and other cargoes which normally move in ship loads and have a low value. These demand a low transport cost.

Frequency of service is most important when goods can only be sold in small quantities at frequent intervals. This is a very strong selling point in favour of the air freight operator, particularly in long distance markets and is relevant as frequent schedules coupled with fast transits enables stocks to be quickly replenished thereby avoiding excessive stockpiling. Deep-sea container services offer frequent schedules often on a regular time interval basis such as every week or fortnight from specified ports. Ro/Ro services found particularly in the UK/Continental trade operate daily between specified ports and, on more popular routes, up to six sailings daily. The overnight services are the most practicable to the TIR road haulier as it enables the driver to have a good night rest in preparation for the next day's driving. The shipper of perishable fruit and vegetables also relies on frequent as well as fast ships to obtain maximum benefit from the season's crop.

To the tramp charterer, frequency of sailings is not of paramount importance. He must not, of course, allow his stocks to run down too fast, but he will have a margin within which he can safely operate, and will come in to buy and ship when conditions suit him.

Reliability is an essential requirement to the shipper whose goods are sold against expiry dates on letters of credits and import licences. Furthermore, the shipper relies upon the operator to deliver his traffic in good condition, which is now becoming a very important factor in very competitive overseas markets. To the shipper, therefore, reliability infers that the ship, air freighter, TIR road haulage unit, etc. will depart and arrive at the advertised time; the ship or air freight operator will look after the cargo during pre-shipment throughout the voyage or flight and after discharge; and finally, the operator can be relied upon to give adequate facilities at the docks or airport and at his offices to enable the appropriate documents and other formalities to be satisfactorily completed. In short, prestige in the liner cargo or air freight trades goes with the reliance which the shipper can place on any particular operator. Reliability infers service quality and, in recent years, this has been a very competitive area amongst both ship and air operators. The shipper has come to expect the merchandise to arrive in accord with a predetermined schedule and in a good mercantile condition, otherwise the product will be very vulnerable to competition. This has been achieved through the development of unitized consignments, particularly under the aegis of ISO containerization and air freight.

Transport costing of individual services is fast becoming an important aspect in transport management today. It is a commodity which is difficult to cost, particularly when a multifarious service or joint supply is offered, for example, a vehicular ferry conveying passengers, motorist, car, lorries and/or trailers etc. The position is more complex when on one sailing, the vessel conveys motorists with their cars, whilst on another it is simply lorries/trailers with their drivers. The same applies to an aircraft which may be exclusively used for passengers on one flight and for a mixture of passenger and cargo on another. The operator endeavours to devise a tariff which will maximize revenue and optimize fleet use. This involves market pricing whereby the rate is pitched at the level which will attain high load factors on individual sailings or flights. Such a philosophy is developed more extensively in Chapter 5. Therefore, one sees the rate in one direction differing from the one in the reverse direction with the sole aim to attain good capacity utilization. Such an example is found in the commodity air freight rates found on the North Atlantic services. Moreover, for similar reasons, rebates are given on most Ro/Ro services between UK/Continent to encourage regular shipments in substantial quantities throughout the year. In very broad terms, the operator will formulate tariffs which will cover all his direct or variable cost and make a contribution to indirect or fixed cost. The direct cost represents expenses actually incurred in the service provision including fuel, day to day maintenance, dues or tolls, crew cost etc. Indirect cost embraces administration, depreciation, sinking fund asset replacement provision, insurance, annual overhaul/survey cost etc. The indirect cost is apportioned by flight/voyage relative to the transport user throughout the year. In situations where traffic flows are imbalanced, producing differing tariffs in each direction, an element of cross subsidization takes place to produce overall a long term profitable service. Tariffs on scheduled services tend to be rather more rigid compared with chartered vessels or aircraft which are influenced by the economic market forces of supply and demand. It must be recognized that the foregoing analysis deals only with the freight cost assessment and excludes ancillary expenses viz. Customs clearance, handling cost, collection and delivery etc.

The shipper marketing goods of relatively low value must seek the lowest possible transport charge, as the freight percentage of the total value may have a direct bearing on the saleability of the commodity. This involves the tramp vessel which is most ideal for this market. He has thus a prime interest in the availability of tramp shipping space at any particular time by reason of the fact that freight and chartering rates will vary reflecting the economic forces of supply and demand. In a market situation where there are plenty of vessels, the shipper will be able to charter at a rate which will be only marginally above the operating costs of the vessel. In the opposite situation, he will be forced to pay more but there is a limiting factor on the price of the commodity at the point of sale to the rate which the shipowner may receive. In these conditions, the premium returns are earned by the operators of the most efficient ships. In weak market conditions their relative efficiency ensures a small profit while others just break even. Where the market is strong, the proven reliability shown before will ensure that the services of such vessels will be sought out before opportunities are taken up. To conclude, the tramp operator will endeavour to cover his direct cost and contribute to indirect cost in the overall fixture rate concluded. A similar criteria applies to the chartering of an air freighter.

In the liner trade and scheduled air freight services, the tariffs are more stable and controlled primarily under the aegis of the liner conference system or IATA. Both the ship and air operator are able to hold their rates at a fair level to show a very modest profit margin based on a fairly high load factor. They must be careful not to hold their rates so high that they price the goods out of the market. At this point, there is need for joint consultation between the shipper and carrier.

The freight forwarder, container operator and TIR road haulier operator in the liner trades and scheduled air freight markets, offer facilities for consolidated consignments at very competitive rates and transit times. This market is fast expanding particularly in air freight and ideal for the small exporter.

To conclude it is fair to say that service standards will continue to improve to the benefit of the shipper and international trade development. Likewise unitization will continue to expand both in sea and air transport services.

EVALUATING THE SUITABILITY OF TRANSPORT MODES OF AN INTERNATIONAL CONSIGNMENT

Transport distribution analysis to the exporter/shipper involves the process of deciding which is the most ideal mode(s) of transport and route for the particular consignment. The ultimate selection can vary seasonally and by quantity. Some services vary considerably summer and winter due to market demand and climate conditions. Moreover, the despatch of a small quantity urgently required may be ideal for air freight, but a larger consignment less urgent for later despatch may be suitable for a deep sea container schedule under consolidation arrangements.

In a world where countries are trying to improve continuously their overall trade balance, an increasing number are insisting on shipment by their own national airline or shipping service irrespective of the commercial/economic advantages there may be from competitive services. This is a difficult situation to combat, but the UK exporter must strive to sell his goods under CIF terms to maximize payment to the UK balance of payment account and thereby have much influence on the transport mode/routing of the consignment.

Today more and more exporters are setting up their own shipping office which should be more than self-financing. This means that the cost of running such a department should more than offset the savings realized through international distribution cost. In some companies, such a department has it own TIR road fleet.

To conclude, the exporter must continuously review his international distribution arrangements and the following are the more important aspects to consider in the evaluation of transport mode/routing suitability etc.

(1) The customer's choice is the prime consideration and this is usually found in the export sales contract. It is inter-related with the delivery trade terms. Moreover, there is increasing evidence of the importer insisting on the goods being conveyed on his country's

national shipping or airline to save hard currency.

(2) The nature of the commodity, its dimensions, weight and whether any special facilities are required for it during transit, for example, livestock requires special facilities, gold requires special security or a strong room and meat requires refrigerated accommodation. This is a major consideration, and one must establish through research/enquiry whether the actual dimensions are ideal in the interest of maximizing the use of the available container capacity and lessening the risk of broken stowage. Moreover, one must bear in mind broken stowage usually attracts additional freight payments.

(3) The degree of packing and cost thereof. Packing cost can form a very significant proportion of the overall distribution expense. For example, a consignment sent under 'tween deck tonnage usually requires very extensive packaging possibly involving a wooden case, whereas cargo despatched by train ferry wagon, containerization and air freight requires less — particularly the latter two. In the case of air freight, packing needs are very much reduced and numerous consignments are conveyed affixed to a pallet with the cargo enveloped in a plastic cover to protect it from scratching, dust, moisture etc. Likewise, an examination of the type and quality of the packing used can often produce favourable results to the exporter/shipper. One must endeavour to ensure the packing needs are adequate and not overgenerous thereby incurring increased packing cost without justification. Numerous specialized packing companies exist and the exporter new to the business is strongly advised to consult them.

(4) The degree to which the consignment presented aids handling. For example, palletized cargo facilitates handling by fork lift truck employment whilst cartons are ideal for containers etc. Conversely, the awkwardly shaped cargo may require special facilities/handling arrangements and may be subject to a freight surcharge. Additionally, such consignments encourage broken stowage and tend to be more prone to damage which increases their premium level. In the ideal situation the consignment should be easy to handle from the time it leaves the factory premises until it reaches the retailer. Accordingly, much progress has been made to develop a code of standardized package sizes internationally which will aid distribution and optimize use of containers and other forms of unit distribution, that is, stillages, pallets etc. A point to bear in mind is the growing tend-

ency to stack cargo to make the best use of warehouse cubic space and accordingly the consignment needs to be adequately robust to combat this situation.

(5) Any statutory obligations imposed relative to the transit. Certain products need special facilities both in the transport mode and terminal. This in itself restricts route/service and transport mode choice. For example, the movement of meat, offal etc. requires special facilities both by the operator to ship it and inspection facilities at the import terminal. Additionally, most countries have weight restrictions on road vehicles together with their length. This is particularly relevant to containerization regarding overall weight. Likewise, there are restrictions on road haulage driver's hours and some EEC countries restrict road haulage movement at weekends. Statutory obligations also influence the type of packaging, for example, as found in the Australian trade in the use of straw and marking of cargo.

(6) Dangerous cargo. Again regulations are stringent regarding its packaging, stowage and mixture with other cargoes during stowage. This can restrict service/routing/schedules. International distribution of dangerous cargo requires the most careful evaluation as controls are tending to become more stringent.

(7) Suitability of available transport services. For example, air freighters have limited capacity/weight/dimensions and the cargo may require extensive collection and delivery arrangements. Additionally, it offers fast transits and reduced packaging needs. In contrast, the deep-sea container service will have a much slower transit, probably less collection and delivery expense (if it is a consolidated consignment), slightly more packing expense, less frequent service, but lower freight rate. The Ro/Ro operator will have similar features as the containerized consolidated consignment except that in the UK/Continental trade the transit time is likely to be more competitive with air. Overall, this aspect requires very careful consideration and one must bear in mind that an increasing number of exporters are now using thier own vehicles to distribute their products in the UK/Continental trade. In exceptional circumstances, the shipper may resort to chartering an aircraft or vessel if sufficient cargo is available. One must bear in mind that some services may be so popular as to have no cargo space available for the next few sailings/flights.

(8) The transit time and related urgency of consignment. To deter-

mine the transit time overall one must bear in mind the periods of collection and delivery of the cargo. Moreover, one must not discount any likely custom clearance delays evident in some countries. Air freight services offer the fastest schedules and are particularly suited to the urgent consignment.

(9) Quantity of cargo and period over which shipment is to be made. In broad terms, the greater the quantity available for shipment, the lower the overall distribution cost per tonne/kg. For example, if the exporter can originate a full container or train ferry wagon load, the overall freight will be much cheaper than despatching the cargo under consolidation arrangements. Furthermore, a guaranteed substantial quantity of cargo conveyed over a period of time could attract a concessionary tariff. This is particularly relevant to sea transport. Again, if the circumstances are favourable, it may be advantageous to charter an aircraft or ship.

(10) Insurance of cargo. The premium is determined by numerous factors but primarily by nature of cargo and mode of transport plus type of packaging. Air freight cargo insurance with its quick transits and low risk of damage and pilferage tends to have the most favourable premium rates. Container shipments also are competitive bearing in mind the longer transit involved.

(11) Terms of export contract. The most important quotations in exporting are CIF and FOB. Under a CIF (cost, insurance, freight) contract of sale, the seller provides the goods, engages cargo space on the vessel, pays freight to the buyer's port which is normal, for example, CIF Singapore, insures the goods on behalf of the buyer against normal marine and fire risk to that port and pays all charges incidental in getting the goods onto the vessel. He is liable for any loss or damage before the goods reach the ship. Under these terms, which UK exporters should strive to attain, it maximizes the income to the balance of payments from the sales contract subject to the insurance and freight being undertaken by British based companies.

FOB (free on board) implies that the duty of the seller is to present the goods to the sea port/airport and see they are actually placed on board the vessel/aircraft which the buyer provides. The seller meets all charges incidental to placing the goods on the ship/aircraft such as collection, handling, insurance, but once the goods are on board and he has obtained a receipt for the goods, the exporters responsibilities cease. Thereafter, the buyer pays all the charges. The buyer or his agent would thus insure the goods from the sea port or airport of departure to destination and pays the freight. Other terms of contract include FOR, FAS, Loco, Ex-works which are explained fully in Chapter 13.

(12) Freight and documentation. In broad terms, the actual sea freight tends to be very much lower than air freight but it is not practicable to consider such cost in isolation as one must bear in mind the total overall distribution cost to embrace all the elements viz. packing, insurance etc. to obtain a fair assessment. Air freight tariffs, compared with road and rail, likewise tend to be high, but the margin lessens significantly the larger the transit. Documentation cost between various transport modes do not vary a great deal but, with the development of the combined transport concept in recent years involving particularly road, through ISO container and the long established train ferry, it has tended to become simplified on the basis of through rates/consignments notes with no intermediate Customs examination in transit countries.

(13) Emerging from the foregoing it is necessary to produce an overall distribution cost and evaluation of realistic alternatives to arrive at a firm conclusion. The four most decisive factors are terms of export sales contract, commodity specification, freight and overall transit time, including service quality. Other factors embrace cost of packaging — very significant in air freight; convenience/reliability of service; insurance; documentation; warehousing, that is, frequent service requires less storage in warehouse; reduced risk of product obsolescence; less working capital; facilitates smoother production flow and better customer relations; and service quality, particularly the risk of pilferage/damage and marketing condition of goods on arrival — the latter one is becoming of greater importance as competition intensifies. A significant aspect will be the cargo quantity and, in exceptional circumstances, it may be economic to charter an air freighter or vessel. Alternatively, for the small exporter the consolidated air freight container services, or Ro/Ro services are the most ideal.

Finally, one must bear in mind in any transport distribution analysis the existence of the parcel post systems which operate throughout the world with a maximum of 10 kg for any one parcel except to India and Philippines. Customs formalities are simplified. An air and surface service is provided. Likewise British Rail have an international express parcels service operative within Europe. Both systems are reliably competitive, and ideal for the small consignment with the minimum of Customs and other formalities.

TRANSPORT DISTRIBUTION ANALYSIS

Transport distribution analysis is the technique by which alternative methods of distribution are analysed and the optimum pattern of transportation selected. It is often called physical distribution management.

In the home market, it is possible to retain overall control of sales outlets and related distribution arrangements. However, where exports are involved problems of greater complexity arise. Sales made on an FOB basis are bound by the philosophy of 'lowest freight cost' often lead to a reduction of control over marketing efficiency overseas. Distribution costs build up at home and abroad and, with the distribution function being so far reaching, not one manager, but several, will have a direct interest in one or more aspects of distribution efficiency. Yet production planning, cash flow, release of capital and the level of sales can be substantially improved if the most ideal pattern of transportation is selected.

We will now examine the various elements involved and ultimately look at some case studies of actual international consignments. Details of the transportation distribution factors are given below:

(1) Quantity and type of packages. This must specify the quantity of cargo available for despatch and the method of packaging. The latter may be in cartons, in pallets, in wooden cases, or simply bundled. One must bear in mind excessive packing increases the weight and volume of the consignment which in turn raises freight cost. Usually, packing cost by air is less than by sea transport. Additionally, the shipper must remember quantity discounts exist in some forms of transport.

(2) Total weight of consignment. This should be quoted on net or gross weight basis usually in kg.

(3) Total volume of shipment. This should be given on a m³ or ft³ basis. One must bear in mind that different tariff structures apply to air and sea transport. Usually, for certain high volume commodities, there is an advantage in despatching by air, whereas for sea transport

weight/measurement rates (whichever produces the greatest revenue) will apply.

(4) Value of goods ex-works. This is the value of the consignment in leaving the factory gates.

(5) Packing cost. In sea transport, packing cost can represent a formidable percentage of the total distribution cost but, with air freight, it is much reduced and a strong marketing point in persuading the shipper to use this mode of transport.

(6) Inland charges at point of origin. This incorporates all the cost incurred in transporting the consignment from, for example, the factory production site to the nominated airport or seaport for despatch overseas. It embraces cartage, handling charges, etc. Air ports in many countries tend to be closer to both the exporter and importer than sea ports. Moreover, air freight documentation tends to be simpler and handling less expensive compared with sea transport. Much depends on circumstances and overall cargo quantity. In some countries, special fees are raised for only maritime shipments. This includes Brazil port tax — 2% on CIF value; Kenya wharfage — 1.25% on CIF value; and South Africa wharfage — 1.49% on FOB value. Overall, the latter are not commonplace but one must bear in mind the increasing practice of flag discrimination. This arises when governments, irrespective of commercial considerations, direct cargoes export or import, primarily the latter, to be shipped in their own national maritime fleet. (See Chapter 19 of *The Elements of Shipping* for more details).

(7) Freight. This embraces the air and sea freight comparisons. Usually, air freight rates are more expensive than sea transport, but each has a differing tariff structure as fully explained in Chapter 5. For goods shipped by air, there are no *ad valorem* rates applicable as for certain high-priced sea shipments, so that valuable merchandise can sometimes be forwarded more cheaply by air. A comparison of minimum charges per air waybill and bill of lading may show only a small difference, or an advantage for air transportation in some areas, if the consignment weight does exceed approximately 10 kg.

Additionally, there is an advantage in shipping high volume goods by air when sea weight/measurement rates are applicable. For goods with a volume up to 7×10^{-3} m^3 or 427 in^2/kg (194 in/lb) air rates are calculated on the basis of the actual weight. Sea rates usually are based on the actual volume as a basis for calculating the cost of goods whose volume is more than 1 m³/1000 kg (40 ft³/2240 lb or 2000 lb). This corresponds to 68 in²/kg or 31-35 in³/lb. Thus the air cargo shipper can make use of additional volume without additional cost.

Nevertheless, the decision about the most profitable method of distribution, however, cannot be based on pure freight cost alone. The related costs and revenues must be also evaluated. Overall, this involves, when applicable, transhipment cost either at the airport or sea port to another aircraft or vessel to ultimate airport/sea port destination.

Basically, the most critical management decision in distribution is the selection of the transport mode. It determines two elements - transport costs and transit time. In general, there is an inverse relationship between transit time and transport costs. The quicker the transit, the higher the transport cost. Conversely, the slower the transit, the cheaper the transport cost.

(8) Inland charges at destination. This includes cartage, handling charges, Customs clearance, agency expenses and demurrage. Overall, it includes the transportation cost from airport or sea port to ultimate destination. Insofar as shipping is concerned, it could involve transhipment to lighterage.

(9) Duty and taxes. This includes VAT or its equivalent. Likewise it includes import duties.

Advantages for air distribution may materialize if duties are based on FOB value (value at the place of exportation). This arises from reduced packing costs and reduced costs to the airport of departure. Duties, for example, are assessed on FOB value in USA, Canada and South Africa. Conversely, it may be a disadvantage to air freight if the duties are based on CIF value (value at place of importation/destination) as the pure air freight is likewise subject to duty. Similar advantages/disadvantages arise relative to sea transport. Some Customs duties are assessed on the gross weight which is particularly advantageous to air freight with less packing needs producing lower tare weight. Mexico and Switzerland are applying this policy.

(10) Insurance. Faster transits involving reduced risk of damage/pilferage on air freight tend to produce more favourable insurance premiums compared with sea transport.

(11) Unpacking/refurbishing. The inherent advantages of air freight tend to favour such a shipper insofar as unpacking/refurbish-

ing is concerned when compared with maritime transport. Reduced packing tends to make unpacking less expensive. Moreover, any special refurbishing process for the goods before use is not necessary such as degreasing of machinery/apparatus, ironing of textiles etc.

(12) Cost of capital tied up in transit. During the time of transportation from door to door either the exporter or importer has invested money into the merchandise without receiving an equivalent interest or deriving profit from it. The longer the transit and the higher the merchandise value, the greater the capital investment involved. This factor may be of minor importance for a single shipment, but greater significance for all consignments during a specified period.

(13) Inventory and storage costs. The cost of keeping stocks at the place of production and consumption involves four basic elements as follows:

(i)   Cost of capital tied up in inventories.
(ii)   Obsolescence, deterioration, insurance, taxes etc.
(iii) Administration and handling.
(iv)   Warehouse etc. accommodation.

The cost percentage on the average stock value may be as high as 25% per year, but much depends on warehouse location and size, plus type of commodity. The specific advantages of air freight viz. speed, safety, reliability and frequency may result in a reduced lead time for the importer and enable him to increase the shipping frequency for the fast moving items. Instead of shipping quantities covering the demand for several months, it might be more favourable to air freight more frequently, covering only several weeks demand. This produces a lower working stock, less warehouse accommodation and reduced risk of stock deterioration/obsolescence. The consignment itself should be of optimum size to contain transportation cost.

Both the high quality of air freight and the shorter lead time considerably lower the risk of stock piling, commodity deterioration or obsolescence to the importer, thereby reducing his financial risk. A reduction of working and reserve stocks results in a reduced average stock level for the importer so that the turnover rate is increased and the inventory/storage cost decreased.

(14) In regard to marketing, many export orientated companies find themselves in great difficulty in achieving marketing objectives because insufficient consideration is given to distribution. Sales and

communication combine to stimulate demand for a product unless — by planned distribution — the product is at a point of sale when the consumer decides to purchase, a sale is often lost. Even if the sale is not lost, customer service standards fall in that the customer is forced to delay purchase and, while the demand may be so strong that the delay is suffered, the likelihood of a repeat purchase at a later date is reduced. A similar situation applies to 'after sales service', a good example being a spare part. The speed with which the customer can obtain a replacement part for a machine strongly influences his opinion of the supplier, and therefore the likelihood of repeat purchase.

Quick delivery is often vital in providing a high level of customer service which would otherwise only be achieved by holding prohibitively high levels of stock. In fact, situations do exist where setting up of a stock-holding could be uneconomic and dependence is totally upon rapid transit. A good example, is test marketing, where a company testing a new product whose success is uncertain will meet demand direct from production without expensive stock-piling.

(15) A high speed transport mode reduces stock levels — both static and transit — and the financial implications are, therefore, apparent. In effect, the average lead time between manufacture and sale is shortened and this must mean a saving in financial resources. In reality, it improves a company cash flow or liquidity.

(16) Other cost and revenue factors. In addition to the transportation and distribution cost already mentioned, the specific performance criteria of a transport mode have an influence on other cost and revenue factors in ordering, production and administration. These 'hidden' advantages are often difficult to evaluate but they require consideration by both the exporter and importer to find the most profitable way of distribution.

We will now examine a couple of case studies of transport distribution analysis, which appear on pages 195 and 196.

The following points are relevant in the foregoing transport distribution analysis including the two examples given:

(a) With the growing development of maritime container services and Ro/Ro services in UK/Continental trade, the advantage differential, particularly in terms of packing cost, reduced transit times and service quality, are being moderately reduced in comparison with air shipment. Conversely, the air freighter is becoming larger

DISTRIBUTION ANALYSIS EXAMPLE A

Textiles for London to Japan

Gross weight for surface transportation: 1024 kg (165.97 ft^3)

	Air transportation Cost in UK £s	Surface transportation Cost in UK £s
Value ex-works	5500	5500
Transportation cost		
Packing	12	60
Transportation to air/sea port of departure, handling	15	50
Air/sea freight	725	130
Transportation from air/sea port of destination, handling	9	14
Import duties	1020	940
Insurance	14	46
Cost price	£7295	£6740
Cost of capital tied up in transit	7	67
Unpacking/refurbishing	Not	Not
Storage	evaluated	evaluated
Total cost	£7302	£6807
Cost difference	+ 7%	
Time advantage	38 days	
Cost determinants		
(a) Value per kg ex-works	UK £6.00	
(b) Freight proportion air/sea	5.5:1	
(c) Density	238 in^3/kg	

with bigger capacity containers thereby reducing unit costs.

(b) The differential between air/surface transit, particularly in terms of overall cost, freight rates and packing expenses, tend to be very narrow on relatively short distance transit experienced in the UK/Continental trade.

To conclude, transport distribution analysis forms an important

DISTRIBUTION ANALYSIS EXAMPLE B

Electrical appliances from London to South Africa

Gross weight for surface transportation 173 kg (21.89 ft³)

	Air transportation Cost in UK £s	Surface transportation Cost in UK £s
Value ex-works	2600	2600
Transportation cost		
Packing	19	53
Transportation to air/sea port of departure, handling	5	20
Air/sea freight	117	12
Transportation from air/sea port of destination handling	13	43
Import duties	130	134
Insurance	6	7
Cost price	£2890	£2869
Cost of capital tied up in transit	4	34
Unpacking/refurbishing	Not	Not
Storage	evaluated	evaluated
Total cost	£2894	£2903
Cost advantage	+ 0.3%	
Time advantage	41 days	
Cost determinants		
(a) Value per kg ex-works	UK £15.00	
(b) Freight proportion air/sea	9.9:1	
(c) Density	219 in³/kg	

evaluation today in deciding for the exporter/importer the best method of transportation. Airline operators particularly British Airways and Lufthansa, together with some maritime cargo operators, provide cargo consulting or distribution advisory services which the shipper is well advised to use. Alternatively, the freight forwarder can always help in this regard.

CHAPTER 12

Export Documentation

Air waybill. Bill of exchange. Bill of lading. Cargo insurance policy and certificate. Certificate of origin. Certificate of shipment. Charter party. Convention on the contract for the international carriage of goods by road (CMR). Dock receipt. Export invoicing. International convention concerning the carriage of goods by rail (CIM). Letters of hypothecation. Mates receipt. Parcel post receipt. Veterinary certificate/health certificate.

An important part of export practice is a good comprehension of the various documents involved to process the export consignment. Moreover, the need to understand the role of such documents and their limitations together with likely problems which they may encounter is likewise important. If an exporter has any doubt over the role or query over a particular document, the best course to follow is to contact his bank or freight forwarder.

This chapter, in the main, excludes documentation relating to Customs, insurance and finance, which is covered respectively in Chapters 7, 8 and 9. A study of the various documents now follows.

AIR WAYBILL

The air waybill is the consignment note used for the carriage of goods by air. It is often called an air consignment note and is not a document of title or transferable/negotiable instrument. It is basically a receipt for the goods for despatch and is prima facie evidence of the conditions of carriage. Overall, there are usually 12 copies of each air waybill for distribution to the shipper, sales agent, issuing carrier (airline operator), consignee, delivery receipt, airport of destination, third carrier (if applicable), second carrier (if applicable), first carrier, extra copy for carrier (when required), invoice and airport of departure. Copies 1, 2 and 3 are the originals. Each copy is not always used but merely as circumstances demand. For example, the second carrier's copy would be used only if the consignment was conveyed on another airline to complete the transit such as British Airways conveying it for the first leg of the journey and Air Canada the remainder. The conditions of carriage are found on the reverse of the air waybill document and are subject to the Carriage by Air Act,

1961. This is based on the Warsaw rules and a number of other conventions. Overall, it is subject to the supplementary provisions in the Carriage by Air Act, 1962. Actual liability to the IATA airline carrier is based at 250 gold francs per kg.

The air consignment note contains the following information:

(1) The place and date of its execution.

(2) Names of the departure and destination air ports.

(3) The names and addresses of the consignor, consignee and the first carrier (airline).

(4) A description of the goods.

(5) The number of packages with marks, weights, quantity and dimensions.

(6) The total freight amount pre paid and/or to pay is precisely defined and the rate.

(7) The declared value for customs purposes, likewise for carriage and the currency.

(8) The date of the flight.

(9) Details of any special route to be taken.

(10) The signature of the shipper or his agent.

(11) The signature of the issuing carrier (airline operator) or his agent.

Where more than one package is involved, the carrier can require the consignor to make out separate air waybills. The air consignment note must be printed in one of the official languages of the country of departure, for example, French, German, etc. Erasures are not admissible, but alterations can be made provided they are authenticated by the consignors signature or initials. If quantities, weights, or values are altered, they must appear in words as well as figures.

An example of an air waybill is found in Appendix E.

BILL OF EXCHANGE

A bill of exchange is an unconditional order in writing addressed by one person to another, signed by the person giving it, requiring the person to whom it is addressed to pay on demand, or at a fixed or determinable future time, a certain sum in money to, or to the order of, a specified person or bearer. Drafts can be drawn either at sight, payment to be made on demand or on presentation; or, at a particular 'tenor' ('usuance'), payment to be made at a fixed or determinable future date, usually within 180 days of sight of the bill of exchange by the drawer, or within 180 days of the date of the draft. Special Bank of England approval is needed for credit periods exceeding 180 days under an export sales contract. The general procedure for letters of credit is for drafts to be drawn on a bank, but some credits require them to be drawn on the importer. Drafts can be drawn in pairs called 'first' and 'second' bills of exchange.

The bill of exchange contains the following data:

(1) The date.

(2) A specific sum, which should agree with the amount on the export invoice.

(3) The tenor, that is, whether at sight or at a stated period after sight or at a fixed date.

(4) The name of the drawee.

(5) The name and signature of the drawer.

(6) The name of the payee or order or bearer.

(7) The endorsement of the payee where applicable.

Overall, the bill of exchange should be so worded to conform to what is laid down in the credit.

The following discrepancies tend to arise in processing bills of exchange and should be avoided.

(a) Document drawn incorrectly or for a sum disportionate to the credit amount.

(b) Designation of the signature on the document not specified e.g. director or partner.

BILLS OF LADING

A bill of lading, is a receipt for goods shipped on board a vessel, signed by the person (or his agent) who contracts to carry them, and stating the conditions in which the goods were delivered to and received by the ship. It is not the actual contract, which is inferred from the action of the shipper or shipowner in delivering or receiving the cargo, but forms excellent evidence of the terms of the contract. It is a document of title to the goods which is the subject of the contract between the buyer (importer) and seller (exporter).

Before examining the salient points, function and types of bills of lading, we will first of all consider two Acts which have played an important role in the development of this document, namely the Bills of Lading Act, 1855 and the Carriage of Goods by Sea Act, 1924. More recently, in fact from 1977, the Carriage of Goods by Sea, 1971 has emerged and succeeded the Carriage of Goods by Sea Act, 1924.

The Bill of Lading Act, 1855 established the following relevant to this document:

(1) It preserved the right of the original shipper to 'stoppage in transitu' (in transit). Moreover, not only did it give the right of conditional endorsement and of reserving the 'jus disponendi' (law of disposal) but also the unpaid seller could resume possession of the goods by exercising the right of 'stoppage in transitu'.

(2) It established the principle of transferability, permitting the transfer of a bill of lading from the holder to a person to whom the property in the goods passes, together with any rights and liabilities incorporated in the document.

(3) It provided that once the bill of lading has been issued, it is prima facie evidence that the goods have been shipped.

Under the Carriage of Goods by Sea Act, 1924, the carrier is under obligation to properly and carefully load, handle, stow, carry, keep, care for and discharge the goods carried. It was laid down that, in cases to which the Act applies, the carrier should be able to avoid liability in certain circumstances defined in the Act. In general, the extent of the carriers immunity is laid down by the Act and cannot be increased by contract. Any clause or contract purporting to relieve a carrier of his liabilities under the Act is expressively declared void.

The basic object of the 1971 Act is simply to amend the Hague Rules relating to the Bills of Lading Act, 1921, which it will be recalled were appended as a schedule to the Carriage of Goods by Sea Act, 1924. A diplomatic conference was held in Brussels in 1967 on Maritime Law which examined the Visby Rules intended for amendment of the Hague Rules of 1921. A number of the proposed amendments were accepted at the conference with two noticable exceptions: the limitation of the carriers liability, and the scope of the Application of the Rules. In the following year, at the same place another conference was held at which agreement was reached and emerged the rules known as the Hague-Visby Rules. These Rules now form the schedule to the 1971 Act under the title 'The Hague Rules as amended by the Brussels Protocol, 1968.'

The main provisions of the 1971 Carriage of Goods by Sea Act are given below:

(1) It only applies to outwards bills of lading, that is, from a British port, as compared with many national enactments adopting the rules

such as United States Carriage of Goods by Sea Act, 1936, which applies to both inward, as well as outward bills of lading.

(2) The 1971 Act covers the coasting trade — a feature not common to the 1924 Act.

(3) It applies both to shipments under bills of lading and those under 'any similar documents of title'. Moreover, a forwarder's receipt such as a house bill of lading or container receipt would be subject to the Rules if so endorsed. The bill of lading still provides prima facie evidence of receipt by the carrier of the goods viz. identification of cargo marks, condition of cargo, number of packages and their weight. An addition, however, is that the bill provides conclusive evidence when the cargo has been transferred to a party acting in good faith.

(4) It clearly defines the extent of the carriers liability on container traffic.

(5) The 1971 Act permits the carrier and the ship to be discharged from all liability in respect of goods, unless legal proceedings were started within one year of delivery of the cargo or the date when they should have been delivered. The Rules now indicate that the one year limit shall not embrace a third person provided that proceedings against him are commenced within the time — allowed by the law of the Court seized of the case — for bringing an action against such a third person which must never be less than three months.

(6) It limits the carrier's liability to the maximum amount of 10 000 gold francs per package or unit, or 30 gold francs/kg gross weight of the goods lost or damaged, whichever is the higher. It also confirms the maximum limitation does not apply if the damage resulted from an act or omission of the carrier done with intent to cause damage, or recklessly and with knowledge that damage would probably result.

The salient points incorporated in a bill of lading can be conveniently listed as follows:

(1) The name of the shipper (usually the exporter).

(2) The name of the carrying vessel.

(3) Full description of the cargo (provided it is not bulk cargo) including any shipping marks, individual package numbers in the consignment, contents, cubic measurement, gross weight etc.

(4) The marks and numbers identifying the goods.

(5) Port of shipment.

(6) Port of discharge.

(7) Full details of freight, including when and where it is to be paid — whether freight paid or payable at destination.

(8) Name of consignee or, if the shipper is anxious to withhold the consignee's name, shippers order, or order.

(9) The terms of the contract of carriage.

(10) The date the goods were received for shipment and/or loaded on the vessel.

(11) The name and address of the notifying party (the person to be notified on arrival of the shipment, usually the buyer).

(12) Number of bills of lading signed on behalf of the Master or his agent, acknowledging receipt of the goods.

(13) The signature of the ship's Master or his agent and the date.

There are several types of bills of lading and these include the following:

(1) Shipped bill of lading. Under the Carriage of Goods by Sea Act, 1924, the shipper can demand that the shipowner supplies bills of lading proving that the goods have been actually shipped. For this reason, most bill of lading forms are already printed as shipped bills and commence with the wording: 'Shipped in apparent good order and condition'. It confirms the goods are actually on board the vessel.

This is the most satisfactory type of receipt and the shipper prefers such a bill as there is no doubt about the goods being on board and, in consequence, dispute on this point will not arise with the bankers or consignee, thereby facilitating earliest financial settlement of the exported sale.

(2) Received bill of lading. This arises where the word 'shipped' does not appear on the bill of lading. It merely confirms that the goods have been handed over to the shipowner and are in his custody. The cargo may be in his dock warehouse/transit shed or even inland. The bill has, therefore, not the same meaning as a 'shipped' bill and the buyer under a CIF contract need not accept such a bill for ultimate financial settlement through the bank unless provision has been made in the contract. Forwarding agents will invariably avoid handling 'received bills' for their clients unless special circumstances obtain.

(3) Through bills of lading. In many cases it is necessary to employ two or more carriers to get the goods to their final destination. The on-carriage may be either by a second vessel or by a different form of

transport (for example, to destinations in the interior of Canada). In such cases it would be very complicated and more expensive if the shipper had to arrange on-carriage himself by employing an agent at the point of transhipment. Shipping companies, therefore, issue bills of lading which cover the whole transit and the shipper deals only with the first carrier. This type of bill enables a through rate to be quoted and is growing in popularity with the development of containerization. Special bills of lading have to be prepared for such through-consigned cargo.

(4) Stale bills of lading. It is important that the bill of lading is available at the port of destination before the goods arrive, or failing this, at the same time. Bills presented to the consignee or his bank after the goods are due at the port are said to be stale. A cargo cannot normally be delivered by the ship owner without the bill of lading and the late arrival of this all important document may have undesirable consequences such as warehouse rent, etc.

(5) Groupage bill of lading. Forwarding agents are permitted to 'group' together particular compatible consignments from individual consignors to various consignees, usually situated at the same destination (country/area), and despatch them as one consignment. The shipowner will issue a groupage bill of lading, whilst the forwarding agent, who cannot hand to his principals the shipowners' bill of lading, will issue to the individual shippers a certificate of shipment sometimes called 'house bill of lading'. At the destination, another agent working in close liaison with the agent forwarding the cargo will break bulk the consignment and distribute the goods to the various consignees. This practice is on the increase, usually involving the use of containers and particularly evident in the continental trade and deep-sea container services. It will doubtless increase with containerization development and is ideal to the shipper who has small quantities of goods available for export. Advantages of groupage include less packing; lower insurance premiums; usually quicker transits; less risk of damage and pilferage; and lower rates when compared with such cargo being despatched as an individual parcel/consignment.

(6) Transhipment bill of lading. This type is issued usually by shipping companies when there is no direct service between two ports, but when the shipowner is prepared to tranship the cargo at an intermediate port at his expense.

(7) Clean bills of lading. Each bill of lading states 'in apparent good order and condition', which of course refers to the cargo. If this statement is not modified by the shipowner, the bill of lading is regarded as 'clean' or 'unclaused'. By issuing clean bills of lading, the shipowner admits his full liability of the cargo described in the bill under the law and his contract. This type is much favoured by banks for financial settlement purposes.

(8) Claused bills of lading. If the shipowner does not agree with any of the statements made in the bill of lading he will add a clause to this effect, thereby causing the bill of lading to be termed as 'unclean', 'foul', or 'claused'. There are many recurring types of such clauses including inadequate packaging; unprotected machinery; second-hand cases; wet or stained cartons; damaged crates; cartons missing etc. The clause 'shipped on deck at owner's risk' may thus be considered to be a clause under this heading. This type of bill of lading is usually unacceptable to a bank.

(9) Negotiable bills of lading. If the words 'or his or their assigns' are contained in the bill of lading, it is negotiable. There are, however, variations in this terminology, for example, the word 'bearer' may be inserted, or another party stated in the preamble to the phrase. Bills of lading may be negotiable by endorsement or transfer.

(10) Non-negotiable bills of lading. When the words 'or his or their assigns' are deleted from the bills of lading, the bill is regarded as non-negotiable. The effect of this deletion is that the consignee (or other named party) cannot transfer the property or goods by transfer of the bills. This particular type is seldom found and will normally apply when goods are shipped on a non-commercial basis, such as household effects.

(11) Container bills of lading. Containers are now playing an increasing role in international shipping and container bill of lading are becoming more common in use. They cover the goods from port to port or from inland point of departure to inland point of destination. It may be an inland clearance depot or container base. Undoubtedly, to the shipper, the most useful type of bill of lading is the clean, negotiable 'through bill', as it enables the goods to be forwarded to the point of destination under one document, although much international trade is based on free on board (FOB) or cost, insurance, freight (CIF) contracts and, with regard to the latter, the seller has no further interest in the movement of the goods once they reach their

port of destination.

Basically the bill of lading has four functions. Broadly, it is a receipt for the goods shipped, a transferable document to the goods thereby enabling the holder to demand the cargo, evidence of the terms of the contract of affreightment but not the actual contract and a quasi negotiable instrument.

Once the shipper or his agent becomes aware of the sailing schedules of a particular trade, through the medium of sailing cards or some form of advertisement, he communicates with the shipowner with a view to booking cargo space on the vessel or container. Provided satisfactory arrangements have been concluded, the shipper forwards the cargo. At this stage, it is important to note that the shipper always makes the offer by forwarding the consignment, whilst the shipowner either accepts or refuses it. Furthermore, it is the shipper's duty, or that of his agent, to supply details of the consignment; normally, this is done by completing the shipping company's form of bill of lading and the shipping company then signs the number of copies requested.

The goods are signed for by the vessel's chief officer or export wharfinger and, in some trades, this receipt is exchanged for the bill of lading. If the cargo is in good condition and everything is in order, no endorsement will be made on the document and it can be termed a clean bill of lading. Conversely, if the goods are damaged or a portion of the consignment is missing, the document will be suitably endorsed by the Master or his agent and the bill of lading will be considered 'claused' or 'unclean'.

Bills of lading are made out in sets and the number varies according to the trade. Generally, it is two or three — one of which will probably be forwarded immediately — and another by a later mail in case the first is lost or delayed. In some trades, coloured bills of lading are used, to distinguish the original (signed) bills from the copies which are purely for record purposes. The reverse of the bill of lading bearing the terms and conditions of the contract of carriage. The clauses on most bills of lading are similar in effect if not in wording.

Where the shipper had sold the goods on a letter of credit terms established through a bank, or when he wished to obtain payment of his invoice before the consignee obtains the goods, he will pass the full set of original bills to his bank, who will in due course arrange presentation to the consignee against payment. The financial role of the bill of lading is explained in Chapter 9.

The shipowner or his agent at the port of destination will require one original bill of lading to be presented to him before the goods are handed over. Furthermore, he will normally require payment of any freight due, should this not have been paid at the port of shipment. When one of a set of bills of lading has been presented to the shipping company, the other bills in the set lose their value.

In the event of the bill of lading being lost or delayed in transit, the shipping company will allow delivery of the goods to the person claiming to be the consignee, if he gives a letter of indemnity. This is normally countersigned by a bank and relieves the shipping company of any liability should another person eventually come along with the actual bill of lading.

Many bills of lading are consigned to 'order' and in such situations are endorsed, normally on the reverse, by the shipper. If the consignee is named, the goods will only be released to him, unless he transfers his right by endorsement subject to the bill of lading providing for this.

The following items are common discrepancies found in bills of lading when being processed and should be avoided:

(1) Document not presented in full sets when requested.

(2) Alterations not authenticated by an official of the shipping company or their agents.

(3) The bill of lading is not clean when presented, such as, when it is endorsed regarding damaged condition of the specified cargo or inadequate packing thereby making it unacceptable to a bank for financial settlement purposes.

(4) The document is not endorsed 'on board' when so required.

(5) The 'on board' endorsement is not signed or initialled by the carrier or agent and likewise not dated.

(6) The bill of lading is not 'blank' endorsed if drawn to order.

(7) The document fails to indicate whether 'freight pre-paid' as stipulated in the credit arrangements viz. C & F or CIF contracts.

(8) The bill of lading is not marked 'freight pre-paid' when freight charges are included in the invoice.

(9) The bill of lading is made out 'to order' when the letter of credit stipulates 'direct to consignee' or vice versa.

(10) The document is dated later than the latest shipping date speci-

fied in the credit.

(11) It is not presented within 21 days after date of shipment or such lesser time as prescribed in the letter of credit.

(12) The bill of lading details merchandise other than that prescribed.

(13) The rate at which freight is calculated, and the total amount is not shown when credit requires such data to be given.

(14) Cargo has been shipped 'on deck' and not placed in the ships hold. Basically, 'on deck' claused bills of lading are not acceptable when clean on board bills of lading are required.

(15) Shipment made from a port or to a destination contrary to that stipulated.

(16) Other types of bills of lading presented, although not specifically authorized. For example, charter party to forwarding agents bills of lading are not accepted unless expressly allowed in the letter of credit.

Our study of the bill of lading would not be complete without consideration of the common short form liner waybill and national standard shipping note (NSSN).

The use of negotiable bill of lading which has to be surrendered to the carrier at a destination in order to obtain delivery of the goods is traditional — but not without disadvantages. The document has to follow the goods and often, for commercial or financial reasons, passes through a variety of hands, resulting in the goods being held up at destination pending arrival of the document — and thereby expenses and additional risks are incurred and customer goodwill is possibly lost.

The General Council of British Shipping with the co-operation of SITPRO (Simplification of International Trade Procedures Board) have developed the concept of a non-negotiable type of transport document — a waybill — in place of the negotiable traditional bill of lading. The waybill provides for delivery to the consignee named in it without surrender of the transport document.

A common, short form liner waybill is now in process of adoption in the UK for exports — a document already used in Scandinavia. It has the following features:

(a) Liner waybill. As a non-negotiable document, with the goods consigned to a named consignee, it does not require production to obtain possession of the goods at destination.

(b) Short form. As it uses a standard clause to incorporate the conditions of carriage by the actual carrier involved, it removes the mass of small print from the back of the document.

(c) Common form. As it is not pre-printed with the name of a specific carrier, the same form can be used for any carrier accepting the system merely by the shipper or agent entering the appropriate carriers name.

It is also a received for shipment document and should, therefore, be available to the shipper earlier than a 'shipped' bill of lading.

In 1975, a national standard shipping note (NSSN) was introduced in UK. It is available for use of all export consignments delivered to container groupage reception points as well as to conventional dock receiving areas.

A specimen bill of lading and standard shipping note is found in Appendix E.

CARGO INSURANCE POLICY AND CERTIFICATE

The cargo insurance policy may only be issued by the insurer and is usually in a standard form covering the customary risk for any voyage or flight. The form of policy in general use today is Lloyd's SG (ships and goods) policy and this is fully explained in Chapter 8. Individual policies for single shipments are rarely used by regular exporters because a new policy would have to be obtained for each shipment. However, insurance certificates based on the overall policy may be issued and are far more common than the policy.

The insurance certificate must contain the same details as the policy with the slight difference that it will carry a shortened version of the provisions of the policy under which it is issued and should be signed by the policy holder.

Overall, the insurance policy/certificate must contain the following:

(1) The name and signature of the insurer.

(2) The name of the assured.

(3) The endorsement of the assured when applicable so that the rights to claim may be transferred.

(4) A description of the risk covered.

(5) A description of the consignment.

(6) The sum or sums to be insured.

(7) The place were claims are payable together with the name of the agent to whom claims may be directed.

Basically, the insurance policy/certificate must embrace the following relative to the processing of the international consignment.

(1) Cover the risk detailed in the credit arrangements.

(2) Be in a completed form.

(3) Be in a transferable form.

(4) Be dated on or before the date of the document evidencing despatch, for example, bill of lading.

(5) Be expressed in the same currency or that of the credit.

The insurance policy/certificate must avoid containing the following discrepancies when presented under a letter of credit.

(1) The amount of cover is insufficient or does not include the risks mentioned in the credit.

(2) The insurance is not issued in the currency of the credit.

(3) The insurance policy/certificate is not endorsed and/or signed.

(4) The certificate or policy bear a date later than date of shipment/despatch.

(5) The goods are not correctly described.

(6) The alterations on the insurance policy/certificate are not authenticated.

(7) The insurance policy/certificate is not in a transferable form when required.

(8) The carrying vessel's name is not recorded.

(9) The insurance policy/certificate does not cover transhipment when bills of lading indicate it will take place.

CERTIFICATE OF ORIGIN

The certificate of origin specified the nature of quantity/value of the goods etc. together with their place of manufacture. Such a declaration stating the country of origin of the goods shipped is required by some countries often to simplify their Customs duties. It is often incorporated in the Customs invoice. In a minority of cases, the declaration has to be authenticated by a Chamber of Commerce. It could also incorporate the selling price of the goods termed the current domestic value (CDV) in which case it is likely to be embraced in the invoice.

The certificate of origin is also required when the merchandise is imported to a country that allows preferential duties on British Goods owing to trade agreements. In order that goods from UK may enjoy the lower schedule of duties, the Customs Authorities of the importing country must be satisfied as to the value of the goods and they substantially represent British labour and British material.

Details of the four types of certificate of origin or their equivalent are given below:

(1) Those issued by a Chamber of Commerce or other official body. Only required when specificially called for by the creditor.

(2) Commonwealth preference certificates of origin and/or EEC documentary evidence for Commonwealth EEC Associates — usually contained on the back of a special invoice form or obtainable from outside approved bodies.

(3) Exporters own certificate of origin — may be used for any case where no special form is required by the creditor.

(4) Movement certificate for the EEC.

CERTIFICATE OF SHIPMENT

This certificate is issued by a freight forwarder and is merely a document confirming the goods have been shipped on a specified vessel and date. It is often associated with groupage or consolidated container shipments and is also known as the 'in house' bill of lading under groupage arrangements.

CHARTER PARTY

A charter party is a contract whereby a shipowner agrees to place his ship, or part of it, at the disposal of a merchant or other person (known as the charterer), for the carriage of goods from one port to another port on being paid freight, or to let his ship for a specified period, his remuneration being known as hire money. The terms, conditions and exceptions under which the goods are carried are set out in the charter party.

A very large proportion of the world's trade is carried in tramp vessels. It is quite common to find that one cargo will fill a whole ship and, in these circumstances, one cargo owner or one charterer will enter into a special contract with the shipowner for the hire of his ship. Such a contract is known as a charter party. It is not always a full ship, although this is usually the case. There are basically two types of charter parties: demise and non-demise.

A demise or 'bareboat' charter party arises when the charterer is responsible for providing the cargo and crew, whilst the shipowner merely provides the vessel. In consequence, the charterer appoints the crew, thus taking over full responsibility for the operation of the vessel, and pays all expenses incurred. A demise charter party is for a period of time which may vary from a few weeks to several years.

A non-demise charter arises when the shipowner provides the vessel and her crew, whilst the charterer merely supplies the cargo. It may be a voyage charter for a particular voyage, in which the shipowner agrees to carry cargo between specified ports for a pre-arranged freight. The majority of tramp cargo shipments are made on a voyage charter basis. Alternatively, it may be a time charter for a stated period or voyage for a remuneration known as hire money. The shipowner continues to manage his own vessel, both under non-demise voyage or time charter parties under the charterer's instructions. With a time charter, it is usual for the charterer to pay port dues and fuel costs, and overtime payments incurred in an endeavour to obtain faster turn-rounds. It is quite common for liner companies to supplement their services by taking tramp ships on time charter, but this practice may lessen as containerization develops.

There are several types of non-demise voyage charter and these are given below. It will be seen that they all deal with the carriage of goods from a certain port or ports to another port or ports and the difference between them arise mainly out of payment for the cost of loading and discharging and to port expenses.

(1) Gross form of charter. This is probably the most common form of charter used by tramp ships today. In this form, the shipowner pays all the expenses incurred in loading and discharging and also all port charges.

(2) FIO charter. Under this charter, the charterer pays for the cost of loading and discharging the cargo, hence the expression of FIO (meaning 'free in and out'). The shipowner is still responsible for the payment of all port charges.

(3) Lump sum charter. In this case, the charterer pays a lump sum of money for the use of the ship and the shipowner guarantees that a certain amount of space (that is, bale cubic metres) will be available for cargo, along with the maximum weight of cargo that the vessel

will be able to carry. A lump sum charter may be on either a gross basis or an FIO basis. Such a charter is very useful when the charterer wishes to load a mixed cargo — the shipowner guarantees that a certain amount of space and weight will be available and it is up to the charterer to use that space to his best advantage.

The above forms of charter are all quite common today and, in each case, the ship owner pays the port charges.

(4) Net form. In this charter, in addition to paying for the cost of loading and discharging, the charterer also pays all the port charges for the time the vessel is ready to load up until the completion of discharge, that is, the charterer pays the outward port charges at the first port of loading and the inward port charges at the last port of discharge, plus all port charges at any intermediate ports. This form of charter is very useful to a shipowner, if he is arranging for his vessel to go to ports about which he knows very little, as his voyage expenses should not vary much from his original estimate. It is also advantageous for the shipowner if there are several ports of call to be made — it is the charterer who will bear the expense of those calls. Net form, however, is very seldom used these days, although occasionally a vessel is fixed on these terms.

There are, of course, numerous variations that may be made to the above broad divisions and this is a matter for negotiation when the vessel is being 'worked' for future business. For example, the gross and FIO charters may be modified to an FOB charter (free on board) meaning that the charterer pays for the cost of loading and the shipowner pays for the cost of discharge, or alternatively the charter may be arranged on the basis of free discharge, that is, the charterer pays for the cost of discharging. The same general terms of contract are found in all the above types of charter.

A substantial proportion of the charters in this country are negotiated through a shipbroker on the Baltic Exchange situated in London. The role of this exchange has been explained in Chapter 14. The negotiations are carried out by word of mouth in the exchange, not by letter, and when the contract has been concluded the vessel is said to be 'fixed'. The charter party is then prepared and signed by the two parties or their agents. In addition to the trade to and from this country, a large number of cross voyages, that is, from one foreign country to another, are fixed on the London market, quite often to a vessel owned in yet another foreign country. There is no compulsion to conduct negotiations through a shipbroker on the Baltic Exchange. Many negotiations are conducted direct between charterer and shipowner. It is a matter for the shipowner's judgement whether he engages a shipbroker to conduct his negotiations direct with the charterer. Obviously, when the shipbroker is negotiating a series of voyage charters for his principal, the shipowner will endeavour to reduce to an absolute minimum the number of ballast voyages. These arise between termination of one voyage charter for example at Rotterdam, and commencement of the next voyage charter, for example, at Southampton, involving a ballast voyage Rotterdam-Southampton.

It will be appreciated that the terms and conditions of a charter party will vary according to the wishes of the parties to the contract. Nevertheless, the former Chamber of Shipping of the United Kingdom — now designated General Council of British Shipping — together with the Baltic and International Maritime Conference have approved a number of charter parties (about 50) for certain commodities in specified trades. These include primarily the tramp trades viz. coal, wheat, timber, ore etc. The parties to the contract are free to make any amendments to such charter parties to meet their needs and there is no obligation to use any particular charter party for a particular trade.

CONVENTION ON THE CONTRACT FOR THE INTERNATIONAL CARRIAGE OF GOODS BY ROAD (CMR)

The International Convention concerning the carriage of goods by road (CMR) came into force in the United Kingdom in October 1967. It permits the carriage of goods by road under one consignment note under a common code of conditions applicable to 26 countries. These include Austria, Belgium, Bulgaria, Czechoslovakia, Denmark, Finland, France, Federal Republic of Germany, Greece, Hungary, Italy, Luxembourg, Netherlands, Norway, Poland, Portugal, Romania, Spain, Sweden, Switzerland, United Kingdom and Yugoslavia. Additionally, by Orders in Council, the convention has been extended to cover the Isle of Man, the Isle of Guernsey and Gibraltar. It applies to all international carriage of goods by road for reward to or from a contracting party. It does not apply to traffic between the United Kingdom and the Republic of Ireland.

The contract of carriage, found in the CMR consignment note, is established when it is completed by the sender and carrier with the appropriate signatures/stamp being recorded thereon. The senders and the carrier are entitled respectively to the first and third copies of the consignment note and the second copy must accompany the goods. If the goods have to be loaded in different vehicles, or are of different kinds or are divided into different lots, either party has the right to require a separate consignment note to be made out in respect of each vehicle or each kind or lots of goods. The CMR consignment note is not a negotiable/transferable document or document of title.

The consignment note must contain the following particulars: the date when and the place where it is made out; the names and addresses of the sender, the carrier and the consignee; the place and date of taking over the goods, and the place designated for delivery; the ordinary description of the nature of the goods and the method of packing and, in the case of dangerous goods, their generally recognized description; the number of packages and their special marks and numbers; the gross weight of the goods or their quantity otherwise expressed; charges relating to the carriage; the requisite instructions for customs and other formalities; and a statement that the carriage is subject, notwithstanding any clause to the contrary, to the provisions of the convention.

Further, the consignment note must contain the following particulars where applicable: a statement that transhipment is not allowed; the charges which the sender undertakes to pay; the amount of 'cash on delivery' charges; a declaration of the value of the goods; a declaration of the amount representing any special interest in delivery; the sender's instructions to the carrier regarding insurance of the goods; the agreed time limit for the carriage; a list of the documents handed to the carrier; where the carrier has no reasonable means of checking the accuracy of the statements in the consignment note as to the number of packages and their marks and numbers, or as to the apparent condition of the goods and their packaging, he must enter his reservations in the consignment note specifying the grounds on which they are based; and where the sender requires the carrier to check the gross weight of the goods or their quantity otherwise expressed or the contents of the packages, the carrier must enter the results of such checks; and any agreement that open unsheeted vehicles may be used for the carriage of the goods.

The parties may enter any other useful particulars in the consignment note.

The sender is liable for all expenses, loss and damage sustained by the carrier by reason of the inaccuracy or inadequacy of certain specified particulars which the consignment note must contain, or by reason of the inaccuracy or inadequacy of any other particulars or instructions given by him.

The carrier is liable for all expenses, loss and damage sustained by the person entitled to dispose of the goods as a result of the omission of the statement that the contract is subject to the convention.

For the purposes of the convention, the carrier is responsible for the acts and omissions of his agents and servants and any other persons whose services he uses for the performance of the carriage as long as those agents, servants or other persons are acting within the scope of their employment.

There is a duty on the carrier:

(1) To check the accuracy of the statements in the consignment note as to the number of packages and their marks and numbers, and the apparent condition of the goods and their packaging.

(2) If the sender so requires him, to check the gross weight of the goods or their quantity otherwise expressed or the contents of the packages.

(3) To check that the statement that the contract is subject to the convention is properly included in the consignment note.

The sender is responsible for the accuracy and adequacy of documents and information which he must either attach to the consignment note or place at the carrier's disposal for the purposes of customs or other formalities which have to be completed before delivery of the goods.

There is a duty on the sender:

(1) To ensure that the goods are properly packed.

(2) In the case of dangerous goods, to inform the carrier of the exact nature of the danger and indicate, if necessary, the precautions to be taken.

(3) To ensure the accuracy and adequacy of certain specified particulars which the consignment note must contain and of any other particulars or instructions given by him to the carrier.

The statutory provisions are embodied in the Carriage of Goods by Road Act, 1965. An example of a CMR consignment note is found in Appendix E.

DOCK RECEIPT

This may be issued by a Port Authority to confirm receipt of cargo on the quay/warehouse pending shipment. It has no legal role regarding processing financial settlement of international consignments.

EXPORT INVOICING

Export documents are never static — there is a continual stream of new overseas import regulations along with new developments and a constant issue of new forms etc. Accordingly, the requisite invoice for a particular market should be checked to ensure the correct one is used otherwise serious delays will be encountered in processing the export order through Customs. Moreover, the exporters invoice should be carefully and accurately completed. Details of the various types of invoices are now examined.

(1) Commercial invoice. The commercial invoice gives details of the goods and is issued by the seller (exporter). It forms the basis of the transaction between the seller and buyer, and is completed in accord with the number of prescribed copies required. Usually it bears the exporter's own headed invoice form stationery. The invoice gives a description of the goods, stating prices, and terms exactly as specified in the credit, as well as shipping marks. Overall, it contains the following information:

(a) Name and address of buyer (importer) and seller (exporter).
(b) Buyers reference, that is, order number, indent number etc.
(c) Number and types of packages.
(d) Weights and measurements of the consignment.
(e) Place and date of issue.
(f) Details of actual cost of freight and insurance if so requested.
(g) Total amount payable.
(h) The export and/or import licence number.
(i) The contents of individual packages.
(j) The method of despatch.
(k) Shipment terms.

Basically, it is a document rendered by one person to another in regard of goods which have been sold. Its primary function is a check for the purchaser against charges and delivery. With regard to insurance claims and for packing purposes, it is useful evidence to verify the value and nature of the goods and in certain circumstances, it is evidence of the contract between the two parties, for example, packing not up to specification may give underwriters redress against the sellers. The invoice is not necessarily a contract of sale. It may form a contract of sale if it is in writing containing all the material terms. On the other hand, it may not be a complete memorandum of the contract of sale and, therefore, evidence may be given to vary the contract which is inferred therefrom.

In particular circumstances, the commercial invoice can be certified by the Chamber of Commerce and/or legalized by the resident consul in the UK.

(2) Consular invoice. Consular invoices are mandatory when shipping goods to certain ports of the world particularly to those countries which enforce *ad valorem* import duties. This applies particularly in South America. The invoices are specially printed documents which must be completed exactly in accordance with requirements and certified by the consul of the country to which the goods are consigned. This is done at the nearest convenient consular office to the port/airport/ICD of departure. The invoices are issued at the consular office and a fee is payable on certification which is often based on a percentage value of the commercial invoice value of the goods. The consul of the importing country retains one copy, returns one copy to the shipper, and forwards further copies to the Customs authorities in his own country. The consular invoice may be used in some circumstances as a certificate of origin. The forms are available from consuls or possibly through Chambers of Commerce and freight forwarders.

(3) Customs invoices. Customs invoices may be required by the authorities of the importing country. An adequate number should be provided for the use of the Customs authorities overseas.

(4) *Pro forma* invoice. This type of invoice is prepared by the exporter and may be required in advance for licence or letter of credit purposes. The document includes the date, name of consignee, quantity and description of the goods, marks and measurements of packages, cost of the goods, packing, carriage, freight, postage, insurance premiums etc.

The following discrepancies relating to processing invoices under letters of credit do arise and should be avoided:

(i) Value exceeds credit amount.

(ii) Amount differs from draft amount.

(iii) Prices of goods not as indicated in credit.

(iv) Omission of the price basis and shipment terms, for example, FOB, CIF, C & F etc.

(v) Inclusion of charges not specified in the credit.

(vi) Invoice not certified, notarized or signed as required by credit.

(vii) Buyer's name differs from that mentioned in the credit.

(viii) Invoice not issued by the beneficiary.

INTERNATIONAL CONVENTION CONCERNING THE CARRIAGE OF GOODS BY RAIL (CIM)

The international convention concerning the carriage of goods by rail (CIM) has existed in some form since 1893. It permits the carriage of goods by rail under one document, a consignment note (not negotiable), under a common code of conditions applicable to 29 countries mainly situated in Europe and Mediterranean areas. It embraces the maritime portion of the transit subject to it being conveyed on shipping lines as listed under the Convention. Advantages of the CIM throughout rail consignment involving a container or train ferry wagon includes through rates under a common code of conditions; simplified documentation/accountancy; flexibility of freight payment; no intermediate handling usually or customs examination in transit countries; through transits; and minimum documentation. The convention is revised from time to time to reflect modern needs and the current one is the international convention concerning the carriage of goods by rail with additional protocol, 1970.

The CIM consignment note is completed by the shipper/agent/originating rail carrier and has six copies. It embraces the original of the consignment note; the invoice; the arrival note; the duplicate of the consignment note; the duplicate of the invoice; and a supplementary copy.

The following information must be recorded on the CIM consignment note:

(1) The date and originating rail station of the consignment.

(2) The name and address of the sender and the consignee.

(3) The originating rail station accepting consignment and the station/place designated for delivery.

(4) The ordinary description of the nature of the goods and method of packing and, in the case of dangerous goods, their generally recognized description.

(5) The gross weight of the goods or their quantity.

(6) The charges relating to the carriage.

(7) The requisite instructions for Customs and other formalities.

LETTERS OF HYPOTHECATION

This is a banker's document outlining conditions under which the international transaction will be executed on the exporters behalf, the latter of whom will have given certain pledges to his banker. It may be by direct loan, acceptance, or negotiations of draft thereto.

MATES RECEIPT

This document is sometimes issued in lieu of a bill of lading. It has no legal authority regarding processing financial settlement of international consignments but merely confirms cargo is placed on board a ship pending issue of a bill of lading.

PARCEL POST RECEIPT

This is issued by the Post Office for goods sent by parcel post. It is both a receipt and evidence of despatch. It is not a document of title and goods should be consigned to the party specified in the credit. An airmail label should be fixed to a postal receipt in respect of air parcel post despatch; alternatively the Post Office should stamp the receipt 'air parcel'.

VETERINARY CERTIFICATE/HEALTH CERTIFICATE

These may be required when livestock/domestic animals/agricultural products are being exported. It should be signed by the appropriate health authority in the exporter's country.

CHAPTER 13

Processing the Export Order

Contract of affreightment: terms of delivery. The export sales contract. Receipt of export order. Progress of export order and check list. Presentation of documents to the bank: check list.

An important activity of export practice is the processing of the export consignment through all its numerous procedures. It is an area which must be fully understood by the exporter. However, before examining the procedures involved, we must first consider the contract of affreightment embraced in the terms of delivery which now follows.

CONTRACT OF AFFREIGHTMENT: TERMS OF DELIVERY

The basis of a price quotation depends on the correct interpretation of the delivery trade terms. The export marketing manager will through experience accumulate information which will enable him to quote accurately. It is important to bear in mind each delivery trade term quoted embraces three basic elements: the stage at which title to the merchandise passes from the exporter (seller) to the importer (buyer); a clear definition of the charges and expenses to be borne by the exporter and importer; and finally, the stage and location where the goods are to be passed over to the importer.

The international consignment delivery terms embrace many factors including particularly insurance, air or sea freight plus surface transport costs, Customs duty, port disbursements, product cost, sometimes packing costs, etc. Moreover, the importance of executing the cargo delivery in accordance with the prescribed terms cannot be overstressed and this involves a disciplined process of progressing the export sales contract order dealt with elsewhere in this chapter. In the ideal situation, the sales export contract order embracing also the delivery terms should be undertaken on a critical path analysis programme devised by the export marketing manager in consultation with department colleagues within the company and relevant outside bodies, that is, booking shipping space, processing financial aspects, obtaining export licences, etc.

There must be no ambiguity in the interpretation by either party of the delivery terms quoted particularly in the area of cost and expenses. If such problems arise, much goodwill is lost and the exporter could lose the prospect of a repeat order in a competitive market. Moreover, costly litigation could arise. It is essential, therefore, buyer/seller agree on the terms of delivery and their interpretation. Such a situation could be overcome by quoting the provisions of Inco terms 1953 dealt with in the latter part of this section.

The most important and popular quotations in exporting are FOB and CIF. In regard to the CIF quotation, this encourages the UK exporter to obtain the maximum income to the UK balance of payments account, as it includes not only income from the export sale of the merchandise, but also revenue from the cargo insurance and freight assuming of course the latter two are UK based Companies. Nowadays, however, an increasing number of importers are insisting the goods are carried by their national shipping or air-line.

An examination of the most important and common delivery terms follows:

(1) CIF. Undoubtedly the most popular quotation is cost, insurance and freight. Under a CIF contract of sale, the exporter provides the goods, books cargo space on a flight or ship, pays freight to the buyers air or sea port which is named, that is, CIF Singapore, insures the goods on behalf of the buyer against normal marine and fire risks to that airport or seaport and pays all charges incidental in getting the goods onto the aircraft or vessel. The exporter (seller) liability ceases when the goods enter the aircraft or pass over the ships rail at the air or seaport of loading subject to the buyer's payment being forthcoming.

The seller is entitled to payment in exchange for the documents, including bill of lading or alternative document of title, and insurance policy or certificate, relative to the consignment. Hence the CIF contract is one to deliver documents rather than goods. If any loss or damage ensues after the shipping company has received the goods and given a clean bill of lading, the buyer will take the necessary steps against the shipowner or underwriter. The seller cannot be held liable for any such loss or damage. The buyer will be responsible for the charges incurred in getting the goods off the ship to his warehouse, such as lighterage, deck dues and customs duties. The bill of lading must be marked 'freight paid' thereby confirming the goods have been placed on board the vessel and the requisite commercial invoice is required for this type of contract. Moreover, it is often necessary for imported goods to be accompanied by special forms, for example, Consular invoices. In such cases it is usual for the CIF seller to defray the expenses of preparation.

The CIF contract has many advantages. It permits the seller at the air or sea port of shipment to arrange the shipment and accept such liabilities which overall is a convenient arrangement bearing in mind the exporter is situated in the country of origin. On the other hand, the buyer is responsible for arranging delivery, lighterage, cost of discharge import duties in his own country, and loss or damage of the cargo after the clean bill of lading has been issued.

A number of variations exist relative to the CIF quotation and these are detailed below:

(i) Cost and freight (C & F). Under these terms the buyer/importer arranges his own insurance whilst the seller/exporter pays the freight. Basically, the exporter is responsible for all charges until the goods are discharged at the air/sea port except insurance.

(ii) CIF and E. The quotation cost, insurance, freight and exchange is used to safeguard the buyer against any loss due to fluctuations in exchange. It is sometimes loosely employed to indicate payment of banker's charges.

(iii) CIFCI. The quotation — cost, insurance, freight, commission and interest — is quoted by an agent in the country of export of the buyer. The agent in his quotation would include his commission and interest on the value of the shipment until he receives payment. If commission is not included, the quotation would be CIFI — cost, insurance, freight and interest.

(iv) A franco, 'franco domicile' or 'delivered' quotation is an extended form of CIF contract. It includes all charges incurred on delivery to the buyer's warehouse. Such prices are difficult to quote unless the seller has wide experience of costs at the overseas market. The term franco means free whilst the term domicile confirms free delivery will be effected to the importer's warehouse at the exporter's expense. 'Franco' quotations and 'ex-ship' are most suitable for the buyer and eminently ideal for the manufacturer who sell direct via his branches or agencies abroad.

(2) FOB. This quotation — free on board — implies that the duty of the seller is to produce the goods, get them to the port and see they are actually placed on board the aircraft or vessel which the buyer

arranges. Hence the seller meets all charges incidental to placing the goods on the aircraft or ship such as cartage, insurances, handling and lighterage. When the goods are placed on board the aircraft or ship and the seller has obtained a receipt for the goods, the sellers responsibilities cease. Thereafter, the buyer pays all charges including insurance of goods from the departure air/sea port to destination and pays the freight. Overall, the exporter meets all charges up to delivery on board the aircraft or ship, whilst payment of air freight or ocean freight and insurance is for the importers account. Delivery of the goods by the exporter is concluded when the merchandise is on the aircraft or ship, that is, 'over the ship's rail' at which point title of the goods passes to the importer.

The seller still retains some dominion over the goods in certain circumstances. For example, the right of stoppage 'in transitu' is one which accrues to an unpaid seller when the buyer is insolvent as soon as the transit commences. Hence once the seller has placed the goods in the carriers vessel, the carrier being the agent of the buyer (only for carriage purposes) takes possession of the goods. The seller loses the right to dispose of the goods and other rights of ownership but, in the event of the buyer/importer becoming insolvent before the delivery of the cargo takes place, the seller/exporter can exercise his right of stoppage in transitu. In such circumstances, the seller/exporter can reclaim the goods following payment by him of the requisite freight.

Documents required under the FOB terms are the requisite commercial invoice and a full set of bills of lading evidencing the goods have been shipped on board the carrying vessel and stating the freight is payable at the destination.

(3) FAS. Under the free alongside ship terms, the seller pays all the cost incidental to getting the goods where they can be placed on board the vessel. The custom of the port may give FAS a special meaning such as 'goods placed in steamer's shed' instead of the more usual interpretation. There also should be provision for determining where the loss lies when goods are lost before they are actually taken onto the ship. Under such terms, the exporter accepts all charges up to delivery alongside the ship, but exclusive of loading charges. Actual delivery of the cargo by the exporter takes places when the cargo is placed alongside the specified vessel at which place title of the goods passes to the importer.

(4) FOR. This quotation — free on rail — permits the seller to

include in his price cost of the goods, cartage and placing on railway wagons at the rail head from where the goods are to be despatched. Railway and other transport charges thence are paid by the buyer. Care should be taken to ensure the buyer cannot possibly misinterpret this quotation as free on rail at port of departure or at port of arrival. Thus, if motor cars made at Luton are in question, the quotation would read FOR Luton. The terms FOW — free on wagon, and FOT — free on truck are synonymous with FOR. Hence, under the FOR terms, all charges up to delivery on the train are for the exporter's account but not the rail freight which is borne by the buyer.

(5) Ex-works. This quotation places the exporter's liability for cargo loss or damage and duties at a basic minimum. The seller bears all the cost and risk of the goods until such time as the buyer is obliged to take delivery of the consignment and to assist the buyer, at his request and expense, to obtain the documents issued in the country of origin which the buyer may require either for export or import. The buyer takes delivery as soon as the goods are placed at his disposal, pays all fees/charges of exporting and accepts risk from the factory gate. Title to the goods passes at the factory gates and it is normal to place after the term ex-works the place name, for example, ex-works Birmingham. Hence, under such terms, the exporter merely submits commercial invoices for the cost of the goods. The insurance and freight expenses are borne by the importer. Similar terms/liabilities relative to the exporter/importer apply to ex-warehouse, and ex-store. Overall, the cost of cargo packing is borne by the exporter under such terms.

(6) Loco. This quotation means price of the cost of goods where they lie, including usually cost of packing or carriage of any kind. For example, 'loco London' or 'free packed London' includes the cost of the goods, packing and delivery in London.

It must be appreciated that, regardless of the type of contract the exporter concludes, the actual final price of the specified merchandise to the buyer will be the same. The terms of the export sales contract merely set out the responsibilities for taking certain actions between the buyer (importer) and seller (exporter). Nevertheless, it is most important to ensure that, when arranging whatever delivery terms are chosen, the exporter and importer fully understand them and their interpretation.

To overcome any difficulties in interpreting the chief delivery terms used in foreign trade contracts, a set of international rules have been agreed by the member countries of the International Chamber of Commerce (ICC). These rules are known as 'Incoterms' and embodied in the ICC booklet 'Incoterms 1953' (subtitled international rules for the interpretation of trade terms). 'Inco terms 1953' eliminate the possibility of varied interpretation of the same terms in the same countries. If the exporter wishes to use these rules, it must be specified in the contract that it is governed by the provisions of 'Inco terms 1953'.

THE EXPORT SALES CONTRACT

The formulation of the export sales contract represents the conclusion of some possibly difficult negotiations and accordingly, particular care should be taken regarding the preparation of its terms. It must be borne in mind that an exporter's primary task is to sell his products at a profit and, therefore, the contract should fulfil this objective insofar as his obligations are concerned. Above all, they should be capable of being executed under reasonable circumstances and ultimately produce a modest profit. It is, of course, realized that, in the initial stages of developing a new market overseas, a loss may be incurred, but with the long term marketing plan objective to increase the market share it should ultimately gain a favourable profit level. A further point to bear in mind is that the export sales contract also embraces a further contract as found in the delivery terms which may be CIF, ex-works, FOB etc.

Details of a typical UK export contract is given below, but it must be stressed that they differ by individual country:

(1) The exporter's/seller's registered name and address.

(2) The importer's/buyer's registered name and address.

(3) A short title of each party quoted in items (1) and (2).

(4) Purpose of the contract. For example, it should confirm the specified merchandise is sold by the party detailed in item (1) to the addressee quoted in item (2), and that the latter has bought according to the terms and conditions laid down in the contract.

(5) The number and quantity of goods precisely and fully described to avoid any later misunderstanding or dispute. In particular, one must mention details of any batches and reconcile goods description with custom tariff specification.

(6) Price. This may be quoted in sterling depending on its general stability or some other currency which is not likely to vary in value significantly throughout the contract duration such as American dollars or deutchemarks. To counter inflation, particularly in a long term contract, it is usual to incorporate an escalation clause therein, and to reduce the risk of sterling fluctuations implications, the tendency is to invoice in foreign currencies.

(7) Terms of delivery, for example, CIF Lagos, FOB London, ex-works Luton. There is an increasing tendency for many importers, particularly those situated in Communist states or Third World countries to insist on the goods being conveyed on their own national airline or shipping company. It is important both parties to the contract fully understand their obligations as the interpretation of the terms of delivery can sometimes vary by individual country. The ideal solution is to quote Inco terms 1953 which are generally recognized worldwide.

(8) Terms of payment, for example, open account, cash with order, sight bills or term bills. Again this requires careful consideration, particularly the relevant aspects dealt with in Chapter 9. Many importers today require extended credit and the exporter's local bank manager should be able to give the requisite guidance on this matter.

(9) Delivery date/shipment date or period. The exporter should check with his production department the delivery date quoted is realistic and the shipping or air freight space will be available on the date or period specified. The exporter's obligations regarding the latter will depend on the terms of delivery.

(10) Methods of shipment, for example, container, train ferry, Ro/Ro and air freight.

(11) Method of packing. It is desirable both parties are fully aware and agree of the packing specification to ensure no dispute later arises regarding packing or any variation to it.

(12) Insurance — policy or cover note terms.

(13) Import or export licence details or other instructions. The period of their validity must be reconciled with the terms of payment and delivery date/shipment date or period.

(14) Shipping/freight/documentary requirements and/or instructions. This includes marking of cargo.

(15) Contract conditions, for example, sale, delivery, performance

(quality) of goods, arbitration etc. With regard to arbitration, this tends to speed settlement of any disputes without costly litigation.

(16) Signature. Both parties to sign the contract each by a responsible person which may be at directorial or managerial level, and the date recorded.

A copy of the contract should be retained by each party.

RECEIPT OF EXPORT ORDER

Before dealing with the export order acceptance, it is appropriate to give below the check points which need careful scrutiny in any price list tendered and emphasizes how important it is to ensure all the special costs which may enter into an export order are included:

(1) Adequate clear description of goods usually exclusive of tariff. Use Brussels Nomenclature.

(2) Specification — use metric units.

(3) Quantities offered/available with delivery details.

(4) Price (a) Amounts or per unit. (b) Currency. (c) Delivery terms which may involve part shipments over scheduled period and/or transhipments — Ex-works, FOB, CIF, etc.

(5) Terms of payment including provisions for currency rate variation.

(6) Terms of delivery, ex-stock, forward, etc. relevant estimate.

(7) Transportation mode(s), that is, container, air freight, sea freight and road haulier.

(8) Insurance.

(9) Packaging and packing.

(10) Offer by *pro forma* invoice.

(11) Identity of country of origin of goods and country of shipment.

Prior to receipt of the indent/order, a customer may need a *pro forma* invoice, which is essential before a customer can open a bank credit in the supplier's favour. On receipt of the indent or order from the overseas client, the export marketing manager will check the specification and price in the order with the quotation together with its period of validity. Care must be taken to ensure the client is not trying to take advantage of an out-of-date quotation. For example, where the quotation was FOB, the export marketing manager must note whether the customer wishes the supplier to arrange for freight and insurance cn his behalf. The method of payment will be noted and checked with quotation terms. For example, where payment is to be made under a documentary credit, the documents the banks require must be carefully noted. The required delivery date will be particularly noted. If the delivery date is given and the client has been obliged to obtain an import licence for the particular consignment, the date of expiry must be noted.

Given below is a receipt of order check list:

(1) Goods
    (i)   Quality
    (ii) Quantity
    (iii) Description

(2) Payment
    (i)   Price
    (ii) Method i.e. bill of exchange sight draft
    (iii) Time scale
    (iv) Currency variation provision

(3) Shipment
    (i)   Mode(s) of transport/route/transhipment
    (ii) Any constraints i.e. packing/weight/dimensions/statutory restrictions
    (iii) Time scale
    (iv) Any marks i.e. special marking on cases/cartons to identify them

(4) Additional requirements
    (i)   Insurance
    (ii) Inspection
    (iii) Documentation
    (iv) Specific packing — see item (4ii)
    (v) Commissions or discount

(5) Comparison with quotation. A *pro forma* invoice is a document similar to a sales invoice except that it is headed '*pro forma*'. It is not a record of sales effected, but a representation of a sales invoice issued prior to the sale. As the *pro forma* invoice contains all relevant details, for example, full description of goods, packing specification, price of goods with period of validity, cost of cases and, where relevant, cost of freight and insurance, it is particularly used for quotations to customers and for submission to various authorities. Terms of payment are also always shown but it may not

be possible to give shipping marks until a firm order is received. When used as quotation the *pro forma* invoice constitutes a binding offer of the goods covered by its price and condition shown.

As soon as the exporter receives the letter of credit, he should check it against his *pro forma* invoice to ensure both documents agree with each other. Usually, the contract will be in a more detailed form than the letter of credit, but it is important the exporter should be able to prepare his documents complying with both the contract and the credit. For general guidance the following major points should be noted when the credit is received:

(1) Check terms of letter of credit (examine both sides as it is easy to miss a clause typed on the back).

(2) Closing date }
(3) Shipment date }

Adequacy of time for shipment and document preparation for bank: place — port/despatch and if it concurs with quotation. In the case of Ro/Ro traffic usually no such details are given, but the traffic must be pre-booked with the ferry operator. For air freight it is virtually immediate i.e. next available flight.

(4) Amount — Currency: adequacy if total value concurs with acceptance price.

(5) Draft — terms of letter of credit agree with the contract.

(6) Goods description — terms of letter of credit agree with the contract.

(7) Import licence — is it mentioned — if required?

(8) Bill of lading/air waybill/CIM/CMR/waybill documentation. Ensure the documentation is correct and accords with the terms of contract of sale.

PROGRESS OF EXPORT ORDER AND CHECK LIST

To ensure the complex procedure of preparing the goods, packing, forwarding, shipping, insurance, Customs clearance, invoice and collecting payment do not go wrong, it is suggested a check list or progress sheet be prepared for each export order. A suggested version is given here but it must be borne in mind there are many variations in progressing a given export order.

In regard to items sent by parcel post or air freight, the credit and

Export order progress check list

Order cleared for credit worthiness: terms of payment	Signature	Order cleared for exchange control purposes	Signature	Order cleared for export licensing purposes	Signature

(1) Customer's name and address
(2) Customer's order no. and date
(3) Date of receipt and export department's serial number
(4) Brief details of the order
(5) Import licence no. and date of expiry
(6) Export licence no.
  (a) Date of application
  (b) Date received
  (c) Date of expiry
(7) Method of packing
(8) Shipping or airline — if prescribed
(9) Type of insurance
(10) Terms of payment
(11) Details of letter of credit, including full list of documents required
(12) If FOB, who arranges and pays for freight/insurance
(13) Date order acknowledged
(14) Promised delivery date
(15) Date order put in hand
(16) *Pro forma* invoices sent (often required by customer to open credit)
(17) Production department — completion date
(18) Goods inspected or tested
(19) Packing ordered
(20) Merchandise ready
(21) Shipping bill completed
(22) Consular invoices completed
(23) Certificate of origin or equivalent completed
(24) Application for shipment/air freight space booking despatched/accepted
(25) Shipping marks
(26) Shipment etc. — instructions received/goods called forward/closing date/despatch department instructed
(27) Bills of lading/CMR/CIM/air waybill prepared in requisite quantity
(28) Insured value declared — giving number of certificates required freight paid
(29) Bills of lading/CMR/air waybill received — documents serial no. and date of shipment/despatch
(30) Insurance certificates received — serial no.
(31) Draft and document lodged with bank
(32) Accounts copy of invoice passed through the books
(33) Payment received

despatch arrangements may vary slightly insofar as the foregoing is concerned.

Most exporters today have a separate order date folder for each sale contract order. The folder has a prescribed action chart to follow through for each contract which lessens the risk of any mistakes being made or items overlooked. A specimen is found in DIAGRAM IX (a, b, and c) pages 233 to 235.

Functions/Procedures of Export Documentation
We will now consider the processing of export documentation and the various procedures involved. Details of the salient points follow:

10 March (extracts from original order)	Order received for delivery end April
	All wool tissues
	(Description of goods — wool and worsted piece goods)
	Order No. B 2
	Market: Lebanon
	Port: Beirut
	Packing type: 6 cases Wood, waterproof paper, paper lined cases
	Marking: LAS Beirut 6

Time scale of deliveries

15 March	*Pro forma*
1 April	Payment terms (L/C etc.) received
2 April	Payment terms checked
5 April	Works store promise
18-22 April	Receiving/closing date of shipment
23 April	Insurance dealt with
25 April	Sailing date
28 April	Letter of credit — shipping date
4 May	Bill of lading required by this date
7 May	Completion of documentation to bank
12 May	Proceeds received
15 May	Letter of credit expiry date

Documents required

	Bank	Customer	Agent	Customs Clearance	Consulate	Total
Commercial invoices	—	3	—	—	—	3
Certified invoices	3	1	2	1	— 3	10
Certificate of origin	—	—	—	—	— —	
Bill of lading	2/2	2 copies	—	—	— 2	2/4
Certificate of shipment	—	—	—	—	— —	
Insurance policy	—	—	—	—	— —	
Insurance certificate	—	—	—	—	— —	
Weight and contract note	1	1	—	—	— 1	3
Bank draft statement	1	—	—	—	— —	1

It must be recognized that the number of documents and their type vary by individual consignment, mode of transport, commodity, contract of sale, importing country, customer's country, statutory obligations, financial arrangements etc.

PRESENTATION OF DOCUMENTS TO THE BANK: CHECK LIST

When preparing his documents for presentation to the bank, the exporter should bear in mind the following points which can constitute a form of 'check list' to be adopted:

(1) All the documents are presented within expiry date.

(2) Goods are shipped within the stipulated period.

(3) Documents are presented to the bank within 21 days of the date of shipment/despatch or such shorter time as laid down in the letter of credit.

(4) The aggregate amount of the drawing is within the credit amount.

EXPORT DOCUMENT AND PROGRESS FOLDER

1976/77

OZALID (U.K) LIMITED

Incorporating Nig. Bonda Limited

Cowdray Avenue Colchester Essex CO1 1XU Telex 98296
Registered Office Langston Road Loughton Essex IG10 3TH
Registered in England No. 709483

Vehicle Bkg. Ref.	CAN	Tariff Heading
Invoice No. and Date	Exporter's Reference
Buyer's Reference	F/Agent's Ref.	S.S. Co. Bkg. No.

Consignee (if 'Order' State Notify Party and Address)	Buyer (If not Consignee)

Name of Shipping Line | Port Account No.

Forwarding Agent/Merchant	Coding for H.M. Customs ▶	Destination	ICD	Container	Ro Ro (a) (b)	Flag	Port
	Country of Origin of Goods	Country of Final Destination

NO ORIGINAL DOCUMENTS TO BE REMOVED FROM THIS FILE

Receiving Date(s)	Dock, Container base Etc.	Terms of Delivery and Payment
Pre-Carriage By	Place of Receipt by Pre-Carrier	
Vessel/Aircraft Etc.	Port of Loading	EUR 1 Remarks
Port of Discharge	Place of Delivery by On-Carrier	Insured Value (state Currency)	Name of Receiving Author'ty

Marks, Nos. and Container No.; No. and Kind of Packages; Description of Goods (specify Nature of Hazard if any)	Quantity Ordered / Supplied	& Per Unit	Amount (State Currency)

CUSTOMER STANDING INSTRUCTIONS	LETTER OF CREDIT
	REF.
	EXPIRES

SPECIAL INSTRUCTIONS	
WORKS	READY DATE ....
PACKING	
DESPATCH/CARRIERS	DELIVERY DEADLINE ....
OTHER	
FORWARDING AGENT/SS/AIR	ORDER COMPLETED ....
	FILE DATE ....INT...............

BANDA ALIGNED
EXPORT
DOCUMENTATION
PACKAGE
FORM No. 122

9299E OZALID (U.K) LTD © 1976

IX (a)   Export document and progress folder [by courtesy of Ozalid (UK) Ltd.]

ENQUIRY / ORDER CONTROL SHEET

OP No.	*	ACTION / DOCUMENTATION	DOCUMENT DISTRIBUTION							ACTIONED BY		CHECKED BY		COPY REQUIREMENTS			
			MAST FEW NO	AGENT	BANK	PRINT	SS/AIR	CUS NOTE		DATE	INT	DATE	INT	FORM No	COPIES	DATE	INT
1	D	QUOTATION STAGE ENQUIRY TO CONTROL FOLDER															
2	C	PREPARE COSTING TO SCHEDULE															
3	T	RELEASE QUOTATION NO.															
4	D	ORDER STAGE ALLOCATE ORDER NO.'S, CHECK COSTING, CREDIT, LICENCES, STANDING & SPECIAL INSTRUCTIONS															
5	T	RAISE ALIGNED INVOICE MASTER (ORDER)	2														
6	I / I	RAISE ALIGNED CONSIGNMENT MASTER SITPRO FOREIGN BILL DOCUMENTS FOR COLLECTION	1														
	I / I	WORKS ORDER FEEDBACK OR EXPORT REQ. AVAILABILITY-STOCK PROD. CONTROLLER WITH UNIT PACKING CARDS	2														
7	U	AVAILABILITY TO MASTER	2														
8	I	RELEASE ORDER ACKNOWLEDGEMENT	2														
9	I	RELEASE PREPARING COPY, PACKING INSTRUCTIONS, FEEDBACK	2														
10	D	BOOK FREIGHT SPACE/DATE - PHONE FREIGHT FORWARDING SS. CO. AIRLINE															
11	U	MASTER - WEIGHTS CUBE CASE DETAIL	1														
12	U	MASTER - AS OP. 11 COMPLETE EXTENSIONS	2														
13	I	CONSIGNMENT GOODS CLEARANCE STAGE EXPORT CARGO SHIPPING INSTRUCTIONS (CONFIRMS OPP. NO. 10)	1														
14	I	BILLS OF LADING ORIGINAL.......... COPY..........	1														
15	I	EXPORT CONSIGNMENT NOTE	1														
16	I	ADVICE OF SHIPMENT NOTE - AND/OR CERTIFICATE OF SHIPMENT	1														
17	I	CUSTOMS CLEARANCE C273/1 OR C273/4	1														
18	I	STANDARD SHIPPING NOTE.	1														
19	I	INSURANCE CERTIFICATE.	1														
20	I	MOVEMENT CERTIFICATE EUR 1	1														
21	I	INVOICE STAGE COMMERCIAL INVOICE OR	2														
22	I	CERTIFICATE OF VALUE AND ORIGIN INVOICE	2														
23	I	CONSULAR INVOICE (IF REQUIRED)	2														
24		FINAL STAGE PAY ALL DOCK DUES															
25	I	AGENTS COMMISSION CREDIT															

* D = DRAFT   C = CALCULATE   T = TYPE   I = ISSUE   U = UPDATE

IX (b)   Enquiry/order control sheet [by courtesy of Ozalid (UK) Ltd.]

EXPORT COST SCHEDULE

QUOTE NO.		TERMS OF DELIVERY AND PAYMENT		COSTED BY	
DATED					
CUSTOMER ORDER NO.	WORKS ORDER NO.			CHECKED BY	
		EX WORKS/FOB/C&F/CIF	RATE OF EXCHANGE:		

COST ITEM	DETAILS OF COSTING		COST	
			£ STERLING	CURRENCY:
GOODS (INC. % MARGIN)				
AGENTS COMMISSION				
OTHER COSTS (STATE)				
		TOTAL EX-WORKS		
PACKING, MATERIAL, LABOUR.				
HAULAGE RATE TO DEPOT/DOCK				
PORT DUES — DOCK CHARGES				
OTHER CHARGES				
		TOTAL F.O.B.		
FREIGHT	WEIGHT MEASUREMENT	CUBE AD VAL		
OTHER CHARGES				
		TOTAL C. & F.		
INSURANCE	MARINE & WAR RISK OTHER			
ECGD PREMIUM				
OTHER CHARGES				
		TOTAL CIF		
LANDING CHARGES				
PORT/CUSTOMS CLEARANCE				
HAULAGE TO DOMICILE				
OTHER CHARGES				
		TOTAL DELIVERED DOMICILE		

NOTES

IX (c)   Export cost schedule [by courtesy of Ozalid (UK) Ltd.]

(5) All documents requiring endorsement are correctly endorsed, for example, bills of lading, bills of exchange, insurance documents.

(6) Invoices contain exact credit description.

(7) Invoices are addressed to the importer.

(8) Invoices contain exact licence numbers and/or certifications required by credit and such certifications are signed, and must be worded exactly as specified in the credit.

(9) Invoices show terms of shipment mentioned in the credit.

(10) Quantity, weight both gross and nett, shipping marks, unit price, etc. agree with credit and between all the relative documents.

(11) Bills of lading show goods 'on board' a specified named vessel.

(12) Bills of lading show correct name and address of notify party.

(13) Bills of lading are in a full set of signed originals (that is, 2/2, or 3/3) or as called for by the credit.

(14) If FOB shipment, ensure bills of lading show freight payable at destination.

(15) If C & F or CIF shipment, ensure bills of lading are marked freight paid or freight pre-paid.

(16) Insurance document is in currency of credit.

(17) Insurance is for correct value (for example, as specified in the credit).

(18) Insurance covers all the risks as specified in the credit.

(19) Original letter of credit accompanies the presentation.

(20) The insurance document is dated prior to despatch of the goods or specifically states that cover is effective from shipment date.

(21) Insurance certificate is not presented where credit stipulates insurance policy.

The foregoing check list must not be regarded as exhaustive, but merely dealing with the salient points. To the exporter dealing with a documentary letter of credit, the following data must be contained on it relative to a consignment by sea:

(1) The name and address of the beneficiary.

(2) The type of credit (revocable or irrevocable).

(3) The amount of credit in sterling or a foreign currency.

(4) Whether the credit is available for one or several drawings/shipments.

(5) The expiry date.

(6) The name of the party on whom the drafts are to be drawn and whether they are at sight or of a particular tenor.

(7) Precise instructions as to the documents against which payment to be made.

(8) A brief description of the goods covered by the credit (too much detail may give rise to errors which can cause delay).

(9) Shipping details including whether transhipments are allowed. The names of the ports of shipment and discharge should also be recorded, and the latest date for shipment.

(10) The terms of contract and shipment (that is, whether ex-works, FOB or CIF).

Credits should further state that they are subject to the Uniform Customs and Practice for Documentary Credits (1974 Revision), International Chamber of Commerce Publication No. 290. this is a standardized code of practice formulated by the International Chamber of Commerce.

The following check list must be rigorously adopted by the exporter when handling the letter of credit.

(1) Is it confirmed by a British bank?

(2) Is the quantity described correct?

(3) Is partial shipment permitted or required?

(4) Is the letter of credit irrevocable?

(5) Is the name of the exporter and that of the customer complete and spelt correctly?

(6) Is shipment permitted from any place in the UK, or only one named point?

(7) Does the named destination quoted (port of discharge) agree with the letter of credit?

(8) Are the following needed?

(i) Export licence.

(ii) Import licence.

(iii) Exchange licences.

(9) Is the letter of credit amount sufficient to the quotation? The following aspects should be checked:

(i) Cost of goods plus profit element.

(ii) Inland transport cost to ship, including wharfage and handling charges at port of loading, or similar charges relative to air freight or air freight charges.

(iii) Shipping — sea freight or air freight charges.

(iv) Forwarding fees.

(v) Consular fees.

(vi) Insurance cost.

(vii) Inspection and/or miscellaneous charges.

(10) If it is 'on deck' cargo, does the letter of credit authorize 'on deck' shipment?

(11) Compare the contract of sale with the letter of credit to ensure its compatibility.

(12) If a chartered vessel is involved, does the letter of credit state 'charter party bill of lading acceptable'?

(13) Can the exporter comply with the insurance risk required in the letter of credit and does the credit request a policy or certificate?

(14) Does the expiration and shipping date give sufficient time to assure payment?

(15) Is the letter of credit irrevocable?

(16) Can the exporter obtain the following relevant executed documents to conform with the letter of credit?

(i) Bill of lading	(vi) Certificate of origin
(ii) Air waybill	(vii) Insurance policy/certificate
(iii) Parcel post receipt	(viii) Certificate of inspection
(iv) Invoice packing list	(ix) Certificate of quality
(v) Consular invoice	(x) Certificate of health

Circumstances do arise which make it impossible for the exporter to present documents to the bank exactly as stipulated or within the prescribed time. Moreover, unforeseen circumstances can arise. In such foregoing situations, the following options exist to the exporter after presenting the documents to the bank:

(1) Request the advising bank to cable the issuing bank for permission to effect payment despite discrepancies in the documents. Actual cable cost would be for the beneficiary's account.

(2) Ask the advising bank to accept a guarantee order which the exporter requests payment against an undertaking to hold the bank harmless for any loss or damage incurred through making payment against presentation of irregular documents.

(3) Instruct the advising bank to send draft and documents to the issuing bank on a collection basis, that is, documents to be delivered to the importer against authority to pay.

In circumstances where the documents can be corrected/amended, the exporter should arrange for this to be done ensuring that the documents are returned to the paying bank as soon as possible but within the expiry date of the credit. The exporter should remember to check the reverse of, and any attachment to the credit, as further terms and conditions may appear and do form an integral part of the credit. Basically, the simpler the credit terms between exporter/importer the easier it is for trade to take place and expand between the parties and countries concerned.

Although it is often desirable for the UK exporter to ensure that the credit is opened in sterling, that is, the currency of his country, this may not be possible and a foreign currency may be used. To protect himself from any losses due to rate fluctuations in the period between the time he ships the goods and receives payment, he may wish to sell the foreign currency forward to his bank. The bank will quote him a special rate and, no matter what happens to the exchange rate in the meantime, the importer knows exactly how much he will receive. On the other hand, there may be distinct advantages in invoicing in foreign currencies.

In circumstances where extended credit is granted to the importer, the beneficiary should be contracted to pay interest and will receive an acceptance/usance credit providing for payment at a future date.

At the time of drawing up the contract, the period, rate and method of payment of interest should be agreed with the importer and can be incorporated in the price, or the importer could ask his bank to add a clause in the credit stating that the interest is for the importer's account and maybe claimed accordingly. Alternatively, the term 'discount charges are for buyer's account' could be incorporated in the credit terms. Interest rates fluctuate, sometimes on a daily basis.

Following presentation of documents in order, the accepted bill can be discounted (that is, sold to a discount house) usually by the bank accepting the bill, or by the beneficiary's own bankers. An interest charge is levied by the discount house which, if for buyer's account, will be paid by the importer. In effect, the beneficiary then receives settlement as if the bill had been drawn at sight.

If the credit makes no reference to settlement of the discount charge, the bill can still be discounted at any time, but the interest charge levied should be for the beneficiary's account. Unless the credit specifies that drafts are needed in duplicate, a single draft will be acceptable.

Many credits stipulate the name of the port from which shipment is to be made but in some circumstances it may be advantageous to the exporter for shipment to be allowed 'from any UK port' thereby providing a choice. This must be arranged in consultation with the importer and provides a degree of flexibility. It can be extended to include the port of discharge.

There are three features which are basic for export success in terms of documentation viz. quality of management, quality of staff and effective communication.

Exporters are not just simply selling a product, but also service and efficiency. Of vital importance is the ability to examine each problem as it arises to obtain correct information without delay, to use it effectively and to make correct decisions.

The overseas customer has the same attitude to business detail as the good business in the UK. Hence, he will be impressed by clarity, accuracy and suspicious of the exporter who fails to produce correct documents in the correct sequence. Export documents must be precise and accurate. Documentation is required for the following reasons:

(1) To provide a complete and specific description of the goods including values and all relevant details so that goods can be correctly assessed for customs import and duty purposes.

(2) Documents may be needed for exchange control regulations — quantitative or quote restrictions and also for statistical purposes.

(3) Buyer requires the relevant documents for his own purposes, for example, in order to obtain the goods.

Delay in delivery/despatch of shipping etc. documents has reached serious proportions in recent years and has resulted in excessive delays in despatch of goods. It has arisen for many reasons and these can be summarized as follows:

(1) Non-availability at time of despatch of commercial invoices and packing lists.

(2) Late submission of bills of lading by manufacturers and/or shippers to shipping companies etc.

(3) Delay in releasing bills of lading by shipping companies.

(4) Errors in compilation of bills of lading, insurance certificates etc.

(5) Delays in communication between clerical staff in ports/airports/ICD and shippers.

(6) Delay in obtaining necessary consular invoice.

(7) Inadequate scrutiny at time of receipt of letters of credit.

(8) Delay by banks in processing documents due to discrepancies found in them.

(9) Delay due to one or more of the following:

(i) Letter of credit expired or withdrawn

(ii) Partial shipment i.e. only part of consignment sent

(iii) Stale or incorrectly completed bill of lading

(iv) Insurance certificate not enclosed or dated after shipment, or cover incorrect in terms of value or currency

(v) Incorrect invoices, consular documents or draft drawn incorrectly

(10) Documents sent by surface post when they could be delivered by air.

(11) Documents sent to small local branches of banks when the main or foreign branches deal with shipping documents.

(12) Wrongly completed documents including customs invoice delaying customs clearance. To overcome the foregoing problem, the exporter should do the following:

(i) Employ professional services of a freight forwarder and/or

(ii) Provide an adequate trained staff of good calibre

(iii) Study letter of credit carefully so there is time for amendments to be made if necessary and send copy to freight forwarder.

(iv) Apply the aligned documentation system. This involves use of the simplified method of documentation with standard size forms. By engaging the aligned system and mechanization, and one run series of production, the complete operation is speeded up. Discuss the matter with the freight forwarder/SITPRO.

(v) Maintain a record of documents flow and status reports in order to isolate consistent bottle-necks with a view to correction.

(vi) Use fully the telex and other aids for rapid transmission of information when appropriate which is dependent on the time scale.

CHAPTER 14

Export Facilitation Organizations

Baltic Exchange. British Overseas Trade Board. British Shippers Council. British Standards Institution (THE). Central Office of Information. Confederation of British Industry. Department of the Environment. Foreign and Commonwealth Office. General Council of British Shipping. Inter-Governmental Maritime Consultative Organization. International Air Transport Association. Liner Conferences. London Chamber of Commerce and Industry. National Ports Council. Simplification of International Trade Procedures Board. PIRA. Road Haulage Association.

Our study of export practice would not be complete without consideration of the increasing number of organizations that are available in international trade. It may be either allied to international distribution arrangements or offering direct help to the exporter in the facilitation of international trade.

THE BALTIC EXCHANGE

A large volume of world tonnage is engaged in tramping. These vessels are employed under a document called a charter party wherein a shipowner agrees to the charterer engaging a vessel for a specific voyage or period of time. This process is called chartering and has been described in greater detail elsewhere in this book.

The voyage charter relates to a stated voyage to carry a specified amount of cargo at so much per ton. Time charters contract for the hire of a vessel for a specified period of time. There are two types of time charters (a) when the charterer hires the vessel 'all found' and (b) where the owner hires his ship for a period to the charterers to be operated by them as they wish, the charterers supplying crew and fuel, and paying all costs for one agreed rate of hire known as a 'bareboat' or demise charter. These charter rates fluctuate almost daily in accordance with the conditions of supply and demand operating in the market. The exporter with a shipload of cargo is likely to charter a vessel under non-demise voyage charter party terms engaging the services of a shipbroker.

A considerable amount of the world chartering is undertaken on the Baltic Exchange where the shipowners and charters are able to arrange their business under conditions of reliability through a ship-broker. The Exchange is situated in London, and its work may be divided into four main classes, details of which are as follows:

(1) Purchase and sale of oil seeds and vegetable oils.

(2) Purchase and sale of grains.

(3) Chartering of ships or space in ships for the carriage of all types of cargo to and from all ports of the world.

(4) Chartering of aircraft or space in aircraft for cargo or passengers.

Chartering operations represent the most numerous transactions on the Baltic Exchange, and are mainly concerned with, although not entirely confined to, tramp ships. The dealers on the Exchange are known as chartering agents who represent charterers, that is, the merchants and other interests who charter ships to carry their cargoes. Others known as owners' brokers, represent the shipowners. Additionally, there are many broking firms who have both charterers and shipowners among their clients, who may be in London or anywhere else in the world. Many merchants and shipowners are members of the Exchange and have their own chartering staff in the Exchange, who take the place of chartering agents and brokers but perform the same function.

BRITISH OVERSEAS TRADE BOARD (BOTB)

The role of the British Overseas Trade Board is to provide information, advice and help to British exporters. The Board itself comprises businessmen and industrialists, trade unionists, senior civil servants and others with exporting knowledge and experience; it directs and administers the Government's export promotion policy under the Secretary of State for Trade, who is the Board's President.

In 1975, the British Overseas Trade Advisory Council (BOTAC) was appointed. The Council's function is, as its name indicates, an advisory one: it offers advice about the operation and development of the Board's services to industry and acts as a channel between the Board and industry and commerce. The Council is a larger body than the Board and the interests represented on it include the CBI, TUC and the Association of British Chambers of Commerce.

In addition to the Council, the Board can call for advice from its 16 geographical area advisory groups. Each group covers a particular trading area (for example, the USA and Canada are combined to form the North American Advisory Group) and comprises a number of British businessmen who are knowledgeable about exporting and also about trading conditions in the specific geographical area covered by the group.

BOTB assistance to exporters falls into two main categories: the provision of market information, advice and individual help to firms; and the organization of collective trade promotions which are supported by publicity.

Market information and advice are available either from the Export Services and Promotions Division at Export House in London or from the export sections of the Department of Industry regional office at Glasgow, Inverness, Cardiff, Newcastle upon Tyne, Cockermouth, Manchester, Leeds, Birmingham, Nottingham, Bristol, and the Department of Commerce in Belfast.

Market intelligence comes into Export House in London from over 200 diplomatic service posts overseas. Much of this material goes out daily via the BOTB's Export Intelligence Service (EIS). This is a selective, computerized service which matches incoming export intelligence to a subscriber's specific profile of interest. The spread of information is wide, from calls for tender to revised import regulations. Once an item has been selected for a company, it is despatched by first class post or, if it is particularly urgent, by telephone or telex. The subscriber pays £37.50 for 150 EIS cards over any period.

Material received from overseas posts is also used to brief businessmen before paying a visit to a new market, and to advise firms on such topics as overseas tariff regulations, the development plans of other countries, attitudes to doing business in other markets, and so on. In addition, the Board will call on the commercial post when it is approached by a UK firm looking for an overseas representative. The charge for this Agency Finding Service is £50 (plus VAT), which includes relevant status reports on the business operations and commercial standing of possible representatives.

Also available is information on the technical specifications of products for export from a body called Technical Help for Exporters. The service is run by the British Standards Institution and funded by BOTB. The European Components Service helps put buyers in mass assembly plants in Federal Republic of Germany, France and Scandinavia in touch with British manufacturers of mechanical components. It is dealt with in greater deail on pages 250-252.

The Overseas Projects Group helps UK companies pursuing major contracts in large capital projects by acting as a focal point for consultants, contractors, manufacturers and bankers. Among the sources of specialist information and advice for exporters is the Board's Exports to Japan Unit (EJU) which keeps British industry in touch with opportunities in the Japanese market. EJU is also responsible for planning the programme of exhibitions and seminars at the British Export Marketing Centre in Tokyo.

Help with market research is provided through the Export Market Research Scheme. This scheme offers free advice on the kind of research a firm might need and can provide financial help towards the cost of market research projects which fall within certain criteria.

There are other BOTB services which financially support firms in their overseas selling. The Joint Venture Scheme helps firms to exhibit at overseas trade fairs, when they are sponsored by an approved trade association, chamber of commerce, or similar non-profit making body. The Board's Fairs and Promotions Branch rents a site for the group display at an exhibition and then allocates space to each participant, usually 15 m². The charges (from April 1978) are £15 a m² for inside space (including the shell stand) and £7.50 m² for outside space. Newcomers to an event are entitled to a 50% discount on these rates for the first two participations. For exhibitions outside Western Europe, the Board will help with a firm's travel costs and the cost of returning unsold exhibits to the UK. Similar terms apply to participation in British Pavilions at international trade fairs, and to the occasional all-British exhibition.

The Outward Mission scheme enables British businessmen to obtain a contribution towards the cost of visiting an overseas market. The criteria are that the businessmen travel as a group of at least six people, and that the group is sponsored by an approved trade association or chamber of commerce. The obverse of this is the Inward Mission Scheme which enables companies (again provided they act as a group with appropriate sponsorship) to obtain financial assistance towards the cost of bringing influential foreign buyers to the UK. An inward mission generally represents a particular sector of industry. The Board will also give financial support to companies presenting papers at specialist seminars and symposia overseas.

The latest addition to the range of services administered by the Board is the Market Entry Guarantee Scheme (MEGS). The scheme is designed to help small and medium sized firms in manufacturing industry to deal with the financial risk and problems associated with a venture to develop a new export market. The assistance will take the form of a 50% loan towards the eligible costs of the market venture and will be repaid, with a commercial rate of return, out of receipts from sales in the market. If sales do not materialize as expected, then the firm and the scheme will share the loss and, for this guarantee, the firm pays the scheme an annual premium. The scheme came into effect in 1978.

For firms wishing to do some research of their own, there is the Statistics and Market Intelligence Library in Export House, London, which is open to the public every weekday. The Library contains a great deal of published information on overseas markets including the import and export trade statistics of other countries, foreign trade and telephone directories, the development of plans of foreign governments, overseas manufacturers' catalogues and other material.

Publicity is considered an important promotional tool in overseas selling, and advice can be given to exporters on the best way to publicize a new product, technological process or service. The Board's Publicity Unit in London works closely with the Central Office of Information, with the BBC External Services and with the information departments at British embassies abroad.

The BOTB is concerned to promote the training of competent export staff available to British industry. To this end, the Board, in collaboration with the Institute of Export, the Institute of Marketing, the Institute of Freight Forwarders, and the Society of Shipping Executive, sponsors the Foundation Course in Overseas Trade. This is a one year, part-time course for people of 18 and over and is available at colleges and polytechnics throughout Britain. The author was one of the four subject specialists responsible for the evolution of the course syllabus, which was introduced in 1975. Further information about BOTB services can be obtained from Export House, 50 Ludgate Hill, London EC4M 7HU. (Telephone 01-248 5757).

BRITISH SHIPPERS' COUNCIL

The British Shippers' Council was founded in 1955 to further the interests of importers and exporters in the United Kingdom in all matters concerning the overseas transport of their goods, whether by sea or air. The Council was the first such national body to be formed but, under the stimulus of organizations such as the International Chamber of Commerce and UNCTAD, the movement has spread rapidly in the last 20 years and there are few significant trading countries which do not now possess one. Since the early sixties, the movement has become particularly strong in Western Europe where there are now 14 national councils, many of whose activities are coordinated through an International Secretariat at the Hague.

Until the beginning of 1979, the British Shippers' Council was one of two national transport users organizations in the country. The other is the Freight Transport Association. In 1978, it was decided to effect a merger between the two organizations so as to form a single national transport users organization, embracing all modes of transport of goods, whether by road, rail, inland waterway, sea or air. The merger took effect from 1st January 1979 and will undoubtedly bring about a strengthening of both organizations and of the voice of the user of freight transport by whatever mode. Outwardly the Council will retain its name and separate identity in its relationships with government, shipping and air lines, port authorities, etc.

About 90% by value, and a much higher percentage by volume, of our overseas trade is still carried by sea. The remainder is carried by air. It is thus natural and inevitable that the main emphasis of the Council's work has been with the problems and costs of the sea carriage of our goods but, in recent years, much more attention has been given to the interests of the air shipper. It is fair to say also that the majority of our export trade is sold on CIF or similar terms, and even where goods are sold ex-works or FOB, it is frequently the case that the seller acts as agent for the buyer in arranging the shipment. Thus, no matter what the terms of sale, the exporter nearly always has a direct interest in the cost of the overseas movement of his goods and in the efficiency with which they are handled and carried, so that their delivered price may be competitive in overseas markets and commercial goodwill may be maintained by the assurance that deliveries arrive on time and in good condition. These considerations tend to place the main emphasis of the Council's work on our export trades, though there are aspects of it which also benefit importers.

Nowadays, the exporter has a wide variety of choice in the services available to him to carry his goods, whether by sea or air. Our entry into the European Community has resulted in a much larger proportionate growth in our trade with Western Europe than with other parts of the world. There is an abundance of ferry services from a wide range of ports to all parts of the Continent and, through the use of groupage and through transport operators, goods can be transported quickly from the consignors warehouse in the UK direct to the point of delivery in Europe without ever leaving their trailer. Strictly speaking, the Council is only concerned with the sea voyage part of this operation but inevitably the problems and cost of the whole movement become increasingly under scrutiny as the techniques and services are further developed. At present, the ferry operators consist of individual lines operating a range of routes in competition with each other. They tend to regard their main customers as the road haulage operators rather than the cargo owner himself. It is the latter, however, which the Council represents and the Council, in common with several other Councils on the Continent, has recently been giving much greater attention to the ever rising costs of moving goods to and from the Continent.

The majority of British exports of manufacturered goods to deep-sea destinations is carried by liner shipping operating within the conference system. Relationships with the shipping conferences have lain at the centre of the Council's work for many years and this has developed into a close and continuing process of consultation under a voluntary commercial Code of Practice negotiated within Europe in 1971. This code, which is distinct from that published by UNCTAD in 1974, has undoubtedly served a major purpose over the last 7-8 years in trying to get the interests of shippers and shipowners on a far better mutual understanding to the undoubted benefit of international trade. It is not a perfect instrument since there are several conferences who do not accept it owing, principally, to governmental regulation in varying degree at the far end of the trade routes. It is notable that relationships with these conferences are less constructive than they are in those trades where the code is fully accepted and implemented.

In the last few years the growth of protectionism by national governments over their shipping industries, the inrease in flag discrimination and cargo reservation measures and the impact of the intervention by Soviet Bloc shipping in the Western liner trades have all combined to bring sea transport to a much more prominent position in international political debate. As the representative body of users of sea transport, the Council has of late found itself much more engaged in promoting policies and attitudes towards these developments, often in close consultation with the shipping industry itself, and in offering advice and comment to the Government.

The Council plays a somewhat similar role in the field of air freighting but here the circumstances are notably different from those which attach to the sea carriage of goods. National airlines are themselves in most cases owned or partly owned by governments and the latter, therefore, have a direct interest in their well-being and profitability. The determination of services and rates for the carriage of air cargo has until recently laid almost exclusively with IATA, subject to governmental approval of the former's proposals. Whilst theoretically shippers have had a voice with which to influence IATA through the International Chamber of Commerce this has not been heard with as much strength as air shippers would desire and, in recent years, the Council has, therefore, sought to influence these matters by direct discussion with the Civil Aviation Authority.

The Council can claim to have played a major part in the last few years in influencing official policy to the benefit of those who choose to send their cargo by air. We have been concerned to see that the structure of air freight rates is designed to encourage the maximum utilization of space in passenger carrying aircraft and in the promotion of rating policies to that end. These ideas are now beginning to see fruition, most notably on the important North Atlantic route.

The third, most important role of the Council lies in the field of trade documentation and procedures. By bringing together shippers from many different organizations and backgrounds in committee, the Council is able to offer a body of experience unequalled in the country on these most complicated but vital matters. The Council has had the closest association with SITPRO and it is represented on many of the committees and working groups which that organization has set up. It is similarly represented on the consultative committees of HM customs and Excise and it thus able to exert a very powerful influence on official policy affecting trade documentation generally.

As the representative of the owners of cargo, the Council can claim to be one of the two chief interests in the operation of British ports, the other being the shipowners. The Council has sought to develop more consultative arrangements between port users and port managements so that the latter can make reasoned judgements about future developments and can be kept aware of the effects of their pricing and charges structure in the interests of users. Owing to the large number of British ports, consultative arrangements of a formal character tend to exist chiefly at the larger ports but the Council, through a series of regional committees, has established relationships with all the ports of significance to British shippers. Besides this, shippers have an abiding interest in Government policy towards the ports industry and the Council has played an influential part in recent years in influencing Government policy towards the industry.

Finally, the Council acts as the focus of the shippers' viewpoint in determining changes to international conventions and other legislation affecting the carriage and insurance of goods by sea and air. The growth of international interest through the United Nations Agencies of UNCTAD and UNCITRAL in these matters is reflected in the revision of the Hague and Hague/Visby Rules on the Carriage of Goods By Sea which resulted from the UN Conference at Hamburg in March 1977. Similar preparatory work is being undertaken to prepare a Convention under UN auspices governing multi-modal transport. The Council is represented within the British Maritime Law Association which acts as a co-ordinating body of all interests involved in these matters for advice to HM Government and in the international field.

BRITISH STANDARDS INSTITUTION — TECHNICAL HELP TO EXPORTERS (THE)

In 1966 the Technical Help to Exporters (THE) service of the British Standards Institution was inaugurated. Its purpose was to provide assistance to UK manufacturers on foreign technical requirements. Today, the THE provides a versatile consultancy service identifying relevant documents, supplying them in both the original language and translation, and interpreting them in terms of manufacturer's individual products. In brief, it is establishing the importing country's technical regulations.

Many UK exporters are unaware that a multitude of standards, technical regulations, codes of practice and approval procedures for products is in force in other countries. Failure to produce goods that comply with these requirements can result in expensive delays, costly modifications to equipment, cancellation of orders and perhaps even prosecution.

Ignorance of these requirements is one problem, but finding out where to obtain copies of the regulations and then identifying those that are relevant to a particular product is an even bigger headache that can be very expensive. The British Standards Institution operates an independent service, Technical Help to Exporters (THE), which is geared specifically to supply exporters with information on all aspects of overseas technical requirements, and so help them gain the most favourable marketing situation for their product.

Since its inception, THE's team of qualified specialist engineers has established personal contact and communication with foreign standards bodies, regulative authorities and approval and certification organizations. Knowing where to look and who to speak to enables THE to obtain up-to-date information easily, quickly and cheaply. This, and other information that is constantly being accumulated, is stored in a data bank incorporating a retrieval system that facilitates rapid reference.

Over the years, THE has acquired a wide-based knowledge of overseas technical requirements and procedures and is, therefore, in a prime position to assist exporters with any problems that these requirements may present. Assistance is provided by a number of special services given below:

(1) Enquiries. This service deals specifically with the minor day-to-day queries of the British exporter.

(2) Consultancy. THE engineers are available to visit manufacturers in a consultancy capacity to discuss particular problems and examine equipment to determine whether it complies with the relevant foreign requirements.

(3) Technical research. THE will undertake major investigations on particular subjects to customers' specific requirements. These may involve visits to the relevant country or countries and lengthy discussions with the appropriate authorities.

(4) Translations. Over 5000 English translations of foreign standards, codes of practice and other technical requirements are available. THE will also translate such documents on request.

In addition to these specific services, there is a wide range of THE publications for sale containing essential information on worldwide regulations. THE also sells official standards of overseas authorities, such as the Swedish Pressure Vessel Code, the American Society of Mechanical Engineers (ASME) Code, and the Standards of the American Petroleum Institute (API).

Assistance in obtaining test certificates or approval for products in overseas markets is another important service, and wherever possible, THE can arrange for testing and inspection of products to be carried out in the UK.

THE has an extensive library which contains a unique collection of over 15000 documents covering information on more than 160 countries. Staffed by a team of specialist librarians, the library service is available only to members of THE.

THE membership, which is on a company basis, is open to any UK manufacturer or company for an annual fee. Membership offers exporters distinct advantages. Members' enquiries take priority over others and those which can be answered by telephone are free. Although members may be charged and non-members are always charged for using THE services, charges for members are at a substantially reduced rate and have the advantage of the invoicing facility. In addition, a quarterly bulletin, containing topical news and advance export information, together with a publications catalogue detailing all the publications available from THE, are sent to members free of charge.

The services of THE not only offer exporters the chance to 'get it right' first time. They also ultimately save them from losing their reputation as well as their profit. Exporters can obtain further information on THE services from the Promotion Services Department, British Standards Institution, Hemel Hempstead, Herts.

CENTRAL OFFICE OF INFORMATION (COI)

The Central Office of Information (COI) is the Government's publicity overseas production agency. Acting on behalf of the Foreign and Commonwealth Office and the British Overseas Trade Board, it deploys a variety of publicity media to maintain and increase industrial prestige abroad. The services operated by COI are sent to UK diplomatic missions overseas. This material is handled there by the diplomatic officer responsible for information work, whose purpose is to get the maximum effective publicity for Britain.

Over two-thirds of the COI's overseas output is connected with exports, both visible and invisible. The COI draws not only on the prestige but also on the new products and processes of industry to demonstrate by specific examples the excellence of design, the ingenuity of British industry and the high quality of the end product; in other words, to show that Britain is a good country to trade with. To get this message across, the COI employs professional experts — journalists, photographers, radio and television producers, graphic artists and so on — whose material has to be topical and of professional quality as it is to be used by the world media.

The COI has nine regional offices in England, staffed by professional journalists who can give exporters immediate advice on what help can be offered. The Scottish, Welsh and Northern Ireland Information Offices act similarly on the COI's behalf. The COI headquarters in London is divided into craft or pròduction divisions, each specializing in the provision of a particular kind of material or services. These are outlined below.

Over 15 000 news stories on industry and research are sent out each year by fast transmission and airmail as part of a daily news and information service. These stories are reproduced in newspapers and periodicals throughout the world. A features service provides editors with fuller treatment on important themes. About three-quarters of the material is concerned with particular events or products. Publicity is provided for over 250 of the overseas joint ventures organized by the British Overseas Trade Board and for some 150 outward trade missions each year. Over 3000 new product and processes stories are produced each year for use in trade and technical journals. For those countries which do not have a well developed trade press, illustrated sheets giving technical descriptions of new products and printed in a number of languages are sent direct to individual businessmen, purchasing agencies, chambers of commerce and interested companies.

Several thousand programme items are recorded each year for incorporation in broadcasts by overseas radio stations. This material is used extensively in trade promotion particularly, for instance, in support of outward trade missions. A fast 'newsline' service feeds special short interviews direct by line or satellite into foreign radio stations for use in newscasts or news commentaries.

Nearly half a million black and white and colour prints, as well as 500 colour transparencies are sent out each year in support of trade and industry. These are either taken by the COI's expert staff photographers or obtained from industry itself. Of these nearly a quarter of a million are issued in the form of fully captioned press prints in a targeted daily service to 100 countries. In addition copies of industrial and scientific pictures are given worldwide distribution in the form of colour photoposters. The COI also supplies printing blocks in lightweight plastic (suitable for airmail) to those countries where block making is difficult.

About 1000 major industrial stories are carried each year in the COI's television services, which include a science and technology series and a steady flow of news items and short features. Documentary films produced by industry are acquired by the COI for overseas distribution, and some films can be dubbed in the languages spoken in the target areas.

The COI co-operates closely with the London-based correspondents of other countries and with visiting television teams, providing them with facilities to help them report on British industrial and technical developments.

Reference Division supplies the factual data about Britain — its leaders, institutions, economy and way of life. Nearly one-quarter of its output is concerned with science, technology, industry and related subjects. The annual publication 'Britain' — a compendium of basic facts and figures — is presented free to many influential overseas contacts. Reference papers and fact sheets on key industries are produced regularly for overseas distribution. Regular series on current affairs and technology, serve to keep these updated and diplomatic posts informed of developments in industry.

The COI produces supplements for publication in specialized overseas journals giving in-depth descriptions of British industries and timed to coincide with trade events in which British firms are participating. Booklets, brochures and catalogues are also produced for use at overseas fairs and seminars. Special trade magazines are produced in Farsi for Iran and in Arabic for Middle East countries.

The COI arranges tours in Britian for leaders of opinion from overseas. These visitors, who are sponsored by the Foreign and Commonwealth Office, include politicians, businessmen, senior officials, trade unionists, editors and so on. About 3000 come to Britain each year and COI Tours Division organizes their programmes, escorts them and makes all the necessary arrangements.

Most tours include visits to factories and the research establishments of firms of actual or potential export interests in the countries from which the visitors have come. The aim is to demonstrate Britain's industrial achivements and technology and that she is a good trading partner. Many firms have had new export fields opened up to them as a result of meeting these visitors.

The COI Exhibitions Division is responsible for the design, production and management of official exhibitions (other than trade fairs) overseas. They include prestige/information exhibitions to show the excellence of British design and products, and the planning of British pavilions at world fairs.

It maintains a close liaison with British industry. Overall, it is in contact with over 10000 firms in the country and handles features from about 3000-4000 of them each year. The COI wants to hear from British industry about new or improved products and processes, large export orders, record outputs, membership of outward trade missions and participation in overseas trade fairs, overseas visitors to Britain and visits overseas by British executives. Material accepted for issue in the overseas services is prepared, according to the form in which it will be used, by the appropriate media division. COI publicity does not attempt to replace a firm's own efforts — it is up to British industry to sell the goods — but it does complement it by helping to shape receptivity to British industry and its products.

CONFEDERATION OF BRITISH INDUSTRY (CBI)

The Confederation of British Industry was founded in 1965 and is an independent non-party political body financed entirely by industry and commerce. It is the principal focal point for the British Business community's views and exists primarily to ensure that UK Governments of all political complexions understand the needs, intentions and problems of British business. The CBI has more than 13 000 individual companies and more than 200 trade associations, employer organizations and commercial associations. It covers all sectors of business, from manufacturing to agriculture, construction to distribution, and mining to finance.

The CBI devotes a significant part of its efforts and resources to fostering the overseas business of British industry and commerce. In this respect, its principle overseas role lies in the field of policy and representation as regards the UK's commercial relations with other countries and international organizations concerned with trade and investment. It is less directly concerned with export promotion which is the responsibility of the official Government services. However, the CBI is involved both in advice to those Government services, through active membership of the British Overseas Trade Board, the British Overseas Trade Advisory Council and the area advisory groups, and in support of non-official trade organizations.

The CBI issues a number of publications including a monthly publication on topics of importance to international business. Each issue contains some six reports on selected overseas countries and markets and are based mainly on material obtained from CBI overseas representatives, supplemented by information from the CBI headquarters resources and activities.

DEPARTMENT OF THE ENVIRONMENT

If an exporter decides to provide, without the help and expertise of a freight forwarder or road haulier, a door to door delivery service to overseas customers or to carry exhibition material overseas in his own vehicle, it will be necessary to ensure the operation complies with the road transport requirements of the countries concerned. It is essential to ensure that documentation is satisfactorily completed for both the goods and the vehicle before leaving the country. This should include any arrangements for giving security for duty, for example, in the form of a bank guarantee, to the Customs authorities of the countries through which the goods and vehicles will pass, or any other alternative Customs facilities which can be arranged in advance. This involves particularly TIR and ATA carnets.

If an exporter is carrying goods abroad by road outside EEC countries in a container or a road vehicle, it is often helpful to obtain a TIR (transport international routier) carnet and have the vehicle or container sealed by the Customs before export from the UK. This procedure, prescribed under the TIR convention to which most European countries have acceded, permit goods to be carried from any approved Customs office of departure in the UK to any Customs office of destination abroad, with a minimum of Customs examination and documentation. Under TIR, the payment or deposit of duties in intermediate transit countries is also waived. Detailed information about the TIR scheme is given in HM Customs and Excise Notice No. 464.

To benefit from the TIR procedure, however, the goods must be carried in vehicles or containers which have been approved as meeting the Convention's construction and equipment requirements and which are covered by a TIR carnet issued by an approved guaranteeing association. The Department of the Environment Traffic Area provides leaflets detailing the technical requirements and the procedure for obtaining the necessary certificate of approval for the vehicle or container. Once the certificate has been obtained, the operator can apply for a TIR carnet to one of the guaranteeing associations approved in the UK, such as, the Freight Transport Association or Road Haulage Association. Details of their addresses are found in Appendix B. It must be borne in mind the TIR carnet gives no right to operate — it is purely a Customs facility.

If an exporter wishes to transport dangerous goods by road, for example, explosives, inflammable items, radio active substances etc, it will be necessary to ensure the operation complies with the European agreement in the international carriage of dangerous goods by road (ADR) as explained in Chapter 6, pages 86-94. Further information is available from the Dangerous Goods Division, Department of the Environment, whose London address is found in Appendix B of this book.

Insofar as the ATA carnets are concerned, these are international Customs documents issued by Chamber of Commerce in most major countries throughout the world. The carnets facilitate Customs clearance of certain classes of temporary importations and exportations by replacing the following:

(a) The normal Customs documentation in the country of temporary exportation and

(b) The normal Customs documentation and security, for example, by bond or deposit in the country of temporary importation.

Carnets do not, however, confer immunity from other conditions of temporary exportation or temporary importation. Further details are found in HM Customs Notice No. 104 whose address is found in Appendix B of this book.

Most countries require foreign operators to comply with their domestic laws on, for example, insurance, vehicles loads, vehicle construction, speed limits, and drivers' hours and records. Some countries restrict the movement of commercial vehicles on Sundays and public holidays. It is usually necessary to obtain a licence or permit to operate in each country but where a bilaterial road haulage agreement is in force these permits, where still required, are issued by the International Road Freight Office whose address is found in Appendix B. Where no bilateral agreement is in force it is necessary to apply to the appropriate transport authority in the country concerned.

The foregoing explain the role of the Department of the Environment as a specialist to facilitate international road transport. Mention is also made of related organizations. Further details relative to the British goods vehicles making journeys overseas is found in Chapter 7, pages 129-134.

FOREIGN AND COMMONWEALTH OFFICE

Export promotion is a major function of British Embassies, High Commissions and Consulates abroad, accounting for approximately one third of the staff at overseas posts engaged on operational tasks. Nearly 1500 staff abroad are employed on this work, from small one-man Consulates to large integrated Commercial Departments in major Embassies. These Commercial Officers are the field force of the official network for economic and commercial intelligence and for the promotion overseas of British visible and invisible trade. About three-quarters are locally engaged officers, specializing in export promotion work in the country concerned, and the remainder are United Kingdom-based members of the Diplomatic Service, who may spend up to four years at any one post. Together they operate as integrated and balanced teams combining a breadth of experience in their full-time commitment to fostering, maintaining and developing close and continuous relationships with the local, business, banking and commercial community and with the government, public sector and institutional organizations.

Operating as the overseas arm of the Department of Trade and the British Overseas Trade Board Services for exporters, commercial officers seek out and report back information of every kind from early warnings of prospective openings for UK exports of goods and services to specific and detailed items which supply the reservoir of the Export Intelligence Service and other BOTB services for exporters. Working in close collaboration with Export Services and Promotions Division of the Department of Trade, the Commercial Departments ensure that changes in overseas tariff and import regulations are notified promptly, market appraisals provided and export opportunities discovered and reported. From their everyday contact in the overseas markets, they help UK firms to find suitable agents, representatives, distributors and associates for joint venture partnerships. They assist in the arrangement of seminars to promote the interests of the invisibles sector and, in certain countries, they are charged additionally with promoting inward investment by foreign interests into the UK. Commercial Departments give UK business visitors all possible assistance, advice and introduction and provide servicing points for UK exhibitors at the principal trade fairs abroad. Commercial officers on home duty tours undertake programmes of visits to individual firms interested in their market and, when circumstances allow, are available for consultation at chambers of commerce or export-orientated organizations.

The Information Services (Foreign and Commonwealth Office Information Departments and the Central Office of Information in London, and Information Officers abroad) provide an essential back-up to the export promotion effort. An estimated two-thirds of the current information operation is directed in support of British trade and industry. This is done by projecting an image of the UK as a reliable trading partner with vigorous and forward-looking industries and by precisely targetted work in support of exporters. By these means, working in close co-operation with the commercial services, the information services work to create a climate of confidence in the British economy against which British exporters can sell their goods.

GENERAL COUNCIL OF BRITISH SHIPPING

The General Council of British Shipping was formed in 1975 as the national organization representing British shipowners. Formerly, two organizations existed viz. the Chamber of Shipping and the British Shipping Federation.

The Council discusses and formulates the general policy of the industry, represents the industry in discussion with the Government, deals with a great variety of technical and commercial questions, and seafarers matters on a national level. Its aim is to create and maintain these conditions for the operation of shipping throughout the world. The Council does not deal with the day to day commercial operation of ships or the running of the individual shipping companies. Above all, its aim is to serve the industry in the range, variety and complexity of the problems with which the Council is confronted.

INTER-GOVERNMENTAL MARITIME CONSULTATIVE ORGANIZATION (IMCO)

The Inter-Governmental Maritime Consultative Organization (IMCO) is the specialized agency of the United Nations concerned solely with maritime affairs. Its interest lies basically in ships used in international services. Some 86 states are members of the IMCO including shipowning nations, countries which use shipping services and countries in the course of development.

Its objectives are to facilitate co-operation among governments on technical matters affecting shipping, to ensure the achievement of the highest possible standards of life at sea and of efficient navigation. This entails providing an extensive exchange of information between nations in technical maritime subjects and concluding international agreements.

IMCO is a forum where its members can exchange information and endeavour to solve problems connected with maritime, technical and legal matters. It makes recommendations on maritime questions submitted by its member states or by other members of the United Nations family. IMCO is responsible for covering and preparing international conferences in subjects within its sphere of action for the purpose of concluding international conventions or agreements.

INTERNATIONAL AIR TRANSPORT ASSOCIATION

The International Air Transport Association (IATA) was founded in 1946 by the airlines of many countries to meet the problems created by the rapid expansion of civil air services at the close of the Second World War in 1946. It is the successor in function of the previous International Air Traffic Organization arranged at the Hague at the very dawn of regular air transport in 1919. As a non-governmental organization it draws its legal existence from an act of the Canadian parliament given Royal Assent in December 1945.

In both its organization and activity, IATA has been closely associated with the International Civil Aviation Organization (ICAO), also established in 1945, the international agency of governments which create world standards for the technical regulation of civil aviation.

IATA is a voluntary, non-exclusive, non-political and democratic organization. Membership is automatically open to any operating company which has been licensed to provide scheduled air services by a government eligible for membership of ICAO airlines directly engaged in international operations are active members, while domestic airlines are associate members.

The IATA is the world organization of scheduled airlines. Its members carry the bulk of the worlds scheduled international and domestic air traffic under the flags of some 55 countries. To ensure that people, cargo and mail can move anywhere on this vast global network as easily as though they were on a single airline within a single country, is IATA's commercial objective.

IATA furnishes the medium for negotiation of international rates and fares agreements. It provides the only practicable way of drawing upon the experience and expertise of the airlines. It helps to carry the fast and economical transport of international air mail and make certain the needs of commerce, safety and convenience to the public are served at all times.

The basic source of authority in IATA is the annual general meeting in which all active members have an equal vote. Year round policy direction is provided by an elected Executive Committee and its creative work is largely carried out by its Financial, Legal, Technical and Traffic Committees. Negotiation of fares and rates is entrusted to the IATA Traffic Conferences with separate conferences considering passenger and cargo matters, and establishing agreements valid for periods of two years.

The IATA administration is headed by a Director General and seven Assistant Ditrectors General. The Association has two main offices, one in Montreal and another in Geneva. Regional Technical Directors are based in Bangkok, Geneva, London, Nairobi and Rio de Janeiro, and Regional Directors (Special Assignments) in Singapore and Buenos Aires. IATA Traffic Services offices are located in New York and Singapore.

IATA's most complex role is in the field of traffic — a term which embraces the commercial activities of the airlines. As an airline association, IATA is particularly concerned with facilitating interline arrangements: the standardization of forms, procedures, handling agreements and the like, which allow quick and easy exchange of traffic between airlines. Beyond this, however, IATA is also a quasi-public agency to which many governments have delegated the responsibility for negotiating international agreements on international rates and fares subject to their approval.

To weld its member airlines into a single network, IATA has produced a series of interline agreements between them (to which many non-IATA and domestic airlines and sea carriers are parties as well) covering all phases of passenger, baggage and cargo handling, reservations codes and related matters. In increasingly more of these areas, IATA works to adopt these forms and procedures by computer and teletype.

Such arrangements are normally worked out under the guidance of the Traffic Committee and various expert working groups, and by the Assistant Director General of Traffic and his staff, often with assistance of other standing committees. Actual application, however, comes about mainly through formal resolutions which are subject to the approval of governments.

The Traffic Conferences process arises from the peculiar nature of air transport. Each Government reserves complete control over its own share of the airspace and the right to determine what its air services may charge the public. International fares and rates, and the conditions which underlie them, must therefore be fixed by international agreements in which virtually every country has some direct or indirect concern.

For administration purposes, there are three Traffic Conference areas: No. 1 for the Western Hemisphere, Greenland and the Hawaiian Islands; No. 2 for Europe, Africa and the Middle East including Iran; and No. 3 for Asia, Australasia and South Pacific.

Conference work is organized within the framework of these areas or on an inter-conference basis but, bearing in mind the inter-relation of fare and rates throughout the world, it is generally advisable that all these conference sessions be held at the same time and in the same place.

World wide composite conference meetings are normally held every two years: in the autumn to review rates and fares for passenger operations, and in the spring to consider matters involving air cargo. Special meetings can be called in the interval, however, and action can be taken immediately by mail vote subject to the same rules of unanimity and governmental approval.

The work load of the conferences has been spread since the establishment of the permanent traffic conference committees which deal with traffic handling procedures, and agency matters except for fares, rates and commissions. The resulting structure of the IATA traffic conference agreements now comprises about 1500 resolutions, incorporating specified and constructed fares and rates between some 200 000 pairs of points on the world network, involving some 200 countries of airline operation.

There is no doubt IATA has made an outstanding contribution to the development of International Commercial Civil Aviation and will continue to do so.

LINER CONFERENCES

The Liner Conference is an organization whereby a number of shipowners offer their services in a given sea route on conditions agreed by the members. Conferences are semi-monopolistic associations of shipping lines formed for the purpose of restricing competition between their members and protecting them from outside competition. Conference agreements may also regulate sailings and ports of call, and, in some cases, arrangements are made for the pooling of net earnings. Conferences achieve their object by controlling prices and by limiting entry to the trade. Their chief policy is to establish a common tariff of freight rates and passenger fares for the trade involved, members being left free to compete for traffic by the quality and efficiency of their service. The organization of a conference varies from one trade to another. It may consist of informal regular meetings of shipowners at which rates and other matters of policy are discussed, or it may involve a formal organization with a permanent secretariat and prescribed rules for membership, together with stipulated penalties for violations of agreement. Members are often required to deposit a cash bond to cover fines in respect of non-compliance with their obligations of such conferences which are international in character. For example, the Far East Freight Conference, which operates in the Far East/European trade, comprises British, French, Dutch, Italian, Swedish, Danish and Japanese lines. Shipping lines often belong to several conferences and there are several inter-conference agreements. In most cases, conference policy is decided by the votes of the members. Conference rights have a market value when shipping lines are sold.

In some conferences, there exists a pooling agreement whereby traffic or gross or net earnings in the trade are pooled, members receiving agreed percentages of the pool. The object of such an arrangement is to guarantee to members a certain share of the trade and to limit competition. It leads to the regulation of sailings and may, in some circumstances, enable the trade to be rationalized. Pools are becoming more common, even in the British trades, where shipowners normally prefer to establish an agreed tariff and permit competition in quality of service. An excess of tonnage in a particular trade may very likely lead to an agreed reduction in the number of sailings and pooling of receipts. Often, when conferences perform special services, such as lifting unprofitable cargo or resorting to chartering to cover temporary shortages of tonnage, they pool the losses or profits on such operations.

The objects of the Liner Conferences are to provide a service adequate to meet the trade requirements; to avoid wasteful competition among members by regulating loading; to organize themselves so that the conference can collectively combat outside competition; and to maintain a tariff by mutual agreement as stable as conditions will permit.

The main advantages claimed for the conference system are as follows:

(1) Avoidance of wasteful competition.

(2) The reasonable assurance that members have a good chance of realizing a profit, and there are no rate wars, as freight rates are determined by the conference.

(3) Stability of rates which enables manufacturers and merchants to make forward contracts for goods and so diminishes undesirable risk and uncertainty in international trade.

(4) Regular and frequent sailings which enable the shipper/exporter to plan his supplies to overseas markets and avoid the need to

carry large stocks with the risk of obsolescence, commodity deterioration and the operator to maximize the use of his vessels.

(5) Equality of treatment, that is, the rate quoted applies to all shippers whether they are large or small.

(6) Economies of service which enable operators to concentrate on providing faster and better ships.

The disadvantage from the shipper's point of view arises from the fact that, if he is tied to a particular conference, he cannot take advantage of tramp tonnage when rates are low. Moreover, if he is a large shipper he often cannot use his superior bargaining power to obtain lower rates. Carriers who are not members of a conference object to the system because it prevents their competing successfully with conference vessels.

During 1955, the British Shippers' Council was formed with the object 'to further the interests of exporters and importers in the United Kingdom in relation to the transportation of goods by sea and air'. This resulted in the emergence of a new era of joint consultation between the Shippers' Council and liner conferences. The Council participated in the formulation of the liner conference machinery of consultation between shipowners and shippers, to consider representations from a shipper or trade association which cannot be resolved by an individual shipowner.

In 1963, there was a major step forward when the European Shippers Councils and European Shipowners' Associations (CENSA) agreed a 'note of understanding' to govern their consultation arrangements. It resulted in the setting up of a number of joint European committees and working groups to resolve matters of mutual concern and agree on recommendations to which shipper and shipowners comply.

By 1978, 18 European countries each had National Shippers' Councils and the movement has spread widely overseas. The European Shippers' Councils confer regularly with Council of European and Japanese National Shipowner's Associations (CENSA) in matters of mutual interest, their work being co-ordinated by a small international secretariat at The Hague.

Associated with liner conferences are the deferred rebate and contract systems. The deferred rebate is a device to ensure that shippers will continue to support a conference. A shipper who ships exclusively by conference vessels can, at the end of a certain period (usually six months), claim a rebate, usually 10% of the freight money paid by him during the period. Hence the shipper has an inducement to remain loyal to the conference insofar as he stands to lose a rebate by a non-conference vessel. This system is described as the deferred rebate and has tended to become less popular in some trades in recent years due to the high cost of clerical administration. Accordingly, it has been substituted, under the same code of loyalty conditions, by the immediate rebate system. This is a somewhat lower rebate, maybe 9½%, but granted at the time freight payment is made and not some six months later with the deferred rebate system.

A further way of retaining the shipper's patronage of a conference is by the contract or special contract agreement systems. The contract system is for a shipper who signs a contract to forward all his goods by conference line vessels either in the general course of business, or perhaps associated with a special project over a certain period. The particular contract concerned may be associated with a large hydroelectric scheme, for example, and the goods would then probably be special equipment. Under this system, the shipper would be granted a cheaper freight rate than a non-contract shipper. In addition, there are the special commodity agreements which are specially negotiated between the trade and conference to cover goods shipped in large quantities and often for short duration. The shipper may be forwarding a commodity such as copper, tea, rubber, foodstuffs or cotton, in considerable quantities.

The shippers' criticism of the deferred rebate system is that it enables conferences to build up monopolies tending to keep rates at a high level. Furthermore, the shipper is reluctant to use outside tonnage for fear of loss of rebate and the system thus restricts his freedom of action. Another point is that a record must be kept of all freight paid subject to rebate to enable claims to be made in due course. This involves clerical expenses, and moreover, the shipper contends that he is out of pocket to the extent of the interest on the rebate while it is in the carrier's hands. So far as the carrier is concerned, the retention of the rebate for the appropriate period has the added advantage of an automatic deterrent to shippers using non-conference vessels. In fact, it can be a very strong weapon, as the carrier is the sole arbitrator in deciding whether or not any shipper's rebate should be forfeited. The carrier also finds it easy to maintain rebate records in his manifest freight books and, by virtue of the amount of work involved, finds it convenient to have a small rebate department. He maintains that there is no compulsion on the shipper to remain with the conference, although of course if he chooses to ship outside it, the shipper will forfeit his rebate. A shipper who forfeits his rebate has, after all, had the benefits of conference shipment which he later discards for something he considers better.

LONDON CHAMBER OF COMMERCE AND INDUSTRY

The London Chamber of Commerce was founded in 1881 and today is the largest Chamber in Britain. It has two main functions: to protect the domestic trade interests of commerce and industry in London and the South East, and to develop the international trade of all British companies. An examination will be made of the latter.

The Chamber has a membership of some 8600 firms covering all business sectors. Its operations are divided into departments embracing International, Export Services, Home Affairs, Economic, Press, Administration, Membership, Finance and Trade Sections.

The London Chamber issues export documents and these include primarily certificates of origin, ATA carnets, national standard shipping note, movement certificates, cocoa certificates and the certification of commercial invoices. The Chamber is the UK guarantor for ATA carnets which allow the temporary importation into other countries of certain types of goods.

The Chamber deals with a wide range of enquiries concerning Customs and Regulations, legislation and regulations both in Britain and throughout the world. It also deals with tariffs and the general rules and conditions governing the movement and finance of export and imports.

The London Chamber is one of Britain's most active trade promotion organizations. These activities are the responsibility of the International Division and its 28 market sections. The sections which are grouped together in six area divisions bring together member firms with common interest in a specific geographical market. The five overseas divisions include Africa and Middle East, Asia and Pacific, Eastern Europe, Western Europe and Western Hemisphere. The sixth division deals with requirements of overseas members.

Each of the six area divisions has a separate membership. A fortnightly digest of commercial intelligence is prepared for each of the five overseas divisions, summarising trade developments and acting as a link with members. A full programme of conferences, meetings, missions and other activities is organized, and advice and information on overseas markets and the UK is available.

The information department of the Chamber also gives details on Customs and Regulations; openings for trade; translation bureau; members' libary, telephone enquiry service and special certification. Additionally, the Chamber offers extensive training facilities including conducting its own examinations in many commercial subjects including international trade.

The Exhibition department organizes British participation in overseas trade fairs as joint ventures with the British Overseas Trade Board. Special services for smaller companies going into export include market feasibility studies; small firms trade missions and group market research schemes. A Business Travel Service is also provided which aims to provide a comprehensive service of business travel schemes to all parts of the world.

In tracing the international orientated activities of the London Chamber of Commerce and Industry, it must be borne in mind it is the largest in Great Britain. However, most major cities/towns have a Chamber, but the extent of their services is not so great other than those found in the major cities such as Birmingham, Liverpool, Manchester, Glasgow, Edinburgh, etc. Nevertheless, the exporter is well advised to contact his nearest Chamber if he is seeking advice on any aspect of international trade.

NATIONAL PORTS COUNCIL

The National Ports Council had its origins in the concern expressed in Parliament and elsewhere in the early 1960s, as to the adequacy of Britain's ports to meet the needs of the nation's expanding post-war trade. This led to the decision of Mr Ernest Marples, when Minister of Transport, to appoint a Committee of Inquiry in March 1961, to examine the adequacy of the major ports. Chaired by Viscount Rochdale, the committee reported in 1962. Its recommendations led to the passing of the Harbours Act in 1964 and the setting up of the National Ports Council with Lord Rochdale as its first chairman.

The Committee had found that there was indeed a cause for concern about the adequacy of port facilities to meet national requirements. They pointed out that since World War II capital expenditure had been devoted mainly to minor projects and that, except for facilities under construction on the Tees, no single additional deep-water berth for general cargo had been started since the 1930s. There was a particular and pressing need for additional such berths to be constructed.

The Rochdale Report advocated the establishment of a National Ports Authority whose major functions would be the control and supervision of major port development in accordance with a national plan. Other functions proposed related to the amalgamation of ports, port statutes, port charges, training and research. In the event, the Government of the day preferred to retain in its own hands the final decision on major issues of port organization and development and, instead of the authority envisaged by the Committee, they decided to set up the essentially advisory National Ports Council with only very limited executive powers. The port authorities themselves remained, and still are, operationally autonomous.

The future of the port industry and the Council has been shrouded in uncertainty since 1966, when the Government of the day announced its intention to nationalize the ports. Some form of nationalization remains the declared objective of the Labour Government. However, because of the pressure on legislative time, there are no firm proposals before the industry at the moment. Meanwhile, the Secretary of State for Transport has recently appointed a new chairman to the Council, Mr John Page. After five years as chairman of the Mersey Docks and Harbour Company, Mr Page is well acquainted with the present day problems and needs of British ports and is thus well placed to give effect to the Secretary of State's wish that the future should see still closer collaboration between the Council and the individual port authorities.

SIMPLIFICATION OF INTERNATIONAL TRADE PROCEDURE BOARD (SITPRO)

SITPRO was set up in June 1970 to 'guide, stimulate and assist' the rationalization of international trade procedures and the information flows associated with them. The Board's members come from a wide range of interests and include shippers, carriers, forwarders, insurers, bankers and Government officials. The staff is small, consisting of a Chief Executive and Secretary with directors and their assistants dealing with various areas of SITPRO activities. The Board is financed by the Department of Trade through an annual grant but is independent within its agreed terms of reference.

SITPRO's work falls under several headings. The central problem is that of procedures. Modern transport methods are serviced by information handling systems which have proven to be inadequate to their task. Traditional systems are costly, complicated and prone to delays and errors, which bring in their train delays to goods out of proportion to their own speed of movement.

Procedures, therefore, have to be rationalized and simplified nationally and internationally. Their point of application in a goods movement is based on traditional cargo intervention points. However, the development of through movement techniques requires the repositioning of official and commercial intervention points. This will in itself bring new relationships and responsibilities to the participants. Its achievement calls for painstaking and continuous negotiation with representative organizations for which SITPRO provides an ideal and generally accepted focal point.

The work takes the form of, initially, studies of procedures and subsequent co-operation with the relevant bodies to carry out rationalization programmes. SITPRO co-operates with other organizations in this field, for instance the Joint Customs Consultative Committee, General Council of British Shipping and British Shippers Council. A large part of the UK's exports are manufactured from imported raw materials and SITPRO is actively investigating facilitation possibilities in this side of international trade.

Procedures are, however, generally represented by documents which have created their own problems and costs. Every effort has, therefore, been made to simplify existing documentation and standardize it on the United Nations ECE Layout Key. The UK now has a fully developed aligned export documentation system, although pressure is constantly kept up for the alignment of further forms. As well as developing and maintaining the system, SITPRO provides an advisory service to enable shippers to instal systems suited to their needs.

The aligned export documentation procedure is based on the 'master' document principle. Under the aligned one run system, as much information as possible is entered on a master document so that all or part of this information can be reproduced mechanically into individual forms of a similar design. This method eliminates repetitive typing and checking. The system offers the following advantages: improved accuracy and complete elimination of variations in detailed information shown on documents relating to any one consignment; quicker and cheaper production of paperwork; elimination of repetitive typing of information onto numerous end-documents and related checking; uniformity of information presentation; easier document handling, filing and reference; and finally, Masters provide a reference for all paper work run off. The latter eliminates the need to produce separate copies of individual documents for future references, often with substantial reductions in filing work.

Paper documents are probably a permanent feature of much international trade, particularly for smaller manufacturers and carriers but, where speed of movement of the goods is at a premium as in air-freight, or where data is highly concentrated in time and space as at major seaports, in banks or Customs departments, the computer is an essential tool. Unfortunately, the informal exchange of information possible by old fashioned documents is impossible for computers, which need standard interfacing elements. Without such elements, all users in international trade would be forced into massive inhouse investment without any possibility of general interchange. Clearly national arrangements, for example, national codes, formats or presentations, would only mitigate and perhaps eventually aggravate this misinvestment. SITPRO is giving priority to the establishment of international standards for computer interchange and is concentrating on this work.

It is also important in EDP (electronic data processing) developments generally to take account of the potential reforming effect on procedures as computer usage procedures have to be written down, spelt out and standardized. This is just the sort of reform needed for procedures in the old-style paperwork system and so SITPRO is at pains to link all procedural improvements to EDP on the one side and persisting paper documentation on the other. SITPRO is also developing a technical advisory service designed to ensure that computer users in the UK benefit from the latest practical experience in adapting their computer systems to deal with international trade procedures and documentation.

The potential benefits of these advances would be lost if SITPRO did not ensure that they were brought to the attention of the international trading community. This is not an easy task given the relative novelty of facilitation work. SITPRO is, therefore, mounting a series of seminars and workshops in particular facilitation applications, such as aligned documentation, Customs procedures and related subjects. Further, SITPRO has a role to play in the preparation of detailed material for use by lecturers and speakers. A programme of audio-visual training aids is being prepared, and several kits are already available. These cover areas of exporting which are thought to have priority. SITPRO also has a central role in informing traders of immediate improvements and publishes information bulletins and leaflets according to need.

The basis of real progress in the last ten years has been made by the formation of national organizations — in many countries these now take the form of SITPRO type bodies. In Eastern Europe, Governments or the very official Chambers of Commerce carry out this work. Because of the nature of international trade, which must always by definition concern at least two countries, international co-operation is essential and merely bilateral arrangements would be hopelessly inadequate and complicated. SITPRO has, therefore, given every support to the work of what used to be the Documentation Working Party in the Economic Commission for Europe in Geneva which, over the last decade, has developed into the Facilitation Working Party with much broader terms of reference. SITPRO also supports UNCTAD in its facilitation programme and sends delegates or supplies officers or special advisers to a very wide range of international bodies, for example, the International Chamber of Commerce, the Customs Co-operation Council, the International Standards Organization, the International Association of Ports and Harbours, the International Association of Forwarding Agents and about 20 others. SITPRO has been instrumental in bringing about the formation of national bodies in a number of countries in Europe and in a few developing countries, for example, India, Nigeria, Kenya, the Philippines and Thailand. SITPRO has also helped set up facilitation organizations in Japan, South Africa, Canada and New Zealand.

PIRA

The Research Association for the Paper and Board, Printing and Packaging Industries (PIRA) is located at Leatherhead, Surrey and offers a wide range of export packaging services to the shipper. PIRA is the UK national technical centre for paper and board, printing and packaging, carrying out research work for the benefit of its members. It also undertakes multi-client research projects for groups of members and confidential sponsored work for individual firms. Other services for management include consultancy, technical enquiry, testing, information, training and techno-economic studies.

Given below is a summary of PIRA services available particularly of interest to exporters:

(1) Courses available for export packaging staff at all levels. These can be arranged either at PIRA premises or in the exporter's own works. In the event, they have proved very popular with exporters and beneficial.

(2) Supply of information on packaging suppliers regulations and appropriate standards.

(3) Measure, test or analyse the properties of packaging materials to enable exporters to prepare adequate specifications; to check that the materials conform to packaging requirements or recognized standards; to assess their ability to withstand transit conditions; and finally, to detect and prevent any harmful effects in a product of a specific packaging material.

(4) To evaluate in laboratory conditions at PIRA the performance of filled packages. This service is particularly useful as it determines adequacy of a simulated international transit for a specified commodity.

(5) To arrange consultancy facilities in, for example, (i) the development of packaging for new products, (ii) in techniques to reduce packaging costs and of improving the protection provided by existing packs, and (iii) how to best organize the packaging activity in the exporter's company.

(6) The Association library provides members with English translations of selected articles on packaging extracted from overseas publications. It also undertakes literature searches and the compilation of bibliographies.

Each month PIRA produces three technical journals: *Paper and*

Board Abstracts, Printing Abstracts, and *Packing Abstracts.* A fourth publication also issued monthly is called *PIRA Management and Marketing Abstracts.*

ROAD HAULAGE ASSOCIATION (RHA)

The assistance given by the RHA to its members in relation to international movement of goods is threefold: by the provision of certain customs documents; by general information on the regulations and conditions in different countries both in Europe and the Middle East; and by representing the British international hauliers' point of view to the Government, EEC and other transport associations in Europe.

The RHA is a member of the International Road Transport Union (IRU) in Geneva, which is the guaranteeing body for the issue of TIR carnets and for guarantee vouchers. The TIR carnet is a very important document which allows vehicles, when properly approved, to pass through foreign frontiers, usually without inspection of the goods, and it also acts as a bond. The RHA is able to make these documents available to those of its members who have provided the appropriate indemnity and enables them to participate in international haulage to countries outside the EEC. Within the EEC, the guarantee voucher provided by the Association acts as a guarantee to support 'T' documents. Both these services are invaluable to hauliers.

The RHA has prepared information sheets on all the countries in Europe and many in the Middle East. These information sheets provide basic information on the need for transport authorizations and where they may be obtained, the regulations governing weights and dimensions of vehicles, traffic restrictions, taxes and other relevant matters. These sheets are regularly revised to take account of changes in different countries. The Association also publishes, from time to time, through circulars and its journal *Road Way,* additional information which it is able to acquire through its close contacts with the Department of Transport in this country and through other transport associations in Europe. Comprehensive information on all aspects of international haulage is, therefore, available to members both through documents and through consultation with officials.

Thirdly, the Association represents the views of international members to the Department of Transport on all legislation affecting this type of operation. Moreover, through its connection with IRU, it is able to make its views known to the EEC Commission in Brussels. This is increasingly important with the introduction of more EEC legislation on road transport. In addition, the Association represents the views of its members to other associations in this country including, of course, the Confederation of British Industry.

CHAPTER 15

Export Research and Marketing

Export market research (scope and objectives). Statistics. Export promotion. Marketing plan. Visits to overseas markets.

EXPORT MARKET RESEARCH
(SCOPE AND OBJECTIVES)

Export Market research is a study of a given market abroad to determine the needs of that market and the methods by which the products can best be supplied. It is intrinsic in this definition that the enquirer starts with a certain product or group of products prescribed in his terms of reference by the exporter, such as, a caravan manufacturer who naturally looks for sales openings for his company, for example, in Holland. The electrical engineer will be looking to the market for opportunities to instal his type of equipment while the constructional engineer would be looking for building projects.

The total market in any given product over a prescribed period is the total sales realized in a defined geographical area, usually a region or country. Export research is concerned with a wide range of products and often tends to be less directed to the point of retail sale. It concerns itself with much more intimacy with the chain of distribution, and covers consumers' semi-durable goods (radios, domestic appliances, cars, etc.) and capital goods (for example, building materials, machinery), as well as mere consumer goods.

For a manufacturer or merchant seeking markets overseas, there are numerous factors which arise that are not encountered in the home market. An examination of such features now follows:

(1) Distance. International distribution arrangements involve many features viz. Customs, marine insurance, extensive documentation, specialized packing, etc. Additionally, international transport distribution cost tends to form a much higher proportion of the total produce cost involved up to 15-20%, reflecting the greater distances involved compared with the home market inland transport arrangements. Market research and operational research can help to determine the most ideal distribution method.

(2) Time. The transit time is a critical factor in planning the distribution arrangements of an international consignment. Generally, international consignments tend to have a longer transit time than ones for the home market, so the production department must plan accordingly to ensure the goods arrive at destination on schedule.

(3) Language. Complications can arise from the use of foreign languages involving labelling changes, special publicity and so on. In some overseas countries, more than one language is used. This presents marketing problems which market research may resolve. It can also give rise in many instances to difficulties in the market research process itself, since the most important part of the research must be carried on in a foreign language. In this area, one must ensure the correct words are used in their own language.

(4) Race and religion. In many overseas countries, difference of race and religion have to be borne in mind in relation to the goods themselves, the presentation of them to the buying public, that is, the packaging, and the publicity approach. It is important to secure the advantages of presentation in a favourable light by using predominantly those colours which are traditionally and emotionally associated with happiness and goodwill.

(5) Local preferences. Quite apart from racial and religious preferences local idiosyncrasies must be discovered by the process of market research in order to set up the most telling form of subsequent approach to the market. For example, the Australians are influenced in their outlook by American sales methods which, in practice, means a higher outlay in publicity than, for example, in Ireland or a Scandinavian country. Moreover, some countries are best approached by radio rather than by newspaper publicity. Similarly, in some places the cinema slide is regarded as part of the entertainment whilst in others it is practically ignored. So far as the products are concerned, and their trade marks and packaging, some things are to be avoided and others exploited. For example, the average hen egg in Egypt is very small so egg cups must be smaller than the UK standard size. Such information would be sought out during the process of market research.

(6) Environmental. Export market research must embrace the study of the climate factors — heat and cold, dryness and humidity, atmospheric densities, rainfall and seasonal sequences. For example

the sweet manufacturer would not market some of his products in a very hot humid climate as the sweets would reach the buyer in rather a sticky mess. Climate conditions are best examined alongside such matters as distances from ports, types of communication, gradients, location of population, airports, etc.

(7) Business practices and credit worthiness etc. This embraces enquiry into the code of legal practice regarding the conduct of business in the overseas country. For example, it would include the giving and implementation of guarantees and warantees connected with the suitability of the goods and performance, for a certain period after sale. Additionally, one would confirm the importer administered his business in an honest and fair way without a taint of corruption.

(8) Scope of market research. The extent and area of the market research must be determined. It may be one country or simply an area or region within a country. Cost and remit terms will play a large part in reaching the decision. None of the foregoing items can be taken for granted in any market abroad. Research must be necessarily undertaken to establish the conventions of the market which is not easy to undertake and bring to a successful outcome. The scale of the market research undertaken is influenced by the exporter's budget and his estimate of the market potential. To be effective, the market research must be well planned and executed. It must have a defined objective and it is advised to spend some time on reflecting the terms of the remit to ensure it adequately meets what is required to produce the desired market research results. Ideally, it is desirable to undertake a pilot survey of the assignment to eradicate any unforeseen bugs which may emerge. Ultimately, this also ensures that a more meaningful report is produced.

In some circumstances, it may be preferred to undertake multi-market research which involves conducting market research within several countries simultaneously with the same objective in view. This is complex and can be difficult to administer, particularly when several languages are involved and the countries differ in their local idiosyncrasies.

A further point to bear in mind is the scope of the research which can vary by individual country. Pilot exercises would tend to reduce the risk of misgivings and avoid a simple market research exercise being transformed into an enquiry.

To conclude, the following points must be evaluated, ideally by a manufacturer, to decide whether or not to enter an overseas market.

(1) Growth trends, particularly embracing production and apparent consumption aspects.

(2) Details of leading competitors, market shares, promotion techniques, services and facilities offered.

(3) Actual channels of distribution and destination cost.

(4) Legal requirements, standards etc.

(5) Adequacy of transportation, particularly bearing in mind speed, frequency, and overall service cost.

(6) Degree to which product subject to official technical regulations or standards.

(7) Tariffs, quotas and import licences impositions/obligations.

(8) Estimate of market size segregating production, imports and export elements.

(9) General political/economic stability of the market.

(10) Adequacy of products currently available.

Various methods of conducting market research exist and the final choice depends on many factors particularly the nature of the product and the money available to conduct the assignment. The latter will be much determined by the likely market share potential of the product etc. to be researched.

One technique is to use desk research. Usually, this simply involves a study/evaluation of public/trade statistics and reports/surveys. This may concern data produced by HM government, agencies, trade associations, international organizations, the press etc, and the more important sources are detailed below:

(1) The major banks, particularly Barclays International, Midland, National Westminster and Lloyds, produce booklets on trade prospects in various countries. Additionally, some of them produce quarterly bulletins through their economic and commercial departments dealing with economic trends, fiscal policy and world trade prospects. All such publications are usually free.

(2) *The Times* and *Financial Times* produce surveys from time to time in various countries highlighting trade prospects particularly to the British exporter.

(3) The Economic Intelligence Unit produces reports on various industries/countries and long term developments.

(4) The various trade associations produce useful reports on their

commodities and opportunities for the exporter.

(5) The EEC and OECD, particularly the former, produce numerous reports on trade prospects and related subjects.

(6) The Department of Trade and Industry weekly journal contains much statistical data and overseas trade news.

(7) The Confederation of British Industry produce a monthly report on overseas markets.

(8) The major UK based Chambers of Commerce and Industry produce monthly journals on overseas markets and related matters. Moreover, British Chambers of Commerce are situated in many countries overseas to encourage trade and have available extensive data on trade prospects.

(9) The Central Statistical Office produce regularly extensive international trade statistical data.

(10) The Central Office of Information circulates details of British achievements overseas and gives data on British products available for overseas importers.

(11) A computerized intelligence service is also operated under the aegis of the British Overseas Trade Board detailing overseas contracts available for which the UK exporter can tender.

(12) The *Economist* produces much useful statistical and international Trade data.

Finally, the exporter can if he wishes ask the British Overseas Trade Board (Export Services Division) to undertake a survey in a particular commodity/country. Advice can also be sought from the local Chamber of Commerce.

Another method is the official overseas Trade Mission, for example, a 'British Week' in Utrecht. The British Overseas Trade Board encourages such assignments which helps the businessman in two ways. Firstly, it enables him to meet Government officials and local businessmen to ascertain at first hand the market opportunities available together with its constraints. Secondly, it is a means of obtaining actual business by taking Exhibition space. This technique is much on the increase and many small exporters have started their overseas markets in this way. The local Chamber of Commerce can also help and the BOTB provide financial assistance to British businessmen to visit overseas markets or official trade missions.

Another technique, which is not always recommended, is the personal visit. An ill-planned visit/programme overseas can produce indifferent results to appraise market potential. A much better assignment is a visit to the trade fair or exhibition, which can provide a useful insight into the overseas market to establish product market potential. It could be a book fair or furniture exhibition. Much export business through the skilful entrepreneur exporter is secured by exporters visiting overseas markets themselves, defining/identifying the market and then exploiting it. Details of such trade fairs are available from BOTB and the local Chamber of Commerce.

The businessman planning such a trip is well advised to obtain one of the 'Hints to Businessmen' booklets issued by the British Overseas Trade Board for individual countries and available at £1 per copy.

The final method is, of course, the properly planned and correctly executed market research assignment. It can be in four ways as detailed below:

(1) It can be undertaken by the merchant. Advantages of this method include: relative secrecy (only the merchant and the manufacturer know research is proceeding); speed of execution and report presentation; and convenience, which facilitates collaboration between the two parties and, if the merchant has a resident agent or branch manager in the territory, time and money can be saved in that part of the enquiry which must be made into the market. Major disadvantages include absence of any market research skill or technical knowledge of the product; the merchant may be biased in sales outlook towards the producer; and ultimately, such an exercise could result in friction between manufacturer and merchant.

(2) The director or senior executive of the manufacturing company may be given the task of conducting the survey and submitting the report. In some large companies, market research staff are employed full-time. In others, the export manager or export sales manager is entrusted with the task. Advantages of this technique include: confidentiality of survey and report content (only manufacturer is aware of such facts); speed of compilation, execution and report presentation; and finally, convenience, particularly in keeping cost of assignment to a minimum and avoiding consultants fees. Disadvantages include: absence of adequate market research skill in the overseas product market involved to appreciate all the elements involved; production of a possibly biased report; and finally, when the report is published, it may be treated with suspicion as it is not produced by an independent source.

(3) An independent organization may be engaged to render a specialized service of the market research exercise. This will produce a fairly unbiased report which is well researched, as the personnel are likely to be efficient in their technique. It could result in cost savings of the survey, when compared with advertising agency. Disadvantages include: possible inadequate consideration of technical products, specification and risk of previous research for another sponsor being rehashed.

(4) Advertising agency containing a market research organization. Often the manufacturer who engages an advertising agency tends to form a long association thereby permitting a continuing interest to be made. This encourages a good relationship between the two parties with beneficial results, particularly understanding the technical specification and potential of any products manufactured. Advantages include a completely unbiased approach to the survey, professionally undertaken at a reasonable cost. A major disadvantage is the length of time sometimes taken to produce the ultimate report and the risk that it may stem from ulterior motives towards justifying promotion of their advertising turnover.

Market research is undertaken usually through the technique of question and answer basis from a well thought-out questionnaire. The questions must be explicit and not ambiguous. Ideally the 'yes' or 'no' or pre-choice type of answer produce the best results. Politically loaded questions should be avoided. Overall, the latter technique viz. 'yes' or 'no' tends to aid answer classification and thereby enables a more meaningful report to be produced. Moreover, it is desirable the questionnaire be tested in the field to eradicate any misgivings in its content which later could prove costly. Above all, the questionnaire should be so formed to produce all the relevant data required of the market research remit and confidential in processing.

Basically, three methods of market research exist and these are detailed below:

(1) By personal interview from a questionnaire. This involves engaging trained personnel to conduct field interviews. It is costly but reliable. Moreover, a greater number of questions can be asked to produce an 'in depth' interview. Such a survey usually involves fewer questionnaires being completed but produces a good response rate with genuine answers. The person responding to a field interview tends to give more truthful answers than with a self-adminis-

tered questionnaire. It can be associated with product sampling.

(2) The self-administered questionnaire. This may be despatched to the recipient by post, or picked up at the local retail outlet or other prescribed place. In some cases, it could accompany a company's product to establish the buying market characteristics and what motivated the purchase. This could help in preparing promotions in other areas. The self-administered questionnaire tends to contain no more than ten main questions. Longer questionnaires tend to discourage the person completing it and thereby produce a poor response rate. The questionnaire is usually returned by post. The cost of obtaining this data on each completed questionnaire is modest compared with the field interview but the response rate tends to be low.

The planning of such field interviews and questionnaire distribution is important. It is desirable that a good cross-section of the populace be obtained relevant to the survey remit terms, and techniques such as random sampling be adopted in the household selected, rather than a complete blanket coverage in one area which may produce indifferent results. For example, a survey on baby foods is best directed toward couples of child-bearing age and not amongst old age pensioners. This could be devised by establishing the child-bearing couples in an area and having a random survey conducted.

The completed questionnaires received are edited and processed, usually through a computer to provide a presentation of statistical data in aggregate terms. This forms the basic data on which the report is written. It is for consideration whether all the questionnaires are processed or merely a selection of them randomly assessed. A report promptly produced following the survey is essential as material quickly becomes out of date and thereby loses its significance.

(3) By organized group discussion. In such circumstances up to 15 people led by a chairman would discuss the merits of a particular product. For example, a new car may have been on the market for some 15 months, and the manufacturer may wish to determine in an overseas country the market attitude towards its design, general competitiveness, comfort, reliability, maintenance cost, availability of spares, price competitiveness, etc. Participants in the group must, of course, have some experience of the product and it is usual for them to be all of the same social class/group, that is, A & B. Moreover, each participant would be paid a modest fee and a psychiatrist would

be present to help the discussion form meaningful conclusions. Over-all, such a method determines attitudes and trend of a particular product in a specified market. The discussion usually lasts for up to 30 minutes or longer if required and is taped throughout. It is later analysed by the research company for report writing purposes.

Another market research technique can be of an omnibus nature involving several companies/manufacturers participating in the exercise and each bearing a proportion of the cost thereof. For example, several manufacturers of washing machines may wish to find out more about the market in which they are selling/competing in a specified country. Alternatively, it may involve several unrelated products and companies such as cars, televisions, kitchen furniture, household utensils etc. It may involve price, design, reliability, after sales service, advertising response with individual manufacturers requiring particular but not common questions to thereby form a composite questionnaire. Each company would, therefore, receive only the data in which he requested originally such as answers to questions 1, 4, 5 and 7 of a 10 answer questionnaire. Overall, it helps to reduce cost of such market research and can also be used in items (2) and (3) described in the following paragraphs.

Associated with market research is research conducted into the product, distribution arrangements, customer satisfaction or promotion.

Product research embraces the development, design and testing of products. It also concerns acceptance of the packaging, colour and general identification of the product.

Distribution research concerns testing the adequacy of the transport arrangements of the consignment and its related elements. This includes conducting test transits to establish areas where delays occur and service suitability to the importer.

Customer research establishes what the consumer thinks of the product purchased. It is particularly useful as it determines consumer motivation towards buying the product and the inadequacies of the product. This attitude can vary by country and class of customer.

Promotion research involves establishing how successful an advertising or promotional campaign has been and what were its shortcomings. This includes radio, television, press promotion and leaflets/brochures etc.

To conclude, market research is an essential ingredient in the successful development by the exporter of overseas markets. The product should be well thought out and advice sought when in doubt, particularly through the British Overseas Trade Board or local Chamber of Commerce and Industry.

STATISTICS

Our study of export research would not be complete without consideration of statistics which is tending to play an increasingly important part in the technique of facilitating the development of overseas markets. In our brief evaluation of statistics, it is important to bear in mind that the statistical techniques should be used skilfully and the exercises undertaken should be continuously costed to ensure one obtains 'value for money' in relation to the benefits to be derived from such data, particularly in terms of export trade development/market share potential etc.

An examination of the various statistical aids available to the exporter now follows:

(1) Sampling has become a very popular technique to determine the results of a survey or similar exercise. For example, the market research operator may initiate a self-administered, postal questionnaire programme in a particular area or region overseas to determine the adequacy of a product launched some two years ago. Each questionnaire circulated would be consecutively numbered. To avoid editing and processing all the questionnaires through a computer, a random selection can be taken on a first come, first served basis. Alternatively, one can process every fifteenth questionnaire which would be called selective sampling. In such circumstances, the questionnaire would be so collated as for each one to be bundled in numerical order.

(2) Graphs and diagrams form an important part of statistical presentation today. It aids the viewer to comprehend them better, rather than studying a series of statistical tables. Moreover, it facilitates comparisons being made as, for example, one year's export results compared with another. Details of the various types of graphs/diagrams are given below:

(i) The histogram and bar charts presents statistical data in a bar type of formation with each bar, for example, representing a particular product's results in one year. One could have one bar representing bicycle sales, another motor mowers, another washing machines and so on. Separate bars placed alongside each other could be produced to show one year's results compared with the preceding one.

(ii) The histogram graph is ideal for presenting a time series of statistical information. For example, the monthly results of sales in an overseas territory could be plotted every month on a graph. This could be related to the budgeted forecast.

(iii) The pie diagram is merely a circle split up into various segments proportionate to the statistical data presented. For example, the total cost of running the export office for one year could be assessed and ultimately broken down into components. For example, telephone calls may represent 10%, stationery 5%, wages 70%, and all these elements could be reflected in the pie diagram formation. It is ideal for poster presentation and simple to understand.

(iv) Again suitable for poster presentation is the pictogram where a symbol represents a certain statistical value in the presentation. For example, if the exporter sold 1500 washing machines to a particular country in a month, this could be represented by a one and half washing machine pictogram symbol, each pictogram symbol representing 1000 units. This technique greatly facilitates statistical data presentation comprehension.

Other types of diagram include the 'Z' chart and ogive which, although less common in use, have a specialized role to play.

(3) The word average in statistics has a wide meaning and the more common types of statistical averages in use today are given below:

(i) The mode is regarded as the most popular/representative item in a group. For example, if some ten types of diesel engines are sold in an overseas market, the modal one would be the one which has the largest sales.

(ii) The arithmetic mean (AM) is widely used in statistics and it emerges on the basis of the aggregate of the group divided by the total participating in the group. Hence, if the aggregate totals 1200 and the number of participants is 20, the AM would be 60.

(iii) Allied to the AM is the dispersion of the range of items in the group. This can be measured by using either the mean deviation or standard deviation technique. For example, if the AM is 60 the mean deviation may be 6.7 suggesting the group is not widely dispersed.

(iv) The median is the value of an item situated at the half-way stage in a series. For example, if a group of 49 persons are placed in order of age graduation, the median age of the group would be the age of the 25th person in the group. This may be 34.5 years, although the actual group ages may range from 15-72 years.

(4) Published statistics both by Government and commercial organizations are numerous. This includes trade associations, banks, Central Statistical Office etc. Such data should be used critically otherwise the wrong conclusions can be reached from the data used. In particular, the source and how the statistics are made up should be ascertained if practicable. Particular care should be taken when calculating derivatives and comparing varying sets of figures, some of which may be unrelated and collated in a different way. Usually, the local Chamber of Commerce and Industry or BOTB can help the exporter obtain the requisite statistical data required. This is particular relevant to market surveys.

(5) Management information involves the preparation and presentation of statistical data on a regular basis (perhaps monthly). For example, it could present each month throughout the year, against a budget forecast, the total number of radios sold in a particular country. This data aids management to measure how the business is progressing in a particular market and, in the event of any fall off in the results against budget, remedial measures can be taken. For example, poor local distribution arrangements may be one of the reasons for disappointing sales results or inadequate after sales service.

The foregoing is only a brief review of statistics and the exporter indulging in this field extensively should study closely one of the established statistical textbooks on the market.

EXPORT PROMOTION

Export promotion is an important activity of the development of international trade and to be successful it must be professionally planned and executed. It comprises all those activities undertaken by an exporter, by direct or indirect appeal, with a view to persuading general buyers (the public) or specific buyers to purchase the exporter's products or service in preference to other products, or services offered by other companies, either locally or from overseas.

Various techniques exist regarding such promotion and the more common ones are now examined:

(1) All forms of mass advertising media service selected from those offered in the actual market with a view to securing optimum impact. Each of these is now examined:

(i) Radio and TV. Visual orientated products are ideal for TV advertising but it must be borne in mind that not all countries permit commercial advertising through such a media. Radio, on the other hand, is ideal for products which are easy to describe and do not have a strong visual impact. Moreover, in underdeveloped countries it is often the only means of communication, particularly when illiteracy is high.

(ii) Cinema involving slides or film presentation is tending to become more popular, particularly with local presentation/promotions. It is most effective when the dialogue is limited, thereby overcoming the language barrier and permitting the presentation to have a wider international market appeal. Although the film cost may be high, its cost can be adequately recouped if its shown in several countries.

(iii) Press advertising involving national or local newspapers, consumer or trade magazines and technical journals is a very popular method of promotion. Each newspaper, magazine etc. has a specialized market and this should be evaluated together with its circulation to determine its adequacy for the product promotion. The exporter must establish whether the publication has any political or religious allegiance, its compatability with the product and manufacturer's promotion.

(iv) Advertising on sites situated on hoardings, transport vehicles, public lounges/areas at railway stations or passenger airport terminals. Such sites, some of which can be permanently illuminated, are ideal for a wide range of consumer products.

(2) All forms of sales aids such as leaflets for use at point of sale with supporting posters, price tickets and other display material, stickers and pelmets, and well designed retail support items such as catalogues instruction leaflets. This includes window display material.

(3) All forms of merchandising — more usual with consumer products — such as premium offers, special bonus deals and specimen layouts designed to enhance sales appeal such as showroom displays.

(4) Direct mail which involves sending sales literature direct to

selected potential buyers. This is best undertaken locally rather than by the UK based exporter thereby saving heavy postage charges. Moreover, it needs to be adequately researched to ensure it reaches only householders who can be regarded as potential buyers. It is best used in industrial countries where a high degree of literacy exists.

(5) The use of trade fairs, public exhibitions and any means of displaying products to visitors at such shows. This technique is very much on the increase.

(6) Public relations involving the release to the mass media viz. press, TV and radio items of 'news' about the export company or its products in such a way that free publicity is secured. This includes measures taken to promote the brand image amongst employees, agents and distributors abroad, suppliers and other contacts, and share holders.

(7) Education of personnel having influence on sales of the product, directly or indirectly viz. salesmen, service engineers etc. This virtually constitutes product support — often of a technical nature — involving users, distributors and service engineers.

The first step in planning export promotion is to formulate an advertising budget. An examination of the various methods are detailed below:

(1) The exporter can base the budget on a percentage of the price structure such as 5% of CIF or FOB per unit price. Hence, if the exporter forecasts to sell 10 000 units each at £100 CIF, it would produce an advertising budget of £50 000. The percentage would be higher than 5% when the product is launched and in the initial years thereafter depending on its success and the degree of competition.

(2) As an alternative to the foregoing, the exporter prepares the budget based on a percentage of the previous year's turnover.

(3) A further method is to allocate advertising money to be used when the market opportunities arise. This is usually called the 'task' method. The exporter calculates what expenditure will be necessary to accomplish a given objective. Care must be taken to ensure that tasks are not set which require expenditures way beyond what one can reasonably hope to earn. Such tasks are geared to anticipate sales in order to keep a reasonable ratio between expenditure and earnings.

(4) The investment method regards all expenditure as an investment exactly as if it were new plant or the purchase of shares in an

associate company, that is, an allocation of capital to the project promising an income flow in the future. The accountant might justify this course by adding the amount to the 'goodwill' item in the firms balance sheet at the time it is laid out, for gradual amortisation in later years. Provided adequate sales result, this method can work well if a realistic amount is allocated to the promotional purposes — not a sum so small as to be derisory.

(5) Many exporters have a standard form of agency agreement which requires the agent to contribute to promotion expenditures. This is more common where the agent is in fact an importer/distributor than where he is a commission selling agent. This may require the agent to share in all such expenditure, or it may only relate to advertising in the market with the possibility of sharing 50/50 expenditure for exhibitions or fairs leaving sales aids to be supplied at the exporter's expense. The prime advantage is that the agent, as the 'man on the spot', shares the promotional expenditure and should be able to judge the impact of promotional measures quicker and perhaps more accurately than may the exporter several thousand miles away. It is important the exporter exercises adequate supervision over the agent.

Overall, there are four methods in which export promotion can be handled and each is now examined:

(1) It can be left to the agent to undertake all forms of advertising in his market. This involves making premium offers and bonus deals at his own discretion to exhibit at fairs etc. in his country, if he thinks it worthwhile, and to embark on such public relations activities as may appeal to him.

(2) The principal's publicity department could assume responsibility for promotional activities abroad as well as at home. The smaller type of manufacturer is unlikely to employ enough staff in its publicity department for them to have adequate time to devote to export. Moreover, they are likely to lack adequate expertise. In the larger manufacturing company however, the publicity manager with staff qualified in the foreign field can execute the appropriate promotional measures in accord with the export manager's prescribed objectives. This method can be a viable one although one must be conscious the risk that home market promotional material can partially subsidize the international market.

(3) Where the exporter does not have adequate resources available

for export promotion, an advertising agency can be engaged. It is advocated that one chooses an agency with local offices or associates through which they work. Care needs to be exercised in the choice of agency to ensure it is of repute and capable of carrying out the assignment. It is important for the exporter to check on the effectiveness of the agency by requiring its foreign sales agent to include comments on the promotional efforts in their periodical reports. For example, when the selling agent considers that advertisements launched in his market do not adequately support his sales activities, it must be supported by facts and remedial measures suggested.

(4) When the exporter cannot undertake his own export promotion or does not wish to engage an advertising agency, a further option exists — namely the employment of a part-time consultant. This is ideal for the small exporter.

The services offered to the advertiser by the advertising consultant is somewhat different from that offered by the advertising agency. Although the consultant is unlikely to take part in the physical operation of any advertising plan, his very broad experience of all aspects of advertising enable him to offer a very comprehensive advisory service.

The consultant is normally fee-earning and will prepare the advertising plan and recommend the nature of its execution, leaving the actual detailed work to be effected by the advertiser. The consultants real function, which comes from an in-depth knowledge of his client's business and the markets in which he operates, is the initiation of the advertising plan. However, his advice may extend to areas such as product and package design, and method of distribution as these are influenced by the plan which he has formulated. The consultant is likely to assess the advertising plan during its operation to determine its effectiveness and to suggest remedies for any weaknesses which reveal themselves.

MARKETING PLAN

The marketing plan is the basis on which all the overseas promotion is formulated. To devise the marketing plan involves reconciling the export strategies and objectives of the manufacturer into marketing terms. It should be produced by the export director or most senior person responsible for the export market.

The marketing·plan embraces many elements including market research project, promotion/advertising details, products involved, distribution arrangements, and total volume/value of goods by individual product/country. Where relevant, various costing information should be included particularly the research and advertising budget. An appraisal of the viability of the plan should be given and all the timing of the elements of the plan should be inserted. For example, the actual periods the advertising programme will operate. Overall, the marketing plan must have the approval of all the departments involved. Above all, the plan must be realistic and should have a clear sense of purpose and direction. It should be reviewed perhaps quarterly throughout its one-year life to reflect change in circumstances.

VISITS TO OVERSEAS MARKETS

Our study of export marketing would not be complete without brief consideration of planning an overseas trip. Whenever a foreign trip is planned it is imperative to establish a very clear picture of its object(s) and to prepare a brief accordingly. The trip could be for one or more of the following purposes:

(1) Initial market research — to carry out to completion the prior desk research investigations.

(2) Continuing market research.

(3) To appoint an agent from those shortlisted.

(4) Finding a replacement agent when the existing one retitres, dies, or services are terminated.

(5) Discussing with an agent differing marketing approach, better distribution arrangements, improved documentation arrangements etc.

(6) Examining with agents the prospects of improved sales, better advertising, new opportunities within the market, improved sales training for staff etc.

(7) 'On the spot' investigation with the agent to enquire into customers complaints.

(8) To examine prospects of setting up a local company.

One needs to be adequately briefed before undertaking such a trip and the following points must be borne in mind relative to the overseas visit:

(1) Obtain sound advice on personal conduct. Such information can be found in the 'Hints to Businessmen' series of booklets, which cover most of the markets in the world. This series costs £1 per copy and can be obtained from the British Overseas Trade Board.

(2) Time the visit to ensure one does not arrive during any legal or religious holiday period as most businessmen are likely to be away.

(3) Conclude/confirm as far as practicable all hotel reservations, travel arrangements and currency needs. Credit cards can help with regard to the latter. Air travel is expensive and, in certain circumstances for near Continental countries, the overnight sea journey with cabin accommodation and the accompanied car can prove to be a cheaper and more flexible operation, particularly when the exporter is visiting a number of areas over several days. A modest amount of loose change is desirable for the individual countries to be visited.

(4) Plan the itinerary allowing adequate time for travel and to see the various people with whom contact has to be made. Allow a modest amount of time for any journey delays. All necessary visas must be obtained before leaving including 'transit visas' when merely stopping *en route*. All journeys should be booked in advance through an airline, ship operator or accredited travel agency. A valid passport is essential.

(5) Ensure all the clients on your itinerary are aware of your visit and its purpose so that they are adequately prepared and the senior personnel are available.

(6) Ensure adequate insurance is arranged in all relevant areas, that is, personal. Baggage should be of modest proportions and clothes should be compatible with the climate/circumstances. Always appear smartly dressed when on business. If the exporter cannot speak the language competently, an interpreter should be present at meetings. The visit should allow adequate time for relaxation and the usual health precautions should be adopted include any vaccinations prior to departure.

(7) The export salesman should take an adequate amount of sales literature and when practicable samples.

(8) Prepare notes of all meetings conducted recording salient points within the remit terms of your visit. Report and observe when relevant the customs and idiosyncrasies of the populace. Give particular attention to detail and when necessary have it checked.

(9) Ensure one's family has details of the visit and contact is made

with them, that is, a cable if necessary on arrival. Also the appropriate family arrangements should be made before departure particularly adequate finance and payment of bills.

Arrangements to call on the Commercial Officer at the Embassy should be made though the Department of Trade and Industry. Likewise, to see bankers through the head office in London, if the bank is so organized, or through the exporters usual bankers in the UK.

CHAPTER 16

The Role of the Specialists

Agents and distributors. Chartered shipbrokers. Concessionaires. Confirming houses. Consortia. Export clubs. Export houses. Factoring. Freight forwarders. Group selling. Institute of Export. International credit clubs. Local buying offices. The future.

Export practice is a complex operation and numerous specialists operate in this field to facilitate the development of international trade. Details of the more important specialists are found in this chapter, but the list should not be regarded as exhaustive. The reader particularly should study Chapter 13 which deals with a variety of organizations of a specialist function in many instances. Study in particular the role of the British Overseas Trade Board and Chapter 10 dealing with the Export Credits Guarantee Department. Both these organizations play a major role in the development of UK export trade.

AGENTS AND DISTRIBUTORS

The narrow definition of 'agent' in export practice is that he is a party who acts for the exporter, the latter being the principal. He does not make a profit but is paid a commission on all orders secured, for which his principal obtains eventual payment. It is most usual for such an agent to work for a number of principals offering a cohesive group of products but not so as to be in direct competition with each other.

There are variations in the type of agency which works on a 'commission only' basis according to what the parties consider suitable to the product and the market. Examples are given as follows:

(1) Fee or retainer. When it is clear from the outset that it will take some time before the product gets established in the market, and thus before the agent can earn a worthwhile commission, it is up to the principal to offer some alternative financial inducement so as to motivate him until straight commission becomes a viable proposition. Where the agent is selling a range of products for one principal on a commission basis, the agent may be offered a fee to launch a

new product which, though within the general range, is an untried newcomer to the market, or some entirely fresh range of products being launched by the principal.

(2) Expenses incurred by the agent. These may be paid by the principal or shared between the parties on an agreed basis. This introduces variation from the 'commission only' type of agency. Such expenses may be a 'once only' arrangement such as setting up showroom facilities. Alternatively, they may be continuing, involving the agent being charged with watching local technical journals and buying them for the principal when appropriate. A further situation may be intermittant whereby the agent is required to cable advice over a pre-arranged minimum at the expense of the principal. Some special variation of the commission only arrangement can be introduced to cover the agent's outlays or to share them in special circumstances, such as, an exhibition where it is decided to take a stand or some exceptional venture in local publicity.

(3) Stockist agencies. This arises where the agent sells on commission but undertakes to buy for his own account — or to share in the cost of — stocks of some of the items within the range. This could significantly improve sales turnover where the goods are such that the demand is always for prompt delivery, for example, components for automobile repair services in a foreign country.

(4) Service after sale. Many technical products are such that it is necessary to provide a maker's guarantee. This is undertaken by the agent who sells on commission and may include a repair service outside the maker's guarantee arrangements. This involves stocks or parts being carried in the market by the agent and usually workshop facilities. The details of the arrangement between the parties varies widely according to individual circumstances. The principal may supply free shares, or they may be sent on a consignment basis. Alternatively, the agent may be required to equip a workshop and carry spares at his expense.

(5) Consignment stocks. The market where sales are made must have goods available for immediate delivery as soon as the commission agent concludes the sale. Such stocks can be entrusted to the agent providing he owns or rents suitable warehousing space. Such an agent must be of outstanding integrity and sound financial standing. Moreover, one must ensure the law of the country involved recognizes the continuing legal ownership by the principal of goods

physically held by the agent. The alternative is for the stock to be held by an independent warehouseman in the name of the principal, who then sends buyers delivery orders to enable them to call on the warehouse for release of the goods for which the order was placed through the commission selling agent.

(6) Salaried agent. The agent is resident in the country of operation and is paid a salary, with or without expenses and fringe benefits, by his principal. This may prove suitable where the products are capital goods or when the principal is a firm of consultants such as a consortium. Such an agent could keep the principal in touch with conditions in his territory and advise on local opportunities and official tenders over a period of years. For example, he could tender on behalf of his principal for medical equipment or harbour navigational facilities.

(7) Distributor/agent. In some markets, conditions are such that they are dominated by one large firm which dwarfs its competitors, but the market potential cannot be fully exploited unless the smaller concerns are enticed into the sale of the products. The large firm acting as a distributor can also secure orders for shipment direct to the small ones. Such transactions are remunerated on a commission basis. The contract of agency between the principal and such a firm must be drafted with special care, but even so it may prove in practice that the small firms are squeezed out of effective marketing because of the uplift in the price they pay to cover the agent's commission. At best they are somewhat restricted in their activities. This type of agency has proved effective where the big firm comprised members of ethnical or religious majority group or ruling caste, at least where the small ones belonged to the minority and monopolized sales to other people in the minority grouping.

(8) Export management agency. The function of the export management agent is to act as the manufacturer's export department, either for all markets abroad or for a selected number clearly agreed in advance. He is briefed in regard to the products, both technically and as to future production flows and possible changes in quality and quantity. Price is agreed and a rate of commission fixed, with or without some contribution to the agent's expenses (generally, or for specific purposes such as travel) or a fee plus commission payable on results. It is usual for the export management to be authorized to appoint agents in foreign territories within the agreed

sphere of operation. On the other hand, the management does not usually incur any financial risk — he would not be expected to put through orders from parties of doubtful standing and would advise the manufacturer about financing the business. This avoidance of financial implication is not, however, invariable; thus the merchants who operate manufacturer's agency departments often take over the goods ex-works or FOB.

Some care must be taken to differentiate between the form of agency explained above and the group sales concept detailed on page 309. In the latter case, the manufacturers who form the grouping, whilst in an export management agency situation, the agency takes over the export function and decides what shall comprise his group of products to be marketed overseas.

(9) *Del credere* agent. Where a commission selling agent, whatever his other terms of reference, undertakes that orders passed to the principal will be paid for in due course by the buyers, he is called a *del credere* agent, that is, he undertakes a credit risk. Great care is necessary in defining the responsibilities and rights of this special type of agent, and when and how he is paid his *del credere* commission. Thus, the principal must be certain to instruct the collecting bank when a document is lodged with a *del credere* agent named as 'case of need', that is, if the buyer refuses the bill, is the agent empowered to take possession of the documents and/or the goods.

It must be stressed that there exist a wide variety of different types of agents and the foregoing are primarily the salient ones. Moreover, one must bear in mind that there are certain similarities of the role of the agents, confirming houses and export houses. The latter two have also been explained in this chapter.

It is appropriate, however, when examining the role of the agent, to consider the distributor. For example, the manufacturer markets some of his products in some territories through commission selling agents, but in other areas through importer/stockist/distributors, who buy the goods for their own account and earn a profit (not a commission) as a basis of their remuneration. The role of the distributor in the overseas market has become increasingly significant and the following are the salient points of difference between the distributor and selling agent.

Selling agent	Distributor
(1) Not financially involved.	Buys for own account.
(2) Leaves importation to the buyers whose orders he passes to the principal.	Imports the products.
(3) Is paid a commission at an agreed percentage on orders secured.	Marks up the supply price to cover his profit.
(4) Any service necessary is rendered by the buyer.	Where necessary undertaken responsibility for the service.
(5) Carries no stock except for showroom purposes.	Normally carries a stock.
(6) Unlikely to be involed in publicity except where required to give advice or report on impact.	Likely to be involved in local publicity.
(7) May be authorised to engage sub-agents.	Appoints sub-distributors.
(8) No control of resale prices.	Controls selling prices in countries where retail price maintenance is possible.
(9) Leaves distribution to the buyers.	Undertakes distribution in the market.

To conclude our study of agents, it would be appropriate to detail the salient clauses usually found in an agency agreement which now follows. The clauses may be varied to meet individual circumstances and others may be added as required:

(1) Details of parties to the contract viz. names, registered address and short title of each party.

(2) Purpose of contract. For example, it must state in specific terms that A appoints B as an agent and that B agrees to act in that capacity in accord with the terms of agreement.

(3) Details of the products involved. For example, A will supply and B will sell the merchandise prescribed including any brand names.

(4) Territory. The agreement must outline the geographical area over which the agent is given exclusive sales rights.

(5) Precise duties of the principal embracing any reference to sales outside the agency handling direct enquiries etc.

(6) Precise duties of the agent. This will incorporate situation dealing with other suppliers particularly of a competitive nature. It will also mention association of names of parties in course of marketing, warranties and description of goods by agent.

(7) Exceptions, reservations or restrictions imposed on either one or both parties to the agency agreement.

(8) Method of quoting prices. For example, whether FOB or otherwise.

(9) Agents purchase and resale. This clause will reflect the type of agency agreement involved as earlier described. For example, if the agent is buying for his 'own account' such as, when acting as a distributor, he may appoint sub-distributors subject to the manufacturers approval; fix sale prices and retail list prices; and report back to the manufacturer. This clause requires adequate deliberation/consideration.

(10) Consignments — in particular terms of delivery. This will embrace under what terms merchandise will be delivered, who pays landing charges, duty, Customs clearance, cartage, warehousing, stevedoring, insurance in warehouse/bond and accounting arrangements. Additionally, it should detail property in the goods, arrangements for release to the buyers and disposal of stock on termination of agreement.

(11) Spares for general maintenance and service. It should also outline general arrangements and disposal of the items on termination of the agency agreement.

(12) Cost of cables, air mails, telexes, and unusual expenses — not mentioned elsewhere in the agreement — and responsibility of their payment.

(13) Force majeure. This clause negates responsibility of principal where force majeure prevents delivery from factory or, in respect of goods ready to leave, prevents despatch or causes diversion of cargo carrying ship or aircraft.

(14) Permissive clause. In situations where the products do not meet the competition in styling, suitability to market or price, whether or not the agent can handle other goods of the same category. This clause is usually found in a commission agency rather than sole distributorship.

(15) Commission. The actual commission scale — fixed or sliding rate and how to be credited/remitted. This requires careful deliberation, particularly in an era of floating currencies and devaluation implications.

(16) Accounting. Agent to keep proper books and render periodical statements including consignment stocks where applicable. Provision to be made for accounts to be audited/examined by the principal or his representative.

(17) Overprice. This usually arises in contracts between merchant and agent in raw materials and semi-finished product trades. It embraces general conditions and authority of the agent to try to overprice. Moreover, it details the allocation between the two parties to the agreement of the overprice apportionment.

(18) Publicity. A general agreement regarding sales literature and catalogues, including responsibility for translations, policy in regard to exhibitions, local advertising and special propaganda. It should detail the apportionment of cost between the two parties to the agreement.

(19) Report. The agent to submit reports at prescribed times and likewise the principal to keep the agent informed of product development and trade generally. It will extend to production and marketing policy.

(20) General conditions. Any general conditions not mentioned elsewhere in the agreement either party mutually wishes to introduce. For example, to pledge the principal credit or start legal proceedings without his consent.

(21) The duration of the agreement and notice of termination of agreement by either party — the latter may be one or three months or other prescribed period.

(22) Breach of contract clause. This involves a case of breach or default by either party or by the agent without mention of breach of principle. It also embraces summary of determination upon liquidation or compensation with conditions or attempt to assign benefits of contract.

(23) Laws and arbitration. This must indicate which country's law will apply and disputes will be settled by arbitration in accordance with the terms prescribed in this clause. This will avoid costly litigation and speed up settlement.

(24) Assignment. Neither party has the right to assign the benefits

of the contract without the prior consent of the other. This may be qualified by a merger sub-clause showing what would happen if the original legal entity of party is merged into another legal entity.

The contract document finishes with space for the signature of the parties with an indication of capacity of signatories and witnesses, including formal application of company's seal where applicable.

CHARTERED SHIPBROKERS

The basic function of the shipbroker is to bring together the two parties concerned involving the ship and cargo owners. In following negotiations between them, a charter party is ultimately concluded. The brokers' income is derived from the commission payable by the shipowner on completion and fulfilment of the contract.

A further role of the shipbroker, other than fixing vessels, is acting as agent for the shipowner. As such, he is responsible for everything which may concern the vessel whilst she is in port. This embraces customs formalities, matters concerning the crew, loading/discharge of vessels, bunkering/victualling and so on.

Duties of the shipbroker can be summarized as follows:

(1) Chartering agent whereby he acts for the cargo merchant seeking a suitable vessel in which to carry the merchandise.

(2) Sale and purchase broker acting on behalf of the buyer or seller of ships and bringing the two parties together.

(3) Owners broker whereby he acts for the actual shipowner in finding cargo for the vessel.

(4) Tanker broker dealing with oil tanker tonnage.

(5) Coasting broker involving vessels operating around the British coast and/or in the short sea trade viz. UK/Continent. Additionally, at the same time, he can act for the cargo merchant in this trade should circumstances so dictate. The deep-sea broker, however, will act for the shipowner or cargo merchant but not at the same time.

(6) Cabling agent involving the broker communicating with other international markets.

There is no doubt the shipbroker is a man of many parts. In reality, he is the middle man between the two principals concerned in a charter party.

CONCESSIONAIRES

These organizations operate as distributors with a special authority granted by the manufacturer to work in a particular market area, usually on a basis of exclusivity. They tend to be expert in their field and have good contacts in their particular trades. The advantage to a manufacturer or exporter is that regular business is assured, but there is no direct contact with the buyer and the channels of distribution to that market will be restricted to the activities of the concessionaire.

Thus a manufacturer might make what at first sight appeared to be an opportunist sale to a merchant and then receive a repeat tender, coupled with a request for exclusivity for the particular territory where the merchant is active. This could, in turn, develop into a regular relationship by which the merchant became the concessionaire for that market.

CONFIRMING HOUSES

The basic function of a confirming house is to assist the overseas buyer by confirming, as principal, orders already placed so that the exporter may receive payment from the confirming house as and when the goods are shipped. Any credit period the buyer may require is arranged and carried by the confirming house which takes the credit risk over from the supplier.

The confirming house is an export house and used extensively by the small and medium sized company involved in the export business.

CONSORTIA

These are groups of organizations which work together as a unit in order to achieve a common purpose. The consortium may operate as a group seller or a group buyer and sometimes will use a nominee in order to preserve anonymity during the negotiations of a contract. Consortia tend commonly to be engaged in bidding for large tenders, particularly where the size of the order is feasible only by employing the combined capacity of individual members.

Many consortia of this type have been set up on the initiative of the leading firms of consulting engineers, with the end products in the foreign country ranging from large dams, irrigation projects, railway modernization and extension, hospital projects, dredging undertakings and harbour installations, to such construction works in the electrical field as power generation, sub-stations and television transmitters. Many of these projects can best be financed with the aid of the Export Credits Guarantee Department explained in Chapter 10.

Since each major undertaking of a consortium is likely to be so different in its nature from any other put out to tender by foreign governments, municipalities or other principals, it follows that many of these consortia are set up for only the one project and, when this is accomplished, they are then dissolved. Some of the parties may come together again for another undertaking, possibly then bringing in other members, but it does not often happen that the second venture is so exactly like the first one that the consortium can again function unchanged.

From the very nature of these undertakings it follows that the negotiations between the members of the consortium are protracted, difficult and complicated, before the nominee can submit the tender. This type of operation is always highly technical and, for every tender which is accepted, there is more than one where the contract is not secured. This involves having to write off the heavy expenses incurred.

EXPORT CLUBS

Export clubs are informal associations situated in the UK which are usually formed on a regional area basis by a number of local manufacturers, often with representatives of local freight forwarders, banks, insurance companies, container operators, etc. No rules are laid down as to how these clubs should operate, but in general they draw on the experience of member firms to give advice on overseas markets and export procedure and in some cases practical help in selling through a marketing group or by organizing trade missions and exhibitions overseas.

EXPORT HOUSES

Export houses have three salient functions which are detailed below:

(1) As an export merchant buying goods outright and selling them on their own account. The merchant may buy goods from the exporter against the requirements of an overseas customer. Alternatively, the agent may buy the product and market it overseas. Finally, the agent by virtue of his international trading activities may indulge in compensation trading, switch deals etc. Indeed, in any barter type transaction.

(2) As an agent but retaining the role of the principal throughout the transaction. In such circumstances, the export house will promote the exporter's products overseas; carry the credit risk on the overseas buyer; attend to the physical and clerical work involved; stock goods at home and overseas on the exporters behalf; follow up delivery dates or delays; deal with formalities overseas; and occasionally provide an after-sales service. Basically, the degree to which the foregoing work is undertaken by the export house will vary according to individual circumstances and is a matter for negotiation. In the main, the small or medium sized export business usually find it cheaper and more economic to engage an export house as their agent rather than employ their own export staff or overseas representative to undertake such work.

The payment for the foregoing services may be in the form of commission with the agent quoting the agreed export selling price to customers overseas. Alternatively, there may be some other form of remuneration to the export house negotiated by the exporter. For example, the export house may calculate the export price with the exporter on a 'cost plus profit margin' basis. The profit margin would be for the export house accountant, who is responsible not only for the product sales, but also its advertising, marketing, distribution, etc.

(3) By acting for an overseas buyer in return for which commission is earned. In such circumstances, the export house may find sources of supply or deal with suppliers (exporters) nominated by his principal. In either case, the export house will arrange shipment and insurance; progresses and despatch of orders; and confirm and finance contracts on the buyers behalf.

The export house may be a buying agent or merchant. The role of the export house varies: the large ones undertaking virtually all the foregoing roles and the smaller ones offering a more specialized and less extensive service. Few if any export houses are prepared to handle all goods for all destinations. Most specialize in markets, types of goods, or in certain types of products for particular markets. To the exporter interested further in the export house activity, it is suggested he contacts the British Export Houses Association whose address is found in Appendix B.

FACTORING

The practice of using factoring companies by exporters is very much on the increase. Their prime function is to administer the sales ledgers and collect payments once the goods have been shipped. Such factoring companies provide a complete range of services which cover those aspects of exporting and leave the manufacturer free to concentrate on export production and sales. For a small service charge of between 0.75% and 2% of turnover, they will provide multi-currency and multi-language sales accounting backed up by credit management, which is exercised in the customer's country by the factor's own employees or agents. Also included in this service charge is 100% protection against losses due to the insolvency of the customer and, in some cases, protection gainst political risk and exchange rate fluctuations. Factoring cannot effectively meet the particular needs of every industry and the most suitable companies are likely to have an expanding turnover in excess of £100 000 and to be selling consumer goods, light industrial products or services on short-term credit.

Basically, a factor buys invoiced debts from his client exporter and becomes responsible for sales accounting, collection and credit protection usually guaranteeing payment on a specified maturity date. Additionally, the factor will, if required, make available up to 80% of the value of the goods invoiced immediately on shipment thus financing the credit taken by customers.

Details of factoring companies are available from freight forwarders or major banks.

FREIGHT FORWARDERS

The freight forwarder, formerly called the shipping and forwarding agent, is concerned with the transport arrangements of all kinds of goods across international frontiers. In reality, he is responsible for the co-ordination of the various forms of transport and related ancillary activities embracing documentation, Customs clearance, booking cargo space, packing etc. for any particular international consignment.

The freight forwarder's knowledge must, therefore, be very extensive as he is responsible for the consignment from the time he has secured it through his canvassing to the point it is delivered to the consignee at the final destination. He must be in a position to advise his principal as to the most suitable service available which may be train ferry, road transport throughout, air freight, high capacity container etc; the most suitable packing; compliance with any maritime and other statutory obligations; Customs clearance procedure, including related documentation needs; rates and insurance premiums for individual services, including related conditions of liability; schedule and transit times of the various forms of transport service available; the most satisfactory method of concluding the international financial arrangements for the cargo; all technical aspects of international forwarding; marking of cargo; and any particular circumstances/obligations obtaining in the country of destination with which the exporter must comply. To amplify the foregoing, the freight forwarders role broadly includes the following:

(1) Advice of a financial and trade nature on the special requirements of foreign countries.

(2) Advice on packing, marking and labelling to comply with the requirements of carriers and of the Customs authorities in other countries.

(3) Planning routes and means of conveyance and preparing inclusive estimates of costs.

(4) Reserving freight space and co-ordinating all forms of transport and may be conveying goods from exporters premises to the destination.

(5) Advising on insurance and obtaining cover if required.

(6) Preparing, obtaining or advising on all necessary documentation.

(7) Arranging Customs clearance.

(8) Providing groupage surface transport service or air freight consolidation facilities.

In short, the freight forwarder must have a good knowledge of commerce, the finance of international trade, forwarding practice including Customs, commercial geography, cargo insurance, the Law of Carriage and commercial law.

In more recent years, the freight forwarder has entered such specialized but ancillary fields to international forwarding as packing, warehousing and the actual carriage of goods generally involving road transport to/from the Continent. Today, this forms an important and sizeable part of their business. Additionally, an increasing number of agents own ISO containers for use in international services offering regular consolidated shipments.

There is no doubt that the freight forwarder has an important role in developing traffic for liner cargo services and as such has made, and will continue to make, an important contribution to the UK balance of payments by using his experience to foster international traffic. Indeed, the freight forwarder, by developing groupage traffic, has helped the development of trade for the small emerging inexperienced exporter who often uses the agent's transport throughout.

In common with other sections in shipping, the freight forwarders are tending to merge to raise capital, often for ISO container investment. They operate under their trading conditions, dated 1974, and to facilitate international trade development, operate in conjunction with another freight forwarder in the destination country. Freight forwarders originating cargo for individual liner cargo services receive a commission which varies according to the tonnage forwarded.

During the past few years, the freight forwarder, or forwarding agent as he still tends to be called, has become increasingly involved in the air freight business under consolidation arrangements. This trend is very much on the increase and is ideal for the small exporter who can despatch his merchandise by air freight under very competitive terms. A number of the larger agents tend to have regularly booked capacity on the more important, scheduled, high capacity, air freight flights, particularly to Europe and North America.

Closely associated with the freight forwarders is the Institute of Freight Forwarders Ltd. which is a professional body representing/promoting the freight forwarder. It was formed as a professional body in 1944 with the title of 'Institute of Shipping and Forwarding Agents'. As the only body representative of the freight forwarding agents of the United Kingdom, the Institute is called upon to promote and protect the interest of forwarding organizations and to negotiate on their behalf with Government, port authorities and others, including the providers and users of international transport. In reality, it undertakes a dual role of a professional institute and trade association which led to it being redesignated in 1970 as 'The Institute of Freight Forwarders Ltd.

The Institute's primary object is broadly based, namely to promote the interest and welfare of shipping and forwarding agents, to improve their professional status and to secure uniform standards of professional conduct and practice. In furtherance of this primary objective, to provide a central organization for those engaged in or connected with the profession and form branches and trade sections as required.

Other principal objects include: encouraging freight forwarding organizations to associate in promoting and developing their general interests, and interests of all members of the Institute; to promote friendly relations with others engaged in transport operations; to represent the views of members and, on their behalf, to enter into discussions and negotiations with official bodies and other organizations; and to promote standards of efficient forwarding services and public confidence in the profession.

The establishment of standards of professional qualifications of membership of the Institute and the granting of certificates or diplomas in recognition of achievement of these standards are other important objects. Details of their examination regulations can be obtained from the Institute whose address is found in Appendix C.

GROUP SELLING

Group selling is the system employed when two or more manufacturers engage jointly to market their products. Each principal continues its own individual activity as a manufacturer of the same merchandise or range of products, except that the goods may be modified or the range extended to meet the overseas requirements. Hence, the only continuity of interest between the various manufacturers is in connection with the marketing function.

The various producers will not amalgamate or merge and there is the interchange of shareholding amongst the various constituent members of the group selling organization.

For a group selling organization to be established with any reasonable chance of success, it must have in prospect sufficient turnover to cover expenses and yield a modest profit. Moreover, the constituent manufacturers forming the organization must usually be well established with a good basic trade in the home market, but without a sufficient share or potential share in the export market to warrant operating alone, except on a token basis.

The products dealt in must be either a cohesive group of manufacturers normally handled by a specialist type of marketing channel or a number of different qualities of the same merchandise. Alternatively, the goods must be produced under conditions of competition but marketed by the group-selling organization on a basis which eliminates such competition.

The disadvantage of this type of organization are mainly concerned with the possible future dissolution of the group as a trading body. This type of venture is always prone to this possibility on account of disagreements concerning the general conduct of business; the sharing of unforeseen expenses; failure to make the anticipated profits; turnover lost through delays in delivery; attempts to secure price ruling on date of delivery; and other such points.

Furthermore, if the venture is a success, the more the turnover achieved by any one manufacturer, the more likely he is to want to break away from the group and work alone. If the venture is only a moderate success, there will always be overseas parties who will try to by-pass the group-selling organization and establish direct dealing with one or more of the constituent members.

THE INSTITUTE OF EXPORT

The Institute of Export is a professional body founded in 1924 as the British Export Society and incorporated as the Institute of Export in 1935. The Institute's principal objective is to maintain a continuous supply of export executive staff to British industry and commerce by means of its educational activities.

Membership consists mainly of professional exporters employed in manufacturing companies, export merchant houses and other export organizations. It also extends to certain categories of brokers, civil servants, insurance officials, lawyers, shipowners and other occupations concerned with export trade.

The objects of the Institute are detailed below:

(1) To promote industry and commerce and particularly international trade in goods and services of all kinds.

(2) To examine, research and analyse problems connected with industry and commerce, particularly international trade in goods

and services of all kinds; to publish the results of such work together with recommendations and advice; and to make the same available to all persons, firms or companies whether or not members of the Institute.

(3) To further public education with regard to commerce and industry, and particularly the need for exports and the methods of realising the same; and further, to educate those who are or may become involved or interested in international trade in all aspects of the same.

The Institute of Export assist both its individual and company members through the medium of its employment bureau, which is officially licensed. It aims to provide candidates for job specifications in the export field.

The Institute issues an educational handbook and interested readers are advised to obtain a copy. The Institute of Export address is found in Appendix C.

INTERNATIONAL CREDIT CLUBS

A number of finance houses can arrange finance through associated companies in other countries for imports and exports between their respective countries. Credit can be arranged for all classes of durable goods for periods normally up to two years, but longer in special cases. Credit can also be provided to enable foreign buyers to take into stock goods imported from the UK and to hold them pending their sale.

International credit clubs, which are reciprocal agreements between leading finance houses in Europe, have also been formed to help exporters of substantial items of capital equipment so that foreign customers can obtain instalment credit finance quickly and cheaply. Similar facilities also exist in both customer and industrial hire purchase. Most of these organizations also give many ancillary services such as market research, shipping and forwarding advice on all matters relating to export credit.

LOCAL BUYING OFFICES

Many marketing organizations in foreign countries buy so much from UK sources that they find it financially advantageous to maintain buying offices in UK, particularly in London. In some instances, this office may be part of a chain of buying offices covering Europe. It is usual for the buying office to look after affreightment, insurance and finance.

The advantages of a UK manufacturer to deal with the local buying office is that he can get a prompt acceptance of orders; saves time and cost in visiting the markets; avoids outlay on publicity; and avoids excessive correspondence with foreign markets. Against all this must be reconciled the fact that the buyers 'shop around' so keenly that their prices are highly competitive, leaving little or no margin of profit for the manufacturer, whilst there is seldom much prospect of repeat orders.

THE FUTURE

Our study of the elements of export practice would not be complete without a brief look at the future but before doing so we will examine the recently formed European Monetory system.

One of the aims and objectives of the Treaty of Rome is to move towards complete economic and monetary union. Economic and political behaviour is not so closely involved with monetary policy that integration on all fronts will have to proceed simultaneously. As far back as 1964, the Six thought they had ruled out the possibility of future changes of parities between members but this idea was exploded in 1969 when the French franc went one way and the Deutschemark the other. As a result, a meeting of the Six was held at the Hague to attempt to achieve monetary co-operation. It was agreed to create an economic and monetary union and to draw up a plan by stages. Of the several plans put forward the one most seriously considered was that by M. Barre.

This plan rejected categorically any idea of fluctuating exchange rates between the Six and stressed the need for the EEC to develop a unified front in the international monetary sphere. An interim report in 1970 suggested a completion date of 1980 for economic and monetary union, of which the final goal would be the creation of a single currency. There was basic agreement among the Six about the proposals for a first stage over a period of three years when the Central banks and Ministers of Finance could meet to discuss fiscal and monetary policies. There was, however, strong opposition from the French to the supranational elements in the second stage after 1973.

Despite the differences and problems, the members of the EEC were determined to proceed with monetary unification and economic integration. This determination was strengthened by the fact that they were finding it increasingly difficult to cope individually with the massive financial and industrial influence of the USA. This influence was increased by the international use of the dollar as a reserve currency and by the development of an unregulated Eurodollar market. Moreover, the unsettled conditions in regard to the French and German exchange rates were a danger to the Common Agricultural Policy.

A unified European currency would have a profound effect on the international monetary system in that the importance of a fully integrated Europe would approach that of the USA. The process towards integration is now irreversible and the member states have too much to gain from it to allow nationalistic economic policies to stand in the way.

However, in the next few years, the picture was radically changed. The problems of inflation led the member countries to take their own internal steps to contain it. Many countries, including the UK, allowed their currencies to float; and three more countries had joined the EEC and were not in a position to maintain their exchange rates within the fixed limits. In fact, only West Germany and the Benelux countries remained within the 'Snake'. Now, M. Barre is Prime Minister of France, and West Germany is increasingly worried by the upward pressure on the Deutschemark.

As regards the UK, there would be benefits to be obtained in the field of trade and investment but against these must be set the many problems which would arise in the conduct of the UK's domestic affairs. The monetary and fiscal measures requires to contain inflation and maintain the exchange rate would tend at first to increase unemployment. It might then become necessary to devalue the pound. If the monetary union developed without the participation of the UK it would increase the pressure, which is already growing, for New York, Frankfurt and Amsterdam to take over much of the international operations which have for so long been a monopoly of London — with the consequent loss of much of our important 'invisible' earnings. Provided the UK could ride the early hardships of a stringent deflation and become an equal member of the system then the benefits would be immeasurable.

To deal with the future there is no doubt that international competition will increase in overseas markets and this trend will continue. Not only will product price, durability, advanced technology and general market appeal continue to remain dominant factors in consumer choice, but also the need to ensure the importer receives his goods in accord with the time scale laid down in the export sales contract. Late delivery, damaged or missing merchandise, poor quality goods and, where relevant, indifferent after-sales service will only lead to a loss of much goodwill in overseas consumer markets and, ultimately, a dwindling market share of the product involved. Good professional exporting can maximize customer satisfaction and aid development to improve product market share. It must be based ultimately on a profit motivated policy. Moreover, the availability of credit to the importer remains a dominant factor in many instances but the ECGD can usually help the exporter over this situation.

The trend towards aligned export documentation together with other techniques described on pages 269-272 to aid export efficiency strenuously being developed by SITPRO merit more support/adoption by UK exporters. Moreover, the transport operator will continue to strive for improved distribution methods to reduce transit time, raise service quality, contain cost and overall to stimulate trade. A continuing trend towards more unitization and groupage/consolidation will continue thereby offering the door to door or integrated multi-modal transport service. Examples are found in ISO containerization, air freight consolidation (usually involving the pallet) and the road haulage unit found particularly in the UK/Continental trade.

Regretfully, in all too many UK companies, their degree of involvement in international trade has tended to be rather small, but there are now signs that many manufacturing industries are taking a more positive attitude towards developing overseas markets. This demands competent staff, professionally trained and dedicated to their work. Education can greatly facilitate achieving this objective and readers are particiuarly recommended to consider taking the Foundation Course in Overseas Trade details of which are available from the British Overseas Trade Board.

It is hoped this book will, in a small way, contribute to providing more expertise in the professionalism of exporting and thereby aid to develop trade which, in turn, raises living standards on an international scale.

Appendix A

FURTHER RECOMMENDED TEXTBOOK READING

BRANCH, A.E. (1977). *The Elements of Shipping*. 4th edn. London: Chapman and Hall.

BRANCH, A.E. (1976). *A Dictionary of Shipping/International Trade Terms and Abbreviations*. (2600 entries). London: Witherby and Co. Ltd.

DAY, A.J. (1976). *Exporting for Profit*. London: Graham and Trotman.

SCHMITTHOFF, C.M. (1976). *The Export Trade*. 8th edn. London: Sweet and Maxwell.

WATSON, A. (1976). *Finance of International Trade*. London: Institute of Bankers.

Appendix B

Association of British Chambers of Commerce,
11, Dean Farrar Street,
London SW1   Telephone 01-222 0201

British Export Houses Associations,
69, Cannon Street,
London EC4N 5AB   01-248 4444

British Overseas Trade Board,
1, Victoria Street,
London SW1H 0ET   01-215 7877

BOTB — Publication Sales Unit,
Export Services and Promotions Division,
Export House, Ludgate Hill, London EC4   01-248 5757

British Standards Institution (BSI),
Maylands Avenue,
Hemel Hempstead,
Herts. HP2 4SQ   0442 3111

Central Office of Information (CIO),
Hercules Road,
Westminster Bridge Road,
London SE1 7DU   01-928 2345

Confederation of British Industry (CBI),
21, Tothill Street,
London SW1H 9LT   01-930 6711

Department of the Environment,
Road Freight Division,
2, Marsham Street,
London SW1P 3EB   01-212 7231

Department of Trade,
Export Licensing Branch,
Charles House,
375, Kensington High Street,
London W14 8QH   01-603 4644

Department of Trade,
1, Victoria Street,
London SW1H 0ET   01-215 7877

Exports Credits Guarantee Department (ECGD),
PO Box No. 272,
Aldermanbury House,
Aldermanbury,
London EC2P 2EL   01-606 6699

Freight Transport Association Ltd,
Sunley House,
Bedford Park,
Croydon,
Surrey CR9 1XU   01-681 2611

General Council of British Shipping,
30, St. Mary Ave,
London EC3   01-283 2922

HM Customs and Excise,
Kings Beam House,
Mark Lane,
London EC3   01-283 8911

Institute of Chartered Shipbrokes,
25, Bury Street,
London EC3A 5BA   01-283 1361

Institute of Export,
World Trade Centre,
London E1 9AA   01-488 4766

Institute of Freight Forwarders Ltd,
Suffield House,
9, Paradise Road,
Richmond,
Surrey TW9 1SA   01-948 3141

Institute of Marketing,
Moor Hall,
Cookham,
Maidenhead,
Berks SL6 9QH   06285-24922

Inter-Governmental Maritime Consultative
Organization (IMCO),
101-104, Piccadilly,
London W1V 0AE   01-499 9040

International Chamber of Commerce,
British National Committee,
6, Dean Farrar Street,
London SW1   01-222 3755

International Road Freight Office,
Department of the Environment,
36-42, Low Friar Street,
Newcastle upon Tyne NE1 5XR   0632-610031

(Responsible for all matters concerning road haulage units)

London Chamber of Commerce and Industry,
69, Cannon Street,
London EC4N 5AB   01-248 4444

Road Haulage Association (RHA),
Roadway House,
22, Upper Woburn Place,
London WC1H 0ES   01-387 9711

Simplificiation of International Trade
Procedures Board (SITPRO),
11, Waterloo Place,
London SW1   01-839 3393

Appendix C

PUBLICATIONS AVAILABLE TO HELP THE UK EXPORTER AND FACILITATE UK EXPORT TRADE

ABC Air Cargo Guide

BOTB Export Services Handbook (price £2.50)

Chambers of Commerce Journals and Newsletters

Croners Reference Book for Exporters

Export Daily Gazette

Export Times

Freight News

Handy Shipping Guide

Hints to Businessmen (BOTB publication, £1 per copy for each country) — A series of booklets, covering most countries of the world designed to assist the exporter who intends to visit these markets.

Institute of Chartered Shipbrokers Journal

Institute of Export Journal

Institute of Freight Forwarders Journal

Institute of Marketing Journal

Lloyds List and Shipping Gazette

Systematic Export Documentation, Volumes I and II, including 1979 Supplement, published by SITPRO.

The Economist

Trade and Industry Journal

Various publications and handbooks (usually free) on export practice and export finance available from the major banks — Lloyds, Barclays International, Midland International etc.

Appendix D

PUBLIC HM CUSTOMS NOTICES AVAILABLE AND USEFUL TO THE EXPORTER/IMPORTER

Subject	Public notice number	Title of HM Customs notice
General exports	104	ATA Carnets
	118	Export Trade Samples
	275	Export Documentation
	276	Guide to C273 forms
EEC	750	EEC Community Transit
	751	Notes on completing T forms
	753	Simplified Rail Procedure
	780	CAP Imports
	800	CAP Exports
	811	EEC Preferences: Greece
	812	EEC Preferences: Turkey
	826	EEC Preferences: Imports
	827	EEC Export Preference Procedures
	828	EEC Preferences. Rules of Origin
Temporary importations	118	Export Trade Samples
	213	Exhibitions
	209	Hire or Loan
	46	Professional Effects
	221	Inward Processing
	235	Outward Processing
	236	Returned Goods Relief
General imports	37	Entry Coding List
	462	Entry Check List
	465	Entry procedures
	252	Valuation
	186	Bonded Warehouses
	700	VAT General
	701	VAT Scope and coverage
	702	VAT Imports
	703	VAT Exports
	714	VAT Childrens' Clothing

The above Public Notices are available free of charge from HM Customs and Excise, Kings Beam House, Mark Lane, London, EC2 or from the Exporters' local HM Customs office.

Appendix E

EXPORT DOCUMENTS

  I Air waybill (Air Consignment Note)
  II ATA carnet (issued by London Chamber of Commerce and Industry)
  III Bill of lading
  IV Certificate of origin (issued by Arab-British Chamber of Commerce)
  V Certificate of origin — European Communities (issued by London Chamber of Commerce and Industry)
  VI CIM international rail consignment note
  VII CMR international road consignment note
  VIII Full Comminity transit (EEC) declaration 'T' form
  IX Movement certificate — International Community transit (EEC) document T2L form
  X Movement certificate Community transit (EEC) DD3 form
  XI Letter of credit — revocable credit
  XII Letter of credit — irrevocable credit
  XIII Standard shipping note

125- 1605 7646

125- 1605 7646

For Carrier use only		
Flight/Day	Flight/Day	Flight/Day
	Flight/Day	Flight/Day

British airways

Air Waybill
(Air Consignment note)

Issued by British Airways, London
Member of International Air Transport Association   Not negotiable

Airport of Departure   Execution Date Day/Month/Year   TC   Chgs Code   Currency Code

Airport of Destination

Airport of Departure (Address of First Carrier) and Requested Routing

Routing and Destination

To	By First Carrier	To	By	To	By

Consignee's Account Number

Consignee's Name and Address

If the carriage involves an ultimate destination or stop in a country other than the country of departure, the Warsaw Convention may be applicable and the Convention governs, and in most cases limits the liability of carriers in respect of loss of or damage to cargo. Agreed stopping places are those places (other than the places of departure and destination) shown under requested routing and/or those places shown in carrier's timetables as scheduled stopping places for the route. Address of first carrier is the airport of departure.
SEE CONDITIONS ON REVERSE HEREOF.

Shipper's Account Number

Shipper's Name and Address

The shipper certifies that the particulars on the face hereof are correct, agrees to the CONDITIONS ON REVERSE HEREOF. accepts that the carrier's liability is limited as stated in 4(c) on the reverse hereof and accepts such value unless a higher value for carriage is declared on the face hereof subject to an additional charge, and that in so far as any part of the consignment contains restricted articles, such part is properly described by name and is in proper condition for carriage by air according to the International Air Transport Association's Restricted Articles Regulations.

Signature of Shipper or his Agent

Issuing Carrier's Agent Account Number

Issuing Carrier's Agent's Name and City

Carrier certifies goods described below were received for carriage subject to the CONDITIONS ON REVERSE HEREOF. the goods then being in apparent good order and condition except as noted hereon.

Executed on .... at ....

(Date: .... (Place) ....

Signature of Issuing Carrier or its Agent

Agent's IATA Code

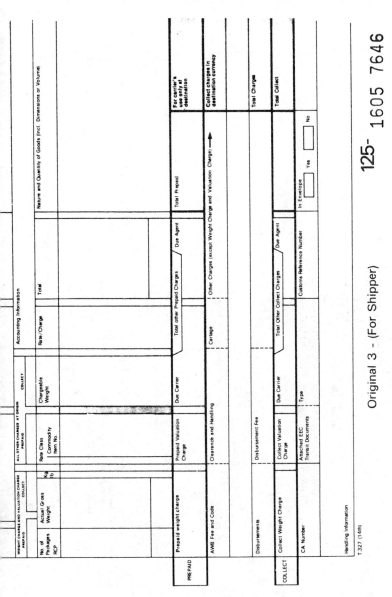

The following is an air waybill (Air consignment note) form.

WEIGHT CHARGE AND VALUATION CHARGE		ALL OTHER CHARGES AT ORIGIN		COLLECT		Accounting Information		

No. of Packages RCP	Actual Gross Weight	Kg / lb	Rate Class Commodity Item No.	Chargeable Weight	Rate/Charge	Total	Nature and Quantity of Goods (incl. Dimensions or Volume)

PREPAID

Prepaid weight charge	Prepaid Valuation Charge	Due Carrier	Total other Prepaid Charges	Due Agent	Total Prepaid	For carrier's use only at destination

AWB Fee and Code	Clearance and Handling	Cartage	Other Charges (except Weight Charge and Valuation Charge) ⟶		Collect charges in destination currency

Disbursements	Disbursement Fee			Total Charges

COLLECT

Collect Weight Charge	Collect Valuation Charge	Due Carrier	Total Other Collect Charges	Due Agent	Total Collect

CA Number	Attached EEC Transit Documents	Type	Customs Reference Number	In Envelope Yes ☐ No ☐

Handling Information

T.327 (14th)

125- 1605 7646

Original 3 - (For Shipper)

I   Air waybill (Air consignment note)

THE LONDON CHAMBER OF COMMERCE & INDUSTRY

(Issuing Association)
(Association Émettrice)

ATA/GB/LO

INTERNATIONAL GUARANTEE CHAIN
CHAINE DE GARANTIE INTERNATIONALE

A.T.A. CARNET No.
CARNET A.T.A. No

CARNET DE PASSAGES EN DOUANE FOR TEMPORARY ADMISSION
CARNET DE PASSAGES EN DOUANE POUR L'ADMISSION TEMPORAIRE

CUSTOMS CONVENTION ON THE A.T.A. CARNET FOR THE TEMPORARY ADMISSION OF GOODS
CONVENTION DOUANIERE SUR LE CARNET A.T.A. POUR L'ADMISSION TEMPORAIRE DE MARCHANDISES

(Before completing the carnet, please read notes on page 3 of the cover)
(Avant de remplir le carnet, lire la notice page 3 de la couverture)

CARNET VALID UNTIL
CARNET VALABLE JUSQU'AU .... INCLUSIVE
INCLUS

ISSUED BY   The London Chamber of Commerce & Industry, 69-75, Cannon Street, London, E.C.4.N. 5AB.
DÉLIVRÉ PAR

HOLDER
TITULAIRE ....

REPRESENTED BY*)
REPRESENTE PAR*) ....

Intended use of good: /Utilisation prévue des marchandises ....

....

This carnet may be used in the following countries under the guarantee of the following associations: /Ce carnet est valable dans
les pays ci-après, sous la garantie des associations suivantes :

AUSTRALIA
The Melbourne Chamber of Commerce, Melbourne.

AUSTRIA
Bundeskammer der Gewerblichen Wirtschaft, Vienna.

BELGIUM & LUXEMBURG
Federation Nationale des Chambres de Commerce et d'Industrie de Belgique, Brussels.

BULGARIA
Bulgaria Chamber of Commerce, Sofia.

CANADA
The Canadian Chamber of Commerce, Montreal 128. Que.

CYPRUS
Cyprus Chamber of Commerce, Nicosia.

CZECHOSLOVAKIA
Ceskoslovenska Obchodni Komora, Prague.

ISRAEL
Tel Aviv-Yaffo Chamber of Commerce, Tel Aviv.

ITALY
Unione Italiana delle Camere di Commercio Industria e Agricultura, Rome.

IVORY COAST
The Ivory Coast Chamber of Commerce, Inc. Abidjan.

JAPAN
Japan Chamber of Commerce, Tokyo.

NETHERLANDS
Kamer van Koophandel en Fabrieken voor 'S Gravenhage, 'S Gravenhage.

NORWAY
Oslo Chamber of Commerce, Oslo.

POLAND

FRANCE
Chambre de Commerce et d'industrie de Paris, Paris

GERMANY
Deutscher Industrie-und Handelstag, Bonn.

GIBRALTAR
Gibraltar Chamber of Commerce, Gibraltar

GREECE
The Athens Chamber of Commerce and Industry, Athens.

HONG KONG
The Hong Kong General Chamber of Commerce

HUNGARY
Magyar Kereskadelmi Kamara, Budapest

ICELAND
Iceland Chamber of Commerce (Verzlunarrad Islands) Reykjavik

IRAN
Iran Chamber of Commerce, Industries & Mines, Teheran.

IRELAND
The Dublin Chamber of Commerce, Dublin.

ROMANIA
Camera di Comert & Republich Socialiste Romanie, Bucarest.

SOUTH AFRICA
The Association of Chambers of Commerce of South Africa, Johannesburg.

SPAIN
Consejo Superior de las Cameras Oficiales de Comercio Industria y Navegacion de Espana, Madrid.

SWEDEN
The Stockholm Chamber of Commerce, Stockholm.

SWITZERLAND
Alliance des Chambres de Commerce Suisses, Geneva.

TURKEY
Union of Chambers of Commerce or Produce Exchange in Turkey, Ankara.

UNITED KINGDOM
The London Chamber of Commerce and Industry, London

UNITED STATES OF AMERICA
U.S. Council of the International Chamber of Commerce Inc., New York.

YUGOSLAVIA
The Yugoslav Federal Economic Chamber, Belgrade.

The holder of this carnet and his representative will be held responsible for compliance with the laws and regulations of the country of departure and the countries of importation./*A charge pour le titulaire et son représentant de se conformer aux lois et règlements du pays de départ et des pays d'importation.*

Issued at/*Emis à* .... **London** .... date ....

....
(Holders signature/Signature du titulair)

(Signature of authorised Official of the Issuing Association ature du *Délégue de l'Association emettrice*)

TO BE RETURNED TO THE LONDON CHAMBER OF COMMERCE AFTER USE.

CERTIFICATE BY CUSTOMS AUTHORITIES/*ATTESTATION DES AUTORITES DOUANIERES*

1. Identification marks have been affixed as indicated in column 7 against the following item Note). of the General List *Apposé les marques d'identification mentionnées dans la colonne 7 en regard du(des) numéro(s) d'ordre suivant(s) de la*

liste *générale* ....

2. Goods examined.*)/*Vérifié les marchandises.*)

3. Registered under reference No.*)/*Enregistré sous le no.*)

....
(Customs office: (Place/*Lieu) (Date/Date) (Signature and stamp)
Bureau de douane) *(Signature et Timbre)*

). Delete if inapplicable./Biffer s'il y a lieu.

II ATA carnet (issued by London Chamber of Commerce and Industry)

BILL OF LADING

JOINT SERVICE BRITISH RAILWAYS BOARD / STOOMVAART MAATSCHAPPIJ ZEELAND
KONINKLIJKE NEDERLANDSCHE POSTVAART N.V.

Hoek van Holland – Harwich

PORT AGENTS :
HOOK OF HOLLAND

N.V. Harwich Ferry Agentuur
P.O. Box 4
Telephone : 01 7 47 - 23 51
Telex : 3 17 26

PORT AGENTS :
HARWICH PARKESTON QUAY

Shipping & Port Manager
British Railways (E.R.)
Telephone : Harwich/Essex 21 41
Telex : 9 82 84

Service: B/Z D/N

Sender

| | C / NC |

Shipped in apparent good order and condition, weight, contents, marks, measure, number, quantity, condition, quality and value unknown by

on board the vessel

now lying in this port, the following goods, viz. :

Marks and numbers	PACKAGES		Full description of contents (Country of origin to be shown)	Gross weight (kg)
	No	Description		

A 'vehicle', 'trailer', 'container' or 'flat' together in each case with its contents constituting for all purposes (including Carrier's liability) one package or unit only.

To be conveyed to the port of HARWICH (PARKESTON QUAY) and there to be delivered subject to the terms and conditions mentioned in this Bill of Lading evidencing the contract of carriage between Shipper and Carrier as defined on the reverse side thereof, to..............

Freight and other charges shall be paid by

....

at ....

and disbursements (including Shipper's charges forward) and any other sums payable hereunder shall be paid by the Consignee at destination, but in the event the Consignee or any other person not paying the aforesaid freight, charges, disbursements and any other sums payable as aforesaid, the Shipper shall remain liable therefor.

In accepting this Bill of Lading the Shipper expressly accepts and agrees to all its terms and conditions on both pages, whether written, printed or incorporated, as fully as if they were all signed by such Shipper.

In witness whereof the Master or Agent of the ship has affirmed to ....Bills of Lading all of this tenor and date, one of which being accomplished the others shall stand void.

Dated at HOOK OF HOLLAND,
this ....day of ....

FOR THE MASTER

Disbursements, including Shippers charges forward

£

		Destination name and address (Rail forwarded traffic only)	Destination station

Prepayment instructions (insert a cross as appropriate)

CHARGES PAID	CHARGES PAID UP TO :	CHARGES TO PAY

Invoiced from	to	route

Advice of Collection (Insert a cross if Advice is attached)		Charges Note (Insert a cross if Note is attached)	

Containers			Control label	
Type	Number		Station No	Consignment No
			....	....
			....	....
			....	....
			....	....

III Bill of lading

CERTIFICATE OF ORIGIN

Consignor: العرسـل : [1]	A/ 768498
	Consignor's ref.: [4]

شهــادة منشــأ

CERTIFICATE OF ORIGIN

Consignee: العرسل اليـه : [2]	تشهد السلطة الموقعة بأن البضائع الوارد بيانها أدناه
	The undersigned authority certifies that the goods shown below
	originated in: منشــأها : [5]

Consigned by: مرسلة بواسطة: [3]	

غرفة التجارة العربية البريطانية

ARAB-BRITISH CHAMBER OF COMMERCE

Marks and Numbers: الأرقام و العلامات	Quantity and Kind of Packages: كمية ونـوع الطرود	Description of Goods: مواصفات البضاعة	Weight (gross & net): [6] الوزن (الصافي والاجمالي)

غرفة التجارة العربية البريطانية

ARAB-BRITISH CHAMBER OF COMMERCE

مكـان وتاريخ الاصـدار Place and Date of Issue	Issuing Authority	سلطـة الاصـدار

861

LONSDALE BUSINESS FORMS LTD

IV Certificate of origin (issued by Arab-British Chamber of Commerce)

<table>
<tr><td colspan="3">

Consignor: (Expéditeur:)

</td><td colspan="2" align="right">

C 995792

</td></tr>
<tr><td colspan="3">

Consignee: (Destinataire:)

</td><td colspan="2">

EUROPEAN COMMUNITIES
(Communautes Europeennes)

</td></tr>
<tr><td colspan="3">

Consignment by: (Expédition prevue par:)

</td><td colspan="2">

CERTIFICATE OF ORIGIN
(Certificat d'origine)

**THE LONDON CHAMBER OF
COMMERCE AND INDUSTRY**

</td></tr>
</table>

THE UNDERSIGNED AUTHORITY certifies that the goods shown below
(L'AUTORITE SOUSSIGNEE certifie que les marchandises désignées ci-dessous)

| Serial No. | Packages | | Description of goods | Weight (1) | |
	Number and kind	Marks and numbers		gross	net

originated in:

(sont originaires de:)

The London Chamber of Commerce and Industry

(Place and date of issue)	(Name, signature and stamp of competent authority)

(1) This entry may, where appropriate, be replaced by others allowing identification of the goods.
DTI/XP/I302.

Netherton and Worth Limited, Truro, Cornwall.

V   Certificate of origin — European Communities (issued by London
Chamber of Commerce and Industry)

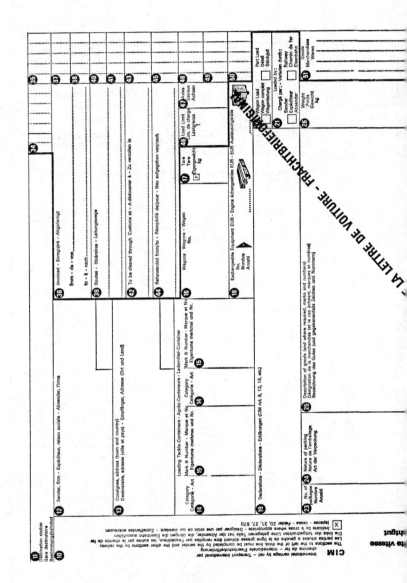

CIM — Internazional carriage by rail – Transport international par chemins de fer – Internationale Eisenbahnbeförderung

The sections to the left of the thick line must be completed by the sender and the other sections by the railway
Les parties situées à gauche de la ligne grasse doivent être remplies par l'expéditeur, les autres par le chemin de fer
Die linke der fettgedruckten Linie gelegenen Teile hat der Absender, die übrigen die Eisenbahn auszufüllen

[X] -Indicate by a cross where appropriate - Désigner par une croix ce qui convient - Zutreffendes ankreuzen
(spaces - cases - Felder 20, 21, 27, 57)]

⑩ ⑪ Destination station / Gare destinataire / Bestimmungsbahnhof

⑫ Sender, firm – Expéditeur, raison sociale – Absender, Firma

⑬ Consignee, address (town and country) – Destinataire, adresse (ville et pays) – Empfänger, Adresse (Ort und Land)

Loading Tackle-Containers – Agrès-Conteneurs – Lademittel-Container

⑭ Category / Catégorie – Art / Kategorie – Art
⑮ Mark & Number – Marque et No / Eigentumsmerkmal und Nr.

⑯ Wagons – Wagons – Wagen No.

⑰ Tare / Tare / Tare kg   P Eigengewicht

⑱ Exchangeable Equipment EUR – Engin échangeable EUR – EUR Austauschgeräte
No. / Nombre / Anzahl

⑲ Declarations – Déclarations – Erklärungen (CIM Art. 6, 12, 15, etc.)

⑳ ㉓ No. of packages / Nombre de colis / Nombre Anzahl
㉔ Nature of packing / Nature de l'emballage / Art der Verpackung
㉕ Description of goods (and where required, marks and numbers) / Désignation de la marchandise (et le cas échéant, marques et numéros) / Bezeichnung des Gutes (und gegebenenfalls Zeichen und Nummern)

㉖ Weight / Poids / Gewicht kg

㉑ Loaded by: / Chargé par: – Verladen durch:
☐ Wagon Load / Wagon complet / Wagenladung
☐ Sender / Expéditeur / Absender
☐ Railway / Chemin de fer / Eisenbahn

㉖ Goods / Marchandises / Waren

㊿ Part Load / Détail / Stückgut

㉟ ㊲ ㊳ ㊵ ㊶ ㊸ ㊹ ㊺
㊱ Invoiced – Enregistré – Abgefertigt
from – de – von
to – à – nach
㊴ Routes – Itinéraires – Leitungswege
㊷ ㊳ ㊵
㊶
㊸
㊹
㊺ To be cleared through Customs at – A dédouaner à – Zu verzollen in
㊼ Reforwarded from/to – Réexpédié de/pour – Neu aufgegeben von/nach
㊽ Wagons – Wagons – Wagen No.
㊼ Tare / Tare kg
㊸ Load Limit / Lim. de charge / Lastgrenze
㊾ Axles / Essieux / Achsen
㊿

LA LETTRE DE VOITURE - FRACHTBRIEFORIGINAL

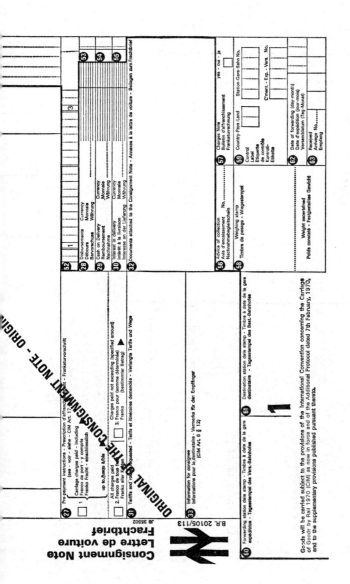

VI CIM international rail consignment note

Exemplaire de l'expéditeur
Copy for sender

1

* En cas de marchandises dangereuses indiquer, outre la certification éventuelle,
* In case of dangerous goods mention: besides the possible certification, on the la

1 Expéditeur (nom, adresse, pays)
Sender (name, address, country)

2 Destinataire (nom, adresse, pays)
Consignee (name, address, country)

3 Lieu prévu pour la livraison de la marchandise (lieu, pays)
Place of delivery of the goods (place, country)

4 Lieu et date de la prise en charge de la marchandise (lieu, pays, date)
Place and date of taking over the goods (place, country, date)

5 Documents annexés
Documents attached

6 Marques et numéros
Marks and Nos

7 Nombre des colis
Number of packages

8 Mode d'emballage
Method of packing

9 Nature de la marchandise
Nature of the goods

10 No statistique
Statistical number

11 Poids brut, kg
Gross weight in kg

12 Cubage m3
Volume in m3

LETTRE DE VOITURE INTERNATIONALE
INTERNATIONAL CONSIGNMENT NOTE

(CMR) **B 66204**

Ce transport est soumis, nonobstant toute
clause contraire, à la Convention relative
au contrat de transport international
de marchandises par route (CMR).

This carriage is subject, notwithstanding any
clause to the contrary, to the Convention
on the Contract for the International Carriage
of goods by road (CMR).

16 Transporteur (nom, adresse, pays)
Carrier (name, address, country)

17 Transporteurs successifs (nom, adresse, pays)
Successive carriers (name, address, country)

18 Réserves et observations du transporteur
Carrier's reservations and observations

Les parties encadrées de lignes grasses doivent être remplies par le transporteur
* The spaces framed with heavy lines must be filled in by the carrier

Classe Class	Chiffre Number	Lettre Letter	(ADR *)

13 Instructions de l'expéditeur
Sender's instructions

19 Conventions particulières
Special agreements

14 Prescriptions d'affranchissement
Instructions as to payment for carriage

☐ Franco / Carriage paid

☐ Non franco / Carriage forward

21 Etabli à
Established in   le on   19

22

Signature et timbre de l'expéditeur
Signature and stamp of the sender

20 À payer par: To be paid by:	Expéditeur Sender	Monnaie/Currency	Destinataire Consignee
Prix de transport Carriage charges			
Réductions Deductions –			
Solde / Balance			
Suppléments Supplem. charges : Frais accessoires Other charges +			
TOTAL :			

15 Remboursement / Cash on delivery

23

Signature et timbre du transporteur
Signature and stamp of the carrier

24 Marchandises reçues / Goods received

Lieu
Place   le on   19

Signature et timbre du destinataire
Signature and stamp of the consignee

Modèle IRU 1976

61   including and
À remplir sous la responsabilité de l'expéditeur   1 – 15   y compris et
To be completed on the sender's responsibility

VII   CMR international road consignment note

| 1 COMMUNITY TRANSIT DECLARATION | | | 4 | | | |

T

1 COMMUNITY TRANSIT DECLARATION		4		
2 Number of sheets T BIS or loading lists	3 Exporter	5 Customs Assigned Number **CAN**		6
		7 F/Agent's reference	8 Exporter's reference	
		REGISTRATION OF DECLARATION		
	11 Consignee	Office of Departure		
		No. and Date		
	21 Principal	22 Country of consignment	25 Country of destination	
		28 Previous Customs procedure		
		39 Licence		
	32 Identity of means of transport	40 Import ship/aircraft		

COPY FOR THE OFFICE OF DEPARTURE

1

Please see Notice No. 751 before completing this form

41 Marks, numbers, number and kind of packages: description of goods		42 Statistical number (1)	43 Gross weight

1

41 Marks, numbers, number and kind of packages: description of goods	49 Net weight (1)	42 Statistical number (1)	43 Gross weight

2		49 Net weight (1)		
53		54		

55 Offices of transit intended (and countries)	
56 Offices of transit used (and countries)	
57 Guarantee	58 Office of destination (name and country)

59 Attached documents

CONTROL BY OFFICE OF DEPARTURE

Results of examination:

Seals affixed: number: identity:

Time limit (date):

Remarks:

At....................................... on ....
(Place of signature)   (Date)

                                    (Signature)

(Stamp)

60 UNDERTAKING BY THE PRINCIPAL

The principal, represented by.................................

hereby undertakes to produce the goods described in this declaration intact and within the prescribed time limit at the office of destination.

At....................................... on ....
(Place of signature)   (Date)

                                    (Signature)

C. 1138

F 4820 (Jan., 1978)

(1) For completion only when required by Community regulations.

VIII   Full community transit (EEC) declaration 'T' form

T2L   No. A 748460

INTERNAL COMMUNITY TRANSIT DOCUMENT FOR
ESTABLISHING THE COMMUNITY STATUS OF GOODS

Please see Notice No. 751 before completing this form.

3 Person concerned

28 Previous Customs procedure

41 Marks, numbers, number and kind of packages; description of goods

42 Statistical number (1)

43 Gross weight

1

41 Marks, numbers, number and kind of packages; description of goods

49 Net weight (1)

42 Statistical number (1)

43 Gross weight

	49 Net weight (1)

CUSTOMS CERTIFICATE

Certified declaration satisfactory   No.

Export Document: type:

Date:

Customs office (and country):

Remarks:

At.................................... on.................
        (Place of signature)   (Date)

                            (Stamp)

        (Signature)

59 Procedure and document used

60 DECLARATION BY THE PERSON CONCERNED

The person concerned, represented by..................

....

declares that the goods described above are Community goods.

At.................................... on.................
        (Place of signature)   (Date)

        (Signature)

F. 3817 (Jan., 1978)

C. 1126

IX Movement certificate — International Community transit (EEC)
document T2L form

DECLARATION BY THE EXPORTER

I, the undersigned ....
(full name and address of exporter)

.... being the exporter of the goods described below:

| Serial number | PACKAGES (1) | | Detailed description of goods | Tariff number | Gross weight | Net weight (kg) or other measure (hl, m³, etc.) |
	Marks and numbers	Number and kind				
1	2	3	4	5	6	7

Total number of packages (col. 3) ....

Total quantities (col. 6) .... in words

declare that these goods ....
satisfy the conditions required for the issue of this certificate.

Place of loading ....

Shipped on .... No. ....
(date)

Country of destination of goods at the time of exportation ....

At .... on ....
(place of signature) *(date)*

....
(signature of exporter)

(1) For goods in bulk give as appropriate the name of the ship or the number of the railway waggon or road vehicle.

X   Movement certificate Community transit (EEC) DD3 form

RESULT OF CUSTOMS EXAMINATION AND INDICATION OF MEANS OF IDENTIFICATION (1)

Declaration certified correct

Export document model .... No. .... dated ....

Customs office ....

Official stamp

Date ....19........

....
(signature of customs officer)

(1) The Customs authorities at the place of exportation should give in this space any relevant details which may facilitate identification of the goods
They should also indicate any special identification measures such as sealing, stamping, etc., which they have taken.

Spaces not used should be crossed through so as to make any later additions impossible.

X   DD3 form, *continued*

Barclays Bank International Limited

date

REVOCABLE CREDIT No. :-
To be quoted on all drafts and correspondence.

Beneficiary(ies)

Advised through

Accreditor

To be completed only if applicable

Our cable of

Advised through

Refers

Dear Sir(s)

In accordance with instructions received from
we hereby issue in your favour a Documentary Credit for
(say)

drawn on

available by your drafts

at

for the   invoice value, accompanied by the following documents :-

Covering the following goods:—

To be shipped from   to

not later than

Partshipment   Transhipment

The credit is available for   until

Drafts drawn hereunder must be marked "Drawn under Barclays Bank International Limited ".
branch, Credit number

We have no authority from our clients to confirm this credit or to guarantee acceptance payment of drafts drawn here against. This credit is therefore subject to cancellation without notice and the above particulars are for your guidance only.

Yours faithfully,

Co-signed (Signature No.   )   Signed (Signature No.   )

CRE 203 (replacing CRE 89, 607 series)   W W Sprague & Co Ltd   PLEASE SEE REVERSE

XI Letter of credit — revocable credit

Barclays Bank International Limited

IRREVOCABLE CREDIT No:-
To be quoted on all drafts and correspondence.

Beneficiary(ies)

Advised through

Accreditor

To be completed only if applicable

Our cable of

Advised through

Refers

Dear Sir(s)

In accordance with instructions received from
we hereby issue in your favour a Documentary Credit for
(say)
drawn on

at
for the   invoice value, accompanied by the following documents:-

available by your drafts

Covering the following goods:—

To be shipped from

not later than

Partshipment   Transhipment

The credit is available for   until

to

Drafts drawn hereunder must be marked "Drawn under Barclays Bank International Limited

branch, Credit number   :".

We undertake that drafts and documents drawn under and in strict conformity with the terms of this credit will
be honoured upon presentation.

Yours faithfully,

Co-signed (Signature No.   )   Signed (Signature No.   )

CRE 202 (replacing CRE 83, 606 series)   Perkins Bacon Ltd London   PLEASE SEE REVERSE

XII   Letter of credit — irrevocable credit

© SITPRO 1976

STANDARD SHIPPING NOTE

Exporter/Shipper (Name and Address)

1 Vehicle Bkg Ref 2 CAN/Pre-Entry No./Other Customs Ref. 3

Exporter's Ref.

Port Handling charges to be paid by *

Exporter   Agent

Other (Name and Address)

F/Agent's Ref.   S.S Co Bkg. No. 4

5

Name of Shipping Line or CTO (if required)   6 Port Account No.

Forwarding Agent/Merchant (Name and Address)

7 For use of Receiving Authority only

Receiving Date(s)   Berth & Dock/Container Base Etc.

8

Ship   Port of Loading

9 This 6 part set is printed on Carrs G-Copy and is suitable for use in spirit duplicators. The sixth sheet is the shipper's file copy. The fifth sheet is to be returned to the haulier by the Receiving Authority.

TO THE RECEIVING AUTHORITY
Please receive for shipment the goods described below subject to your published Regulations and Conditions (including those as to liability.)

Port of Discharge   Destination Depot (LCL only)

10 Name of Receiving Authority (if required)   11

Marks and Numbers; No. and Kind of Packages; Description of Goods; Package dimensions in cm (if required)

◀ Enter Scale (if required)

12   13   For Receiving Authorities Use   Gross Weight (Kg) 14   Cube (M³) 15

This Note must be lodged WITH the vehicle at the receiving point OR at the Receiving Authority's designated office BEFORE arrival of the goods, according to local port practice. Only goods for shipment to one port of discharge on one sailing may be grouped on one Shipping Note. For multi-vehicle deliveries or any further information contact the Receiving Authority.

Cargo Status *	Customs Free Status / Customs Pre-Entry	Special Stowage	16	Reserved for Shipping Company's Use	Total Gross Wt	Total Cube

For Use of Receiving Authority Only

Carrier.. Vehicle Reg. No................................ Name of Company preparing this Note | 17 |

Number of Packages Received..

Condition.. Date

.... (Indicate Name and Telephone Number of Contact)

Signature and Date

1   630   * Mark 'X' as appropriate

XIII Standard shipping note

Appendix F

AAA	Association of Average Adjusters.
A/C	Account current.
Accepting House	Financial house, often a merchant banker, specializing in financing foreign trade.
ACT	Associated Container Transportation Ltd.
Act of God	Any fortuitous act which could not have been prevented by any amount of human care and forethought.
ADR	European agreement on the international carriage of dangerous goods by road.
Ad valorem freight	Freight rate based on percentage value of goods shipped.
Affreightment	A contract for the carriage of goods by sea for shipment expressed in charter party or bill of lading.
Agent	One who represents a principal, or buys or sells for another.
Air waybill	Air freight consignment note.
Aligned Export Documentation System	Method whereby as much information as possible is entered in a 'master document' so that all or part of this information can be reproduced mechanically into individual forms of a similar design.
AMT	Air mail transfer — a remittance purchased by the debtor from his banker in international trade.
Arbitration	Method of settling disputes which is usually binding on the parties concerned.
ASP	American selling price. A Customs term for the retail price of a product in the USA.
ATA carnet	International Customs document to cover the temporary export of certain goods (commercial samples and exhibits for interna-

tional trade fairs abroad and professional equipment) to countries which are parties to the ATA convention. Also covers the re-importation of such goods.

Average bond: Bond in which cargo owners agree to pay their share in the general average losses, each contribution being determined by the average adjuster.

Average deposit: Cash security deposited by the consignee pending assessment of general average contribution.

Back freight: Freight (additional) incurred through cargo being returned from destination port, usually because its acceptance was refused.

Balance of trade: Financial statement of balance of a country's visible trade exports and imports.

Bank rate: The minimum rate at which the Bank of England or a 'national' bank will discount first class bills of exchange.

Bilateralism: Trade between two countries.

Bill of exchange: Written request from a creditor to a debtor ordering the debtor to pay a specified sum to a specified person or bearer at a certain date.

Bill of lading: Receipt for goods shipped on board a ship signed by the person (or his agent) who contracts to carry them, and stating the terms on which the goods are carried.

Bill of sight: Customs import form, used when importer cannot make Customs entry complete owing to insufficient information from the shipper.

Bond: Guarantee to Customs of specified amount of duty to be paid.

BOTB: British Overseas Trade Board.

B/P: Bills payable.

Broken stowage: Space wasted in a ships hold or container by stowage of uneven cargo, that is, irregularly shaped consignments.

Brussels Nomenclature: Internationally agreed tariff classification system containing 21 sections, subdivided in 99

	chapters with 1095 headings for all goods in international commerce.
BTN	Brussels Tariff Nomenclature.
Bulk licence	Licence issued to manufacturers and exporters to cover their requirements for certain bulk quantity or period.
Bulk unitization	Means to consolidate multiple packages or items into a single load device.
CAD	Cash against documents.
CAN	Customs assigned number.
Cargo manifest	Inventory of cargo shipped.
Carr fwd	Carriage forward.
CAP	Common Agricultural Policy.
CB	Container base.
CCC	Customs clearance certificate or Customs Co-operation Council.
CCLN	Consignment note control label number.
CCT	Common Customs tariff (within the EEC).
C & D	Collected and delivered.
CENSA	Council of European and Japanese National Shipowners' Association.
C & F	Cost and freight.
CI	Consular invoice.
CIF	Cost insurance and freight.
CIFCI	Cost insurance freight, commission and interest.
Clean bill of lading	A bill of lading which has no superimposed clause(s) expressly declaring a defective condition of the packaging or goods.
Closing date	Latest date cargo accepted for shipment by (liner) shipowner for specified sailing.
C/N	Consignment note.
C/O	Certificate of origin or cash order.
COI	Central Office of Information.
Collectors office	Customs accommodation where declaration(s) (entries) are scrutinized and amounts payable collected.
Conference	Organization whereby number of shipowners often of different nationality offer their ser-

vices on a given sea route on conditions agreed by members.

Consignee	Name of agent, company or person receiving consignment.
Consignor	Name of agent, company or person sending consignment (the shipper).
Consul	Commercial representative of one country residing officially in another whose duties are to facilitate business and represent the merchants of his nation.
C/P	Charter party.
CTL	Constructive total loss.
Customs clearance	Process of clearing import/export cargo through customs examination.
D/A	Deposit account.
DDA	Duty (Customs) deferment account.
Dead freight	Space booked by shipper or charterer on a vessel but not used.
Deferred rebate	System whereby shippers are granted a rebate on freight for consistent exclusive patronage over a given period.
Del credere	Agent/broker guarantee to principal for solvency of person to whom he sells goods.
Dis	Discount.
Discount market	Process of selling and buying bills of exchange and Treasury bills and providing a market for short bonds.
D/N	Debit note.
D/O	Delivery order.
D/P	Documents against payment.
Dunnage	Wood, mats etc. used to facilitate stowage of cargo.
Dutiable cargo	Cargo which attracts some form of duty, that is, Customs and Excise, or VAT.
DWT	Dead weight tonnage.
ECGD	Export Credits Guarantee Department.
EEC	European Economic Community.
EIS	Export Intelligence Service.
Exchange rate	Price of one currency in terms of another.

Export houses	An export merchant responsible for buying goods outright and selling them on their own account; acting as an export department or agent on behalf of a client; or acting for an overseas buyer.
Exporters acceptance credit	Credit opened by an exporter with his own bank which entitles the exporter to draw bills on his own banker.
Ex quay	Buyer responsible for charges after delivery on quay at bill of lading destination — seller pays landing charges.
Ex ship	Sellers pays freight to port of discharge and the buyer landing and other charges.
Ex Works	Exports sold free of any insurance and freight (transport) charges.
Factoring	Company which administers the sales ledger and collects payments on behalf of an exporter once the goods have been shipped.
FAS	Free alongside.
FCL	Full container load.
FC & S	Free of capture and seizure — insurers are not responsible if the ship or goods are seized by a foreign power.
FIO	Free in and out — charterer pays for cost of loading and discharging cargo.
FIO & stowed	Free in and out — charterer pays for cost of loading and discharging cargo including stowage.
FIW	Free into wagon.
Fixture	Conclusion of shipbrokers negotiations to charter a ship.
Floating exchange rates	Currency rate which varies according to world trade distortions and not subject to exchange control.
Floating policy	Cargo policy which underwrites series of consignments declared.
FOB	Free on board.
FOR	Free on rail.
FOT	Free on truck (rail) — exporter meets all

	charges until cargo placed on truck from which point importer bears all cost.
FPA	Free of particular average — insurers not responsible for partial loss claims with certain exceptions.
Franco pour (French)	Sender undertakes to pay fixed amount in carriage charges.
FSR	Free of strikes and riots — marine insurance policy clause.
G/A	General average.
GIFT	Glasgow International Freight Terminal.
GSP	Generalized system of preferences.
GV	Grande vitesse — fast rail merchandise service.
Heterogeneous cargo	Variety of cargoes.
High stowage factor	Cargo which has a high bulk to low weight relationship, i.e. hay.
IATA	International Air Transport Association.
IBAP	Intervention Board Agricultural Produce.
ICAO	International Civil Aviation Organization.
ICB	International Container Bureau.
ICD	Inland clearance depot.
IMCO	Inter-Governmental Maritime Consultative Organization.
Indemnity	Compensation for loss/damage or injury.
Individual licence	Licence issued for one particular import/export consignment.
Invisible exports	Income from exports embracing tourism, net shipping and air receipts, foreign investments, banking and insurance.
Inherent vice	A defect or inherent quality of the goods or their packing which of itself may contribute to their deterioration, injury, wastage and final destruction, without any negligence or other contributing causes.
Inland clearance depot	Customs cargo clearance depot.

IRU	Union Internationale des Transports Routiers.
ISO	International Standards Organization.
Jus disponendi (Latin)	Law of disposal.
LASH	Lighter aboard ship.
Letter of hypothecation	Bankers document outlining conditions under which international transactions will be executed on exporters behalf, the latter having given certain pledges to his banker.
Letter of indemnity	A document indemnifying the shipowner or agent from any consequences, risk or claims which may arise through 'clean' bills of lading being irregularly issued.
LIFT	London International Freight Terminal.
LNG	Liquified natural gas — type of vessel.
Loading broker	Person who acts on behalf of liner company at a port.
Long room	Customs house office where documentation of goods declared are received and checked, and where ships are reported inwards and cleared outwards at Customs.
Low stowage factor	Cargo which has low bulk to high weight relationship, i.e. steel rails.
Lump sum freight	Remuneration paid to shipowner for charter of a ship, or portion of it, irrespective of quantity of cargo loaded.
Market rate	Rate charged by brokers, discount houses, joint stock banks and other market members for discounting first class bills.
Mates receipt	Document issued to the shipper for ship's cargo loaded from lighterage and later exchanged for bill of lading.
MCD	Miscellaneous cash deposit.
M'dise	Merchandise.
MIFT	Manchester International Freight Terminal. Mail transfer — a remittance purchased by

	the debtor from his banker in international trade.
Negotiable bill of lading	One capable of being negotiated by transfer or endorsement.
NSSN	National Standard Shipping Note.
OBO	Oil bulk ore carriers — multi-purpose bulk carriers.
O/C	Overcharge.
OCL	Overseas Containers Ltd.
OECD	Organization for European Co-operation and Development.
Open policy	One in which a maximum amount is stated and the goods insured are allowed to be shipped in varying amounts in one or more vessels up to a maximum sum, but within the general terms of the policy.
OTAR	Overseas tariffs and regulations.
Overvalued currency	Currency whose rate of exchange is persistently below the parity rate.
Per pro	On behalf of.
PIRA	Research Association for the Paper and Board, Printing and Packaging Industries.
P/L	Partial loss.
Pre-entered	Process of lodging with Customs appropriate documentation for scrutiny prior to cargo Customs clearance and shipment.
Rebate	An allowance made as discount on an account/rate.
Receiving date	Date from which cargo is accepted for shipment for specified sailing.
RHA	Road Haulage Association.
Ro/Ro	Roll on/roll off — a vehicular ferry service.
Shipping invoice	Document giving details of merchandise shipped.
Shut out	Cargo refused shipment because it arrived after closing date.

Sine die (Latin)	Indefinitely — without a day being appointed.
Stale bill of lading	In banking practice, a bill of lading presented so late that consignee could be involved in difficulties.
Subrogation	Process of substituting one person for another in marine insurance matters in which the latter inherits the former's rights and liabilities.
TAN	Transit advice note.
TCM	Draft convention on combined transport.
THE	Technical help to exporters — service of the British Standards Institution.
TIR	Transport International Routier. Bond conditions under which containerized/vehicular merchandise are conveyed internationally under the convention.
T/L	Total loss.
Tramp	Vessel engaged in bulk cargo or time chartering business, i.e. not a liner vessel.
Transferable credit	One which may be transferred by the first beneficiary.
Transhipment entry	Customs entry for cargo imported for immediate re-exportation.
TT	Telegraphic transfer. A remittance purchased by the debtor from his banker in international trade.
UKTOTC	United Kingdom Tariff and Overseas Trade Classification.
ULCC	Ultra large crude carrier.
ULD	Unit load device.
Undervalued currency	Currency whose rate of exchange is persistently above the parity.
Unit loads	Containerized or palletized traffic.
VLCC	Very large crude carrier.
WA	With average.
Warranty	An implied condition, express guarantee or negotiation contained in marine insurance policy.
WPA	With particular average.

Index